T4-AAN-230

Political Insults

POLITICAL INSULTS
How Offenses Escalate Conflict

Karina V. Korostelina

Oxford University Press is a department of the University of Oxford.
It furthers the University's objective of excellence in research, scholarship,
and education by publishing worldwide.

Oxford   New York
Auckland   Cape Town   Dar es Salaam   Hong Kong   Karachi
Kuala Lumpur   Madrid   Melbourne   Mexico City   Nairobi
New Delhi   Shanghai   Taipei   Toronto

With offices in
Argentina   Austria   Brazil   Chile   Czech Republic   France   Greece
Guatemala   Hungary   Italy   Japan   Poland   Portugal   Singapore
South Korea   Switzerland   Thailand   Turkey   Ukraine   Vietnam

Oxford is a registered trademark of Oxford University Press
in the UK and certain other countries.

Published in the United States of America by
Oxford University Press
198 Madison Avenue, New York, NY 10016

© Oxford University Press 2014

All rights reserved. No part of this publication may be reproduced, stored in a
retrieval system, or transmitted, in any form or by any means, without the prior
permission in writing of Oxford University Press, or as expressly permitted by law,
by license, or under terms agreed with the appropriate reproduction rights organization.
Inquiries concerning reproduction outside the scope of the above should be sent to the
Rights Department, Oxford University Press, at the address above.

You must not circulate this work in any other form
and you must impose this same condition on any acquirer.

Library of Congress Cataloging-in-Publication Data
Korostelina, K. V. (Karina Valentinovna)
Political insults : how offenses escalate conflict / Karina V. Korostelina.
   pages cm
Includes bibliographical references and index.
ISBN 978-0-19-937281-2 (hardcover : alk. paper)   1. Intergroup relations.   2. Intergroup
relations—Case studies.   3. Invective—Political aspects.   4. Invective—Social
aspects.   I. Title.
HM1111.K67 2014
302.3—dc 3
2013044963

9 8 7 6 5 4 3 2 1
Printed in the United States of America
on acid-free paper

CONTENTS

Acknowledgments   *vii*

Introduction   *1*
1. Deconstructing Intergroup Insult   *12*
2. Pussy Riot in Russia   *31*
3. Victory Day Violence in Ukraine   *55*
4. Murder and Release   *73*
5. Islands between Two Countries   *94*
6. Declaration of War   *119*
7. Dealing with Insult   *135*

Notes   *167*
Glossary   *189*
Selected Bibliography   *191*
Index of Names   *195*
Index of Subjects   *197*

ACKNOWLEDGMENTS

The volume could not have been completed without Andrea Bartoli, former Dean of my home institution, the School for Conflict Analysis and Resolution, George Mason University. He inspired me to write this book and provided numerous invaluable insights during our discussions. His views on insults as an interruption in the mutual process of the construction of meaning, on intentional and unintentional insults, and on the impact of the perceptions of third parties became very important for this project. It was a great pleasure working with him and discussing ways in which insults are constructed and performed in conflict dynamics.

I also want to express my gratitude to the current Dean of the School for Conflict Analysis and Resolution, Kevin Avruch, all my colleagues who supported me in this endeavor, and to two reviewers who helped shape the book. The help of my graduate assistants, Hilmi Ulas, James Filipi, and Caroline Sarkis, was essential for the success of this project. I offer special thanks to Angela Chnapko and Peter Worger, editors at Oxford University Press, for their support, professionalism, and efficiency at various stages of this work.

I am also very thankful to my family for their interest in my work and support during this project.

Political Insults

Introduction

Thousands of protesters came to the streets in Cairo, enraged over a little-known film posted on the Internet, and threats by a US preacher to burn the Koran sparked deadly riots in Afghanistan. A street vendor, protesting harassment and humiliation by municipal officials, set himself on fire, thus sparking the Tunisian Revolution and the wider Arab Spring. Five women entered the Cathedral of Christ the Savior in Moscow, shed their winter clothing at the altar, and began a performance of a "Punk Prayer," aiming crude language at Vladimir Putin and Kirill I, the Moscow Patriarch of the Russian Orthodox Church. Elderly veterans were assaulted near World War II monuments, and young people fried eggs on the eternal flame near the Tomb of the Unknown Soldier in Ukraine. In a dispute over small islands in the Japan Sea, the Japanese government canceled a currency swap with South Korea and recalled the Japanese ambassador; while the South Korean president visited the disputed islands, 40 South Koreans swam to them, and South Korea's coast guard conducted military exercises nearby. The quick pardon by Azerbaijan's president of the repatriated killer of an Armenian army officer sparked outrage in Armenia and Hungary, as well as a diplomatic maelstrom involving NATO and the European Union.

All these events occurred in different countries, reflect different issues, and involve different participants. But they are united by one common feature that shapes the dynamics of escalation of these conflicts: intergroup insult. While insults are a frequent action in interpersonal and intergroup relations, there are surprisingly few references to insults in the academic literature, especially in literature on conflicts. The absence of the systemic study on intergroup insult is even more notable given the fact that even unintentional insults can result in disproportionate reactions, from dissolution of self-confidence to violent group behavior.

The aim of this book is to create a systemic view of intergroup insults by analyzing their main features, types, forms, and dynamics. My approach to intergroup insult rests on the theories of social identity and power. I posit that intergroup insult is a social act mutually constructed by two social groups on the boundary between them; it is an act that interrupts the shared process of the production of meaning of social reality, reshapes identity, and redefines the balance of power. Both groups—insulting and insulted—can contribute to the construction of insults: the insulting group can produce an insult intentionally, or its actions can be unintentional, while the insulted group can recognize actions of the out-group as an insult or fail to recognize them as offensive. The combination of these actions generates four *types* of insults: *congruous, attributed, futile*, and *potential*.

The insulting side can have different motivation for insults; similarly, the insulted side can attribute various intentions to them. Based on an analysis of identity and power relations between groups, I define six forms of insult. An *identity insult* strips an out-group of positive identity and increases in-group self-esteem. A *projection insult* attributes negative features or intentions to the out-group and justifies in-group actions. A *divergence insult* strengthens intergroup boundaries and provides protection from alien values and rules. A *relative insult* denies rights, opportunities, and abilities to an out-group. A *power insult* redefines a balance of coercive power. A *legitimacy insult* legitimizes the in-group and delegitimizes the out-group.

The book also emphasizes the complex nature of the dynamics of intergroup insult. *Transfer of insult* increases the scope of insult by involving more in-group members in its construction. *Sensitizing* involves enlightening of in-group members about the meaning of an out-group insult and its impact on in-group image. *Learned insult* rests on recognition of a particular insult based on the observation of reactions of other in-group members. *Generalization of insult* unites different actions and words of the insulting side based on their similarity to a previous insult. *Conglomeration of insult* strengthens the reaction to insult based on increasing frequency of insults. A *delayed insult* can be recognized at some time after it is uttered; nevertheless it contributes to conglomeration and generalization processes. *Diffusion of insult* refers to a loss of the offensive effect of an insult over time. *Reactivated insult* can invoke memories of the former diffused insults in situations similar to that in which the old offense occurred.

Through the analysis of five case studies in this book I show that particular forms of insult are indicative of specific drivers of conflicts, and require different approaches by a third party who tries to mediate. This understanding of insult makes it a useful tool in the analysis of conflict dynamics and a resource for practical suggestions in the analysis and resolution of complex conflicts.

INSULTS AS SOCIAL PHENOMENA

Insults are an inevitable aspect of the social relations that face each of us on a daily, or almost daily, basis. Insult is defined as a "behavior or discourse, oral or written, which is perceived, experienced, constructed and, at times, intended as slighting, humiliating or offensive."[1] An insult can be verbal, a facial expression or gesture, or an action. Insults are perceived by the target as both intentional and illegitimate.[2] They exist on different levels in society, including interpersonal, intergroup, and international levels, and they result in production and reproduction of social meaning. They change social relations, provoke violence, and contribute to the worst conflicts of history. "Threatened egotism," a tendency to attack groups perceived as insulting to the in-group, was a major factor in the Holocaust.[3] Whether intentional or unintentional, insults have real and potentially lasting effects on society.

Insults can spark broad social actions and international conflicts. The low-budget movie *Innocence of Muslims*, portraying the prophet Muhammad as a fool and a child molester, was planned by Nakoula Basseley Nakoula as an identity insult to Muslims. He targeted the most sacred beliefs about the Prophet and used the most unacceptable vices in Muslim culture to portray him. Nakoula posted the short version of movie on YouTube; its airing on several Muslim TV stations contributed to a sensitization of insult among Muslims. It immediately sparked a torrent of anti-American unrest in Arab and Muslim countries because it was perceived as offensive insult. The first round of protests occurred on September 11, 2012 in Benghazi, where a militant group used the movie as a diversion to attack the US consulate. Christopher Stevens, a career diplomat named ambassador to Libya in May, together with three other embassy staff members, was killed in this attack. This violent action was planned as an insult to the US government and a country in general on the anniversary of the September 11 attacks. The insult then became more generalized: protests over the video continued in Egypt, where several men scaled the walls of the US embassy and tore down its American flag. In Kana, Nigeria, tens of thousands of Muslims marched to protest the video, shouting threats and projected insults toward the United States and Israel. US and Israeli flags were dragged through the dirt as a symbolic insulting action. Protests continued in London, where thousands of demonstrators marched on the offices of Google, demanding that the company remove the insulting film from the Internet.

Insults also can work as triggering points for social transformations and radical change, including revolutions. Like many young people in Tunis, Mohamed Bouazizi was insulted by the local bureaucracy in many forms. Numerous times police confiscated his scales and his produce, and fined him for running a stall without a permit. One morning, in a small confrontation, a policewoman slapped him and, with the help of her colleagues, forced him to the ground. The officers took away his produce and his scale. The fact that the police officer was a woman underscored this power insult: a slap from a woman is perceived as a complete humiliation in Tunisian culture. Seeking justice, Bouazizi went to the local municipality building and demanded a meeting with an official. When his request was denied, Bouazizi poured flammable liquid over his body and set himself alight outside the local municipal office. This action deeply resonated throughout the country, where people were deeply frustrated with the lack of freedoms and were continuously insulted on all levels by the Tunisian bureaucracy. Many young people had lost any hope of finding a job, and the option to emigrate became an illusion with the European Union states closing their borders to Tunisia. According to official government data, the level of unemployment at the time was 18 percent, but the real situation was much worse, especially in the countryside. Nepotism, corruption, and policies of privatization contributed to the wealth of the president, Zine El Abidine Ben Ali, but impeded the access of young people to jobs and education. Within hours, Bouazizi's self-immolation became a learned insult and gave a rise to protests in Sidi Bou Saïd; police attempts to settle the unrest only fueled more violent actions. After two weeks, Ben Ali, attempting to reduce the tension, visited Mohamed Bouazizi at the hospital in Ben Arous and reached out to his family, inviting them to the presidential palace. But these actions were perceived as a stronger insult because they were too late and were clearly manipulative. After Bouazizi's death, the protests became widespread, moving into the more affluent areas and eventually into the capital, sensitizing more and more people to Ben Ali's insult. The anger and violence became so intense that Ben Ali fled Tunisia with his family on January 14, 2011, and was given an asylum in Saudi Arabia. The revolution spread beyond Tunisia, taking other authoritarian Arab governments down.

Many scholars emphasize that the construction of insult involves the active participation of all involved parties and can be understood as a dialogic process.[4] Every insult involves a perpetrator, target, and audience, even when some insults can be attributed solely to the insulting party.[5]

These intentional and unintentional insults can be displayed in play, humor, ritual, blasphemy, and hate speech. Thus, insult can be determined by both a recipient or insulting party, and this process depends on the particular culture or society.[6]

All insults are formed, maintained, and transformed through social relations and help construct reality through social interaction.[7] These social constructs are written into the fabric of our institutions and practices; thus insults and responses to them are culturally produced. Cultural features such as levels of empathy and social distance influence people's responses to shame, insults, and victimization in general.[8] An audience is a key aspect of insult: it transforms insult from simple annoyance to violent offense and stigma, as judged by others.[9]

Often culture helps produce or maintain power relations that promote one group over another, and this creates special contexts of insult. Through the use of insult, a dominant group labels and defines what it means for a minority group to exist, and thus insults can be a powerful way of creating group solidarity out of once disparate individuals.[10] A dominant group can insult a minority group by emphasizing differences between their cultures and histories. Conversely, any challenge to a dominant group by a minority group (such as questioning the ethnicity of the Christ figure) can be perceived as an insult or threat because stereotypes are deeply embedded in the group's history, culture, and rituals.[11] A history of racism affects interpretations of insult and the production of hate-speech directed toward minorities that can be accepted by the majority.[12]

Liberal societies are committed to free speech but recognize that certain forms of speech are harmful. Through the insult, the intentions to do harm are translated into actual harm. While society builds institutions and practices to protect from certain insults, these attempts, in an almost paradoxical way, contribute to the harming power of the prohibited words.[13] For example, the punitive requirements of the criminal justice system produce a potential insult rather than compassion for the victims of violent domestic assault. An alternative system that focuses on restorative justice and healing rather than shame and punishment is the only way to reduce violence in the home.[14]

Insults are connected with several other social phenomena like impoliteness, humiliation, embitterment, revenge, and incivility. Impoliteness rests on interpretation and the context in which something is said; thus insult can only become offensive through interpretations. Even something uttered politely may be interpreted as an insult given the particular social context within which it occurs.[15] Many social situations are coded with rituals of shame and humiliation. Based on culturally specific codes of honor, reactions to insults are as much about our care for the presentation of self as they are about the "right" interaction with the other.[16] Similar to humiliation, insults result in powerful emotions and enter into a personal or group history. This dynamic creates the experiences of shame, guilt, and anger as fundamental emotions connected to insults.[17] However, while they both produce negative emotions, humiliation and insults differ from one another. Humiliation as "the enforced lowering of a person or group, a process of subjugation that damages or strips away their pride, honor or dignity,"[18] aims to make the insulted side feel inferior. Insults have wider purposes, including creation of the social boundary between people and the redefinition of legitimacy. The categories of insult include exclusion, stereotyping, obliteration of significant identity details, ingratitude, scapegoating, rudeness, broken promises, being ignored or kept waiting, defamation, and despoiling of idealized objects, persons, or ideas.[19]

People can also perceive insult in situations that are not intended to be offensive. Posttraumatic embitterment disorder[20] develops when anxiety-provoking events are "experienced as unjust, as a personal insult, and psychologically as a violation of basic beliefs and values. The psychopathological reaction is a prolonged feeling of embitterment."[21] The insulting event occupies a major place in the thoughts of the insulted person, and memories about it recur in despair. A person wants to fight back, plans revenge and acts of aggression, feeling at the same time helpless and cornered. This feeling of embitterment can also arise in the context of in-group conflict, influencing the relations between two sides.[22] While the concept of embitterment explains why some unintentional actions are perceived as an insult and how these perceptions can lead to a motivation to create new insults, the dynamics of insult itself are not a focus of these studies.

Similarly, a person or group might commits acts of revenge in response to subjective experiences of injustice, victimization, or violation of personal rights and claims,[23] as a response to negative experiences and insults,[24] or humiliation or threat to the sense of identity.[25] The desire for revenge has been cited in many intergroup conflicts, including Kosovo, Afghanistan, Uganda, and the post-9/11 United States.[26] The desire for revenge can be a coping strategy that never results in actions: studies do not show significant interrelations between feelings of revenge and actions of offense and crime.[27] Thus, feelings of revenge as a tool of managing personal traumatic experiences can explain some motivations for insult but do not provide insights into the mechanisms of insulting behavior.

Insult usually represents a low level of intensity of aggressive action, thus being similar to incivility analyzed in work settings. Incivility as an interactive event "involves acting rudely or discourteously, without regard for others, in violation of norms for respect in social interactions."[28] The intent to harm in incivility acts is ambiguous: some acts can be produced with a desire to harm, while others can be a result of ignorance or stress, representing "'milder' mistreatment such as condescending remarks or impolite gestures."[29] A series of acts of incivility will have a more significant effect on people and their well-being than a single act. While the concept of incivility helps to contextualize low-intensity violent acts toward other people, it is mostly connected with the violation of norms (of the workplace, for example), perceptions of justice, and social ostracism. As I argue in this book, the concept of insult has a wider causation.

Insults contribute to the formation and reformulation of self-image and identity of all parties, but are especially influential for the identity of the insulted one. In the face of domination and insult, gay male identity is contracted to resist subjection and reformulated as resistance and freedom.[30] Insults are also influential to a person's identity through the creation of a powerful motivation for actions. An insult to status may be used to manipulate a consumer's motivations to purchase items and increase social status.[31] Several studies show that insult in interpersonal relations is perceived as more offensive if it creates an unfavorable situational identity by making a person appear weak, incompetent, and cowardly.[32] Likewise, a person might aim to dismiss or humiliate another by calling him ugly, ignorant, boorish, boring, or dirty.[33] In intergroup relations more insult-related anger is experienced by people with highly salient in-group identity.[34] Often such an insult will lead to a counterattack or retaliation in an attempt to nullify the imputed negative identity. This is done through a show of one's strength, competence, and courage, or by casting a negative identity on the original aggressor.[35] The latter situation produces a desire to take confrontational action against offending groups,[36] a willingness to take risk, and an inability to thoughtfully take the other side's perspective, reconsider the situation, or think about alternatives to aggression.[37] In addition, the insult of an in-group is typically received more defensively when it originates from an out-group rather than from another in-group member or a representative of a shared, superordinate identity.[38] So the perception of insult as grievously offensive and the readiness of persons to retaliate depends on both the importance and the salience of this identity.

While the meaning of insults is fluid and constantly redefined in different cultural and historical contexts, insults can result in disproportionate reactions, from aggressive and violent behavior to social revolutions. Depending on the nature of conflict, parties can use different forms of insult; these insults are indicative for the core issues of conflict. The study of insults also requires the development of practical suggestions for dealing with the offenses and the conflicts that involve them. Some research suggests that we ought to do two things in life to fend off insults: first, develop a thicker skin, becoming more like Stoic philosophers; second, become "insult pacifists," who try hard not to engage in insults and attempt to diffuse their social power.[39] The language of apology also can help to reduce or intensify the effects of initial insult. If the out-group expresses shame, then this may exacerbate the insult, whereas guilt will begin to repair the damage of insult.[40] As I show in this book, different forms of insult are sensitive to specific types of conflict management and require different approaches by a third party who wishes to intervene.

METHODOLOGY

The cases selected for this book focus on multiple insults that are central to the dynamics of conflict, and all occurred during the years 2012–2013, in which the book was written.[41] Thus, much of the data were collected through examination of newspapers, Internet media, polls, documentaries, official documents, and official reports.

The analysis of the data was based on the conceptual definitions of the forms of insults, the matrix of the types of insults, and the conceptual elements of insult dynamics elaborated in chapter 1. To analyze the creation, employment, and impact of insult and the intergroup relations associated with it, I used the method of process tracing,[42] with events as embedded units of analysis within multiple contexts.[43] I analyzed each case in terms of the sequence and structure of events to reveal the causal connections between certain events, constructed insults, produced effects, and reactions of different groups. I focused on the unfolding of events over time, concentrating on a series of insults and reactions toward them as key steps in the conflict dynamics.[44]

STRUCTURE OF THE BOOK

Chapter 1 of this book, "Deconstructing Intergroup Insult," presents the theoretical foundations of the analysis of intergroup insult, including its main features, types, forms, and specific dynamics. It also includes the conceptual framework for the analysis of the case studies in this book. The chapter stresses that intergroup insult, as a social act constructed mutually by social groups on the social boundary between them, involves (1) the social identity and power positions of both groups; (2) a history of relations between the two groups, (3) awareness of the insult by one or both groups, and (4) the sociocultural meaning of insult accepted in the specific society and culture(s). It also describes insult as an interruption in the mutual process of the production of meaning of social identity and power. Intergroup insult strips the insulted group of a positive identity and decreases its power.

Chapter 2, "Pussy Riot in Russia," discusses a series of scandals around the Russian Orthodox Church that Russian society perceived as insults. It also discusses events connected with Pussy Riot's protests. Pussy Riot, the feminist punk band, stormed the main altar of Moscow's Cathedral of Christ the Savior and performed their "Punk Prayer," containing crude language aimed toward Russia's president and the leader of the Russian Orthodox Church. By using this divergence insult they protested the collusion between the Russian Orthodox Church and President Vladimir Putin. For the Russian government it was a legitimacy insult. The government-controlled Russian mass media were quick to influence public opinion, insisting that Pussy Riot had insulted a place of worship and the Orthodox faith in general. As a result, three members of the band were convicted of "hooliganism" and sentenced to two years in prison.

Chapter 3, "Victory Day Violence in Ukraine," depicts the role of insults in the conflict over history in Ukraine. Insults in this case included diverse verbal statements and actions, the "war" of regional laws, the beating of war veterans, and frying eggs on the internal flame of the Tomb of the Unknown Solder. Verhovna Rada (the parliament of Ukraine) passed a law that supported the official use of red flag replicas during the celebrations of Victory Day. The population of Western Ukraine and pro-Ukrainian movements immediately perceived this decision as an insult, and as a result the local administrations of the western regions banned the use of the red flag because it represented the repression of the people under Soviet rule. They also moved to rename Victory Day the Day of Grief, and to invite veterans of the anti-Soviet, underground Ukrainian Insurgent Army (UPA) into schools to tell pupils about its heroic fights against both Soviet and Nazi regimes. On May 9, 2011, a group of World War II veterans and representatives of NGOs came to L'viv from the eastern and southern regions of Ukraine to celebrate Victory Day. Together with a group of Russian diplomats, they were attacked by a Ukrainian nationalist from the ultra-right-wing party Svoboda. Some of the nationalists were prosecuted, and the attack was officially condemned by the Ukrainian and Russian governments. The chapter also discusses another insult: in the capital of Ukraine, young people fried eggs on the eternal flame near the Tomb of the Unknown Soldier.

Chapter 4, "Murder and Release," discusses the series of insults connected with the murder of an Armenian soldier by Ramil Safarov, an Azeri army lieutenant, during a NATO Partnership for Peace course at a military school in Budapest. Safarov claimed that he had reacted to Armenian officers who laughed at him behind his back and at the general assault on Azeri people in the war over Nagorno-Karabakh. He was sentenced to life in prison in Hungary, but was extradited to Azerbaijan after the Azerbaijani government gave assurances that his sentence would be enforced. Upon his return to Baku, Safarov was given a hero's welcome. He received an official pardon from President Ilham Aliyev, was promoted to the rank of major, and was given a flat and all the pay he had lost since his arrest eight years prior. The Armenian government and people perceived this action as a power and identity insult. Hundreds of Armenians protested outside Hungary's consulates in Yerevan and outside Hungarian embassies in other world capitals by burning Hungarian flags.

Chapter 5, "Islands between Two Countries," analyzes the disputes over islands in the Japanese Sea known as Takeshima in Japan and Dokdo in Korea, which involve a series of evolving power and legitimacy insults. Japan sees South Korea's presence on the islands as an insulting "illegal occupation," referring to historical documents showing that Japan has held sovereignty over Takeshima since the middle of the seventeenth century. South Korea considers these islands its territory and sees Japan's continued claim to them as an insult, especially as it symbolizes, for South Korea, the unwillingness of Japan to condemn its earlier militarism. The South Korean president, Lee Myung-bak, made a statement that the prime minister of Japan should apologize more clearly for his country's harsh 1910–45 colonial rule of the Korean Peninsula. This statement was perceived as combining projection and legitimacy insults by the Japanese leadership. The Japanese government subsequently reneged on an agreement to engage in a so-called currency swap with Korea, recalled the Japanese ambassador to South Korea, and started insulting diplomatic tit for tat behavior. In response, Lee visited the disputed islands, 40 South Koreans swam to the islands to mark the anniversary of the country's liberation from Japan in 1945, and South Korea's coast guard conducted military exercises near the disputed islands, adding a new power insult to ongoing tension in the territorial row.

Another dispute between China and Japan over territory known as the Senkaku Islands in Japan and Diaoyu in China escalated after a Chinese fishing boat crashed into a Japanese Coast Guard vessel in 2010, resulting in the arrest of the Chinese captain. This eventually led Tokyo's controversial nationalist governor Shintaro Ishihara to propose buying the islands.

Undertaking this initiative, Japan's national government signed a contract to buy the islands for ¥2.05 billion ($26 million) from the Japanese family that has been leasing them to the government. The Chinese government immediately sent patrol boats to the nearby waters, which the Japanese government, in turn, perceived as a power insult. The Japanese military arrested 14 Chinese activists who landed on the disputed islands. This retaliation was perceived as a power insult by Chinese leaders, who then sent a Chinese naval flotilla, including two destroyers, to sail near the Japanese islands.

Chapter 6, "Declaration of War," describes unfolding conflict between North Korea and the United States. Reacting to the international nuclear security summit in South Korea and military games in the region, North Korea launched a rocket that malfunctioned and fell into the sea. The next rocket launch, successful in its execution, was followed by nuclear bomb tests despite protests from the international community, the UN, and the United States. Several months later North Korea announced that it was scrapping the 1953 ceasefire agreement and nullifying the declaration on denuclearization of the Korean Peninsula. It also cut direct phone lines with South Korea, released propaganda videos showing a possible missile attack on the United States, and named possible targets on US territory. Finally, North Korea declared that it was "entering the state of war" and was ready to "make a strike of justice at any target any time as it pleases without limit." Although the United States condemned these actions, it did not involve itself in the vicious circle of insults.

Chapter 7, "Dealing with Insult," discusses major results of the case study analyses and provides recommendations on how understanding the types and forms of insult and its dynamics can help third parties in mediating and resolving particular conflicts. These intervention approaches depend on the forms of the core and secondary insults, their use of both or only one party (types of insult), and the specificity of the dynamics of these insults. The chapter also provides practical recommendations for each proposed method and develops ideas for dealing with insults in each of the analyzed cases.

The book argues that insults often serve as essential tools for shaping conflicts, deeply impacting relations between groups. Based on analyses of five conflict cases, the book provides insights into the ways in which insults can be prevented or mitigated to reduce intergroup hostility and conflict. The main task of this analysis is to demonstrate that specific forms of insults are indicative of particular types of conflict. Therefore, the employment of one or another form of insult can reveal the main issues that underline conflict dynamics. To deal with the encounters that involve specific insults, it is important to use appropriate tools of resolution and management of conflict.

CHAPTER 1
Deconstructing Intergroup Insult

INSULT AS SOCIAL ACT

In this book I concentrate on intergroup insult—insult that is produced between social groups: ethnic, religious, national, gender, ideological, and others. An insult of this sort targets a social group as a whole entity, where the majority of members of the group recognizes and acknowledges its effects. An insult changes the dynamics of intergroup interactions, provokes new conflicts or deepens old encounters, reshapes perceptions between groups, and changes relations between them forever. One intergroup insult can lead to another, spiraling into belligerent sequences of insulting social acts and resulting in aggressive actions, social movements, and mass violence. Insult plays an essential role in many intergroup conflicts and may reside at the heart of their dynamics.

My analysis of intergroup insult is based on two main postulates. First, I believe that insult is a social act constructed mutually by social groups on the boundary between them. This social boundary is a perceived frontier between groups that includes distinctive social relations within these groups, inclusive of particular relations between them, as well as shared views on these encounters.[1] It usually exists in narrative form that captures the specificity of relationships within the groups and across the boundary. The narratives of both groups can contradict or complement one another but always have mutual impact. Intergroup insult, like many other mutual acts, is also constructed on this social boundary and involves (1) the social identity and power positions of both groups, (2) a history of relations between the two groups, (3) awareness of the insult by one or both groups, and (4) the sociocultural meaning of insult accepted in the specific society and culture(s). The first component, the social identity and power positions of the groups, reflects their self-images, main values and beliefs, and perceptions of their relative positions and power balance with another group. Thus, a group can perceive itself as a highly spiritual minority with deep traditional values, at the same time seeing another group as individualistic and primarily oriented toward achievements. Another group can see itself as composed of fair and kindhearted "have-nots," while perceiving another group as cold-hearted greedy "haves." Another group can posit itself as an educated, progressive, and hard-working majority, while treating another group as a lazy, ignorant minority with few inspirations.

The second component, a history of relations between two groups, includes narratives about collaborations and conflicts, assistances and counteractions, traumas and glories, supports and treasons. While the history of particular intergroup relations can go back many centuries, only a few events will congeal in historic narratives used by the groups, and these events take on specific meanings that define current interactions between the groups. These historic narratives can vary from very positive to very negative and contain different accounts of insult. In some cases intergroup insults can be central to historic narratives of intergroup interactions. Take for instance the case of Ukraine, where the part of population sees the unification with Russia in 1654 as an insulting for the very idea of Ukrainian independence while the signing of the treaty with Sweden 50 years later is considered as insult for the feelings of brotherhood with Russia by the another part of the population.

The third component, awareness of the insult by one or both groups, reflects the crucial feature of intergroup insult. To produce a specific aggressive reaction, intergroup insult does not need to be intentionally constructed by the insulting group. "The intention to insult is not a necessary ingredient of an insult. Some insults, notably in cases of blasphemy, may result without an intention on the part of the perpetrator, who finds himself/herself unwittingly to have broken a taboo or violated a deep sensitivity."[2] Often people do not believe that statements by others are merely benign and consider them insults. This attribution depends on structural factors and on the fluctuation of meaning from the social to the personal level. A situation is perceived as insulting when adaptability mechanisms are not working well.

If the insulted group views unintended or accidental actions of another group as an insult, this perception is sufficient for the production of antagonistic actions and new insults. At the same time, if the insulted group does not recognize an insult as such, even well-planned and insolent action will not have any effect on the group or on relations between groups, and will be performed in vain. For example, though perhaps meant as a polite gesture and to establish social bonds, if a Westerner asks an Afghan man to show a photo of his wife, the request can be interpreted as an insult, thereby leading to intergroup aggression. Yet a quick, shallow bow performed among Japanese colleagues and intended to insult a business rival can be overlooked by Westerners, yielding no impact on intergroup relations. Later in this chapter I will further examine this interplay of (un) intended and (un)recognized insults.

The fourth component is the sociocultural meaning of an insult. The meaning of insults is fluid and constantly redefined in different cultural and historical contexts. The human capacity to identify insulting situations and produce new meaning from them results in the ever-changing and dynamic meaning of insults. Consequently, some insulting situations congeal in the social fabric and are easily identified, while others have unexpected or novel meaning. For example, a new type of insult—"defriending" on a social network like Facebook—is produced within the context of a new type of interaction, and has offensive meaning only within this specific type of social interaction. Nonetheless, despite the fluidity of the meaning of insults, it is possible to identify the main types and to specify the dynamics of insult.

The second postulate presents insults as interruptions in the mutual process of the production of meaning of social identity and power. Every interaction between social groups involves everyday negotiation and reproduction of connotations of their group identities, translation of their self-images, communication of their values and beliefs, and mutual acknowledgments. It also includes negotiations of the balance of power, compromises and mutual agreements that are essential for collaborative and fruitful relationships. Through insults, parties deprive themselves of the creation of a common meaning, resulting in painful and stressful acts of communication. Intergroup insult strips the insulted group of a positive identity and decreases its power. Like Goffman's "identity politics," which characterize the interactions between the stigmatized and the "normals," an insult requires management of potentially damaging information to preserve positive identity.[3] It is an act of redefinition of the social boundary and power hierarchy between two parties that leads to the disruption of established relationships.

FORMS OF INSULT

These preliminary conclusions lead to the analysis of intergroup insult within the conceptual frameworks of social identity and power. Based on the definition of intergroup insult as an act constructed on the social boundary between the insulting and insulted groups, its scrutiny requires the development of some topology. Based on theories of social identity and power, I identify six particular forms of intergroup insult. In the further discussion I will present the insulting group as "group X" and the insulted group as "group Y."

Identity Insult

The construction of insult is connected with the self-esteem of both sides. The theory of social identity[4] stresses that together with personal identity, an individual has a social identity that is reflected in his or her membership in different groups. This identity is an important part of self-conception and influences the individual's self-perception and perception of society as a whole. Social identity is based on the belief that a person belongs to a particular group, shares common ideas, values, and feelings with other group members, and differs significantly from members of other social groups. This social group provides a person with particular social status, protection and security, emotional and cognitive certainty, and positive self-esteem. One of the central ideas of social identity theory is the individual's need for a positive social identity, which can be achieved in the comparison between groups with positive overestimation of the in-group, otherwise known as in-group favoritism. Such an evaluation often emerges through in-group enhancement rather than out-group derogation.[5] Thus, when members of an in-group compare their own group and other groups, they increase their self-esteem by attributing superiority and higher qualities to their in-group. But in situations of conflict and perceived threat to the in-group, out-group derogation seems more likely to emerge: to increase their self-esteem, members of an in-group attribute negative features to out-group members.[6] The more salient an in-group identity, the stronger the tendency to exaggerate group differences and conflict between groups. Members of groups with strong salient identity are more willing to put down other groups and even support intergroup hostility.[7] Thus, an *identity insult* occurs when group members perceive a threat to their social identity, and thus their self-esteem and sense of dignity, in a situation of conflict with the other group.

To increase or restore positive self-esteem, group X creates an *identity insult* by putting down another group. Group X can attribute negative features, wrong motivations, or foul values to the out-group or accuse it of performing destructive or erroneous actions. An identity insult helps in-group members put their group in a position higher than the out-group and, thus, to increase the self-esteem of in-group members. Group Y recognizes this identity insult if group members feel that their significant values and positive features are under attack and their self-esteem is targeted by the out-group. For example, in Ukraine, a group of young people created an identity insult by frying eggs on the internal flame of the Tomb of the Unknown Solder: they intended to diminish the value and achievements of the Soviet Red Army.

Group Y can also construct an identity insult even if it was not intentionally performed by group X. Group Y can perceive unintentional words or actions by group X as a reduction of the value of the in-group, denial of its goodness, and unreasonable ascription of negative features. In this case, group Y perceives actions or words of group X as threatening to its self-esteem. For example, the use of Soviet symbols during national holidays in Ukraine was perceived by the population of Western Ukraine as an insult to their positive identity as fighters against the Soviet regime.

Projection Insult

Insult can also help preserve positive images through projection. Like a child who wants to "rid itself of un-integrated 'bad' aspects of its world,"[8] people and groups try to project negative images onto others. People have a tendency to split off and externalize negative aspects of themselves—the dimensions they wish not to acknowledge, or for which they will not or cannot take responsibility. Group identity is like a "large canvas tent" that protects individuals as if they were family members.[9] As long as the tent remains strong and stable, held erect by the leader, the members of the group do not pay much attention to it—that is, they do not have the need to constantly prove or express their group identity. If the tent is shaken or disturbed, however, those who are under it become collectively preoccupied with trying to "shore it up" again. The group identity supersedes individual identities and becomes a matter of major concern.[10] In these situations, in-group members project their negative features onto out-group members. Thus, the in-group can justify its aggressiveness by the need for defense provoked by the threatening actions of an out-group. Similarly, the in-group can validate its disloyalty by attributing treason to the out-group. Minorities can easily become suitable targets for the projection of the negative feelings and images of majorities. Thus, a *projection insult* provides an opportunity to justify particular actions or eradicate the negative features of the in-group by imposing them on an out-group.

To construct a projection insult, group X can depict an out-group through negative characteristics or undesirable behaviors that group X does not want to recognize as its own. For example, members of group X can accuse the other group of impoliteness to cover up their own bad manners. Members of group X can also create a projection insult by blaming the out-group to conceal their own inabilities. For example, local governments in Tunisia describe street vendors as lazy swindlers to deflect their own responsibility for the management of street markets. It gives local managers an opportunity to harass street vendors and extract bribes. Group X can also create a projection insult by blaming the out-group for the aggressive intentions and behavior that provoke defensive behaviors of the in-group. For instance, North Korea justifies all its actions, including nuclear bomb tests, rocket launches, and declaration of war, on the aggressive, imperialistic policies of the United States.

Group Y can also construct a projection insult to warrant negative behavior. In these situations, group Y presents their adverse actions as a reaction to the insult committed by group X. Thus, group Y treats unintentional actions of group X as an insult provoking actions of group Y. While feeling embarrassed by particular actions, members of group Y can reduce feelings of guilt or responsibility by ascribing provocative intentions to the out-group. Thus, group Y portrays group X as insulting to justify it own behavior as a simple reaction to this insult. In some cases, the dynamics of projected insult can be similar to the dynamics of the security dilemma.[11] This dilemma arises from uncertainty, mutual suspicion, and fear among people regarding the out-group's intentions toward them. Similarly, the out-group's intention to insult the in-group may not exist at all, but fear and distrust can lead the in-group to view the out-group with suspicion. For example, in their dispute over a small island, the Japanese and Korean sides used a projection insult to blame each other for organizing provocations, which resulted in aggressive actions on both sides.

Divergence Insult

The third function of insults is to protect the claimed uniqueness of an in-group or differences between the in-group and out-groups. If the real or psychological borders between groups are not clear and several groups share similar characteristics, behaviors, and beliefs, the identity of a group can be at risk. A group needs to emphasize its exclusivity to protect its right to sovereignty and autonomy, ability to make decisions, and pursuit of its own goals. A group also needs to protect its uniqueness to be able to project negative images or characteristics onto the out-group: the more similar the in-group and the out-group, the harder it is to distinguish between them and exclusively ascribe negative features to the out-group. If the in-group and out-group are very similar to each other, their members stress minor differences between groups.[12] Thus, in the Ukraine, new words from the Polish language are introduced into the Ukrainian language in order to emphasize differences with Russians; in Croatia, Croatian is written exclusively in the Latin script rather than in Cyrillic, as is the Serbian language. This language-engineering helps to distinguish ethnic and national groups for political purposes. In a situation of conflict, such differences are reinforced by enemy images and the dehumanization of members of other groups. Thus, a *divergence insult* serves to enhance differences and the social boundaries if one group does not want to acknowledge similarity or resemblance.

Group X can use divergence insults to stress the differences between groups by emphasizing the negative characteristics of an out-group. The in-group can be unwilling to accept similarities with out-groups because the in-group members have biases and prejudice against these out-groups; they see the out-group as having lower social status or undesirable features, or the in-group is reluctant to accept common characteristics between themselves and the out-group. If two groups are perceived as similar but the first group does not want to be associated with the second, linking the groups will cause insult to the latter group, stressing the differences between them. For instance, the people of South Korea do not want to be associated with the atrocities and violence of World War II; thus they ascribe violent characteristics exclusively to Japan and blame the Japanese for unforgivable cruelty. Another reason for divergence insults can be a need to protect the in-group from the influence of the out-group and to impose a common identity. If group Y considers group X to be related and wants group X to accept similar values or types of actions, group X can use divergence insults to emphasize the boundary with, and reduce the influence of, group Y. For example, the population of Western Ukraine constructed divergence insults depicting East Ukrainians as totalitarian pro-Stalinists, thus resisting the imposition of pro-Soviet and pro-Russian ideology on the whole Ukraine by the East.

Group Y can construct the divergence insult by claiming that any reference to similarities between the groups, which group X is emphasizing, is insulting to group Y. This treatment of unintentional actions or words of group X as an insult helps group Y to protect itself from the dissolution of the boundary between groups. Thus, the Russian Orthodox Church sees women as mothers and wives above all; the Pussy Riot group in Russia perceives these views as insulting to them and emphasizes the differences in perceptions of women's functions in society.

Relative Insult

Insults can also be constructed in the context of the relative assessment of the in-group and the out-group. Perceptions of deprivation or disadvantage are usually based on comparisons rather than the estimation of in-group positions alone. There are several definitions of relative deprivation, which may be judged according to different standards of comparison. One of them is a comparison with the past or future: a group believes that its current position is worse than it was before. The perception of possible loss or expectations of decreasing status can also influence the emergence of relative deprivation. The second standard of comparison is a group's prospects: a group can feel offense when comparing the actual status of the in-group and expectations regarding its own position.[13] The third basis is intergroup comparison: a perception that the in-group has fewer resources or is in a lower position than other groups. People can compare their in-group with similar groups or with advantaged out-groups; the outcomes of the latter comparisons are called fraternal deprivation.[14] As a result of fraternal deprivation, members of disadvantaged groups perceive more discrimination; have stronger feelings that the other side has more resources, rights, and opportunities;[15] and are greater supporters of social change.[16] Thus, *relative insult* involves presentation of group Y as having fewer rights, resources, and capacities than group X or fewer than previously, or in comparison with group Y's expectations. Relative insult is an attempt to deny certain rights to the out-group and to emphasize the in-group's privileged position and inclusive rights to control a specific territory or group, make a decision, or to define the connotations of historic events and holidays.

Group X can create the first type of relative insult by depriving group Y of rights, resources, and capacities that group X possesses or wants to possess. For example, group X can deny that group Y has a right to make a decision in a particular situation and arrogate this right only to itself. It creates a situation in which group Y will feel relative deprivation of its rights as an insult and be offended by the fact that these rights are not extended to it. Thus, group X creates relative insult by introducing a comparative perspective. For example, representatives of eastern regions of the Ukraine state that they have a right to decide when to use the red flag for the entire Ukraine and that western regions do not have a right to change this decision.

Group X can also construct relative insult by creating reasons for group Y to view itself as in a position lower than its previous position or its expectations. Thus, group X can change its relations with group Y: remove previous support, not fulfill promises, or worsen the state of relations. Group X can change previous conditions of cooperation with group Y, thus offending group Y by worsening existing favorable conditions. For example, Armenians perceived the release of an Azeri officer who murdered an Armenian officer as an insult. In response, Armenia broke off diplomatic relations with Hungary, thus creating another relative insult.

The members of group Y can see relative insult in the actions of the third group that provides some resources to group X or supports group X's particular rights. They feel offense when group X receives something—a political gain for instance—even if they do not actually have a desire for it. For example, the in-group can perceive affirmative action supporting group X as a relative insult even if it does not need this social benefit in their own social position. A relative insult is evident when the population of Western Ukraine perceives that the population of Eastern Ukraine and ethnic Russians are favored by the new Ukrainian government at the expense of the Ukrainian ethnic group.

Group Y can also construct a relative insult by perceiving changes in relations with group X as offensive if these changes worsen its previous position or reduce its expectations. These actions of group X can result from new circumstances or changes in its strategic orientations that do not have any specific connections with group Y. However, group Y may believe that group X intends to insult it by proposing new conditions of cooperation or by setting some limitations on the activities of group Y. Group Y can also perceive as an insult an inability of group X to change its actions or policies to improve the position of group Y or to meet its expectations. For example, in London thousands of Muslim demonstrators marched on the offices of Google, demanding that the company remove the insulting film *Innocence of Muslims* from the Internet.

Power Insult

Concepts of power also help illuminate the nature of insults. The classic definition of power characterizes it as the ability of one party to influence the behavior of the other, and the ability of the other party to achieve its power.[17] Power also involves dependence and coercion against people's will, changing their will and beliefs through norms and social consensus.[18] A group in power can possess two sets of values: welfare values (necessary conditions including well-being, wealth, skill) and deference values whose necessary conditions include taking into consideration power, respect, and reputation. The rest of the people are dependent upon "influencing power" for the satisfaction of their needs and desires or the fulfillments of their goals. These resources depend on the obedience and cooperation of the subjects as well as their contributions to the established system.[19] The perception of a group serves as a precondition of influence rather than simply an outcome.[20] The classic typology of power[21] includes five types: (1) reward power, based on perception that a leader has the ability to mediate rewards; (2) coercive power, based on perception that a leader can produce a punishment; (3) legitimate power, based on perception of the legitimate rights of a leader; (4) referent power, based on identification with a leader; and (5) expert power, based on acknowledgment of the specific knowledge or expertise of a leader. Another approach[22] defines three types of power: institutional power, a capacity to dominate the group; generative power, a group's capacity for mobilizing skills and multiplying resources; and ecological power, which mobilizes and directs activities toward the outside world. Despite differences in typologies, scholars agree that leaders can have power over others by virtue of resources under their control or from mobilization and inspiration to follow the path leaders outline. The former can be defined as a coercive power and the latter as a legitimate power. Thus, a *power insult* occurs in situations where there is competition for coercive power, both real and perceived. A power insult aims to decrease absolute or relative coercive power of the out-group in comparison with the in-group.

Group X constructs a power insult if it perceives a threat to its power vis-à-vis the increasing power of group Y. This occurs if group Y is getting more rights to ownership or influence over some groups; gaining rewards, support, or punishment; or getting wider recognition of its knowledge or skills, or more people identify themselves with group Y (acceptance of an out-group's legitimate authority will be discussed separately below). In this case, the insult aims at restoring a balance of power by decreasing positive social acceptance of group Y by others. A power insult can also aim directly at group Y by stressing its weak abilities or position. For example, the populations of both Eastern and Western Ukraine justify a privileged position in society and impose their power over the other side using insults connected to the history of World War II.

Group Y can construct a power insult by claiming that the other side has overused its power or uses an unacceptable type of power in a given situation. In the former case, the insult is perceived as an imposition of power: group Y blames group X for forcing it to do something or depriving it of something. For instance, Japan believes that South Korea does not have rights to the disputed island and overuses its power to defend its ownership. In the latter, the power insult is constructed because group Y believes that the same aim could be achieved by different means, for example, the use of reward instead of punishment. Another example is that of Armenia believing that Hungary misused its judicial power by transferring a convicted murder to Azerbaijan without ensuring that he serves his time in prison.

Legitimacy Insult

The fight for legitimacy is the most important source of insults based on power relations. Legitimate power depends on internalized values and acceptance of a leader's legitimate rights to influence people who are obligated to accept this influence. Legitimacy is the moral basis of social interaction, resting on certain claims by one group that other groups can accept or reject based on their perceptions of rightfulness or fairness.[23] Thus, legitimacy includes two levels: that of the claim and that of the claimant. Legitimization involves the redefinition of an action, policy, system, or group, in the way that what was previously illegitimate now becomes legitimate, or what was previously optional now becomes obligatory.[24] This process increases the moral acceptance of the claim and claimant, and the acknowledgment of the rights and power of the claimant. Delegitimization likewise diminishes these. Both processes are facilitated by authorities and operate in tandem, decreasing the moral acceptance of one group and policies associated with it and increasing the moral acceptance of the other group. The intensity of this normative shift in perception of groups depends on the congruence of this recategorization with the in-group's interests and preferences. In-group willingness to accept the legitimacy of specific out-groups or their actions plays an important role in the legitimization process. It is also significantly affected by the historic and structural dispositions of the society. Thus, a *legitimacy insult* initiates and promotes a recategorization process that legitimizes one side and delegitimizes the other.

Group X constructs a legitimacy insult by legitimizing itself and/or delegitimizing group Y. A legitimacy insult can increase the claim of group X to make a decision or commit a specific action because it is more capable than group Y. It can also challenge the justifications of group Y's rightful power to obligate or restrict actions of group X. The dual legitimacy insult aims to both increase its own validity and decrease the rightfulness of group

X. For example, some regional Western administrations in Ukraine made the decision to rename Victory Day as the Day of Grief and invite veterans of the anti-Soviet underground organization UPA into schools to tell pupils about its heroic fights against both Soviet and Nazi regimes. By this dual insult they reduced the legitimacy of the Soviet narrative and increased the legitimacy of nationalistic ideology.

The members of group Y construct a legitimacy insult by claiming that the actions of group X are insulting to them. While these actions are completely unintentional and do not target group Y, group Y treats them as an unprovoked offense. It gives group Y an ability to reduce the legitimacy of group X as an aggressor or perpetrator, and at the same time increases the legitimacy of group Y as the innocent victim. In the Ukraine, communists and veterans of the Red Army viewed the ban of the red flag issued in many regions of the Ukraine as a delegitimization of their ideals and a legitimization of Nazi supporters in Western Ukraine.

INSULT AND AGGRESSION

This analysis confirms our definition of intergroup insult as a linguistic or behavioral act constructed by both groups and as an interruption in the mutual production of the meaning of identity and power. It is important to note here that this approach differs from the views on insult as a result of aggression. I believe that both forms of aggression—affective and instrumental—arrive from the six motivations for insult presented above and constitute the emotional foundation of insult as an offensive act. Frustration can result from a threat to self-esteem, the need to acknowledge a negative fact about the in-group, increasing similarity with an out-group, feelings of relative deprivation, or loss of power or legitimacy.

Retaliatory aggression, elicited in response to real or imagined provocation, can be the product of deprivation of positive identity or reduction in legitimacy. For example, group X can feel the threat to its self-esteem or believe that group Y wants to increase its legitimacy and obtain more influence or authority. Thus retaliatory aggression will be the part of *identity insult* or *power insult*. Displaced aggression—offense resulting from frustration caused by the other side—can be the result of an insult by a more powerful group or by the groups claiming influence based on similarity between groups. For instance, group X can feel frustration because group Y wants to impose its values and ideas over it. Thus, displaced aggression will be the part of *legitimacy insult* or *divergence insult*.

Instrumental aggression can be used to increase self-esteem, project negative knowledge about the in-group onto the out-group, increase distance from and differences with the out-group, reduce feelings of relative deprivation, restore a balance of power or obtain more power, or legitimize the in-group and delegitimize the out-group. In these situations, aggression will be the part of insults constructed by group X, which will use them as a tool for achieving its goals. Annoyance with somebody can be an outcome of a threat to self-esteem or positive self-image, boundary intrusion, changing balance of power, illegitimate actions by one side, or enforced delegitimization. In these situations, aggression will be part of the insults constructed by group Y, which will see insults in unintentional actions of group X. Thus, I treat aggression not as a direct cause of an insult, but as its emotional component arriving from the disruption of the processes of mutual production and reproduction of identity and power. As this disruption causes pain in relations, aggression emerges as an inevitable part of insults.

TYPES OF INSULT

As we discussed above, group X can produce an insult intentionally, or its actions can be unintentional. Group Y can recognize actions of group Y as insult or fail to recognize them as offensive (see Table 1.1).

Congruous and Futile insult

An insult produced intentionally by group X and recognized by group Y as an offense can be called a *congruous insult*. A *congruous identity insult* occurs when group X aims to increase its self-esteem or restore a positive identity

Table 1.1 TYPES OF INSULT

		Group X	
		Intention	No intention
Group Y	Recognizes insult	Congruous insult	Attributed insult
	Does not recognize	Futile insult	Potential insult (perceived by a third party or parties)

[24] *Political Insults*

by targeting the identity of group Y, and group Y recognizes the offense to its self-esteem or group image. A *congruous projection insult* occurs when group X aims to eliminate accusations of wrongdoing and blames group Y for the provocation of these actions; group Y sees these actions as unjust and attempts to increase the responsibility of group X. A *congruous divergence insult* occurs when group X intends to increase social distance from group Y, using offense to emphasize distinctions; group Y perceives these foundations for distinction as insulting. A *congruous relative insult* occurs when group X deprives the insulted party of its rights and abilities, which the insulted party perceives as an intentional offense. A congruous relative insult also occurs when group X worsens the position of group Y or reduces its perspectives to meet expectations. Subsequently, group Y sees group X as a source of these relative deprivations. A *congruous power insult* occurs when group X aims to restore the balance of power or increase its power, and employs abuse to decrease the power of group Y; group Y sees this as an offense to its lawful rights to execute different types of power including reward, coercive, referent, or expert power. A *congruous legitimacy insult* occurs when group X legitimizes its own power and delegitimizes the power of group Y; group Y sees offense in the denial or diminution of its legitimacy.

An insult that is produced intentionally by group X but is not recognized as insult by group Y is called a *futile insult*. A futile insult is constructed by group X in six ways, similar to a *congruous* insult, but group Y does not perceive offense in these actions and does not generate any reaction.

Attributed Insult

An insult that is not intentionally produced by group X but is claimed as intentional by group Y is called an *attributed insult*. An *attributed identity insult* occurs when group Y perceives a threat to self-esteem or positive identity in the unintentional actions of the other side. An *attributed projection insult* occurs when group Y presents its adverse actions as a reaction to the insult committed by group X, in spite of group X's actions being unintentional. An *attributed divergence insult* occurs when group Y claims that any references of similarities between the groups, which group X is emphasizing, are insulting to group Y, and that in making this emphasis, group X is imposing its identity, norms, and beliefs onto group Y. An *attributed relative insult* occurs when group Y thinks that group X is depriving it of its rights and abilities; in addition, group Y believes that group X intends to insult it by proposing new unfavorable conditions of cooperation, or by setting some limitations on the activities of group Y. An *attributed power insult* occurs when group Y declares that group X has overused its power or is using a type of power—reward, coercive, referent, or expert—that is improper to the given social context or structure. An *attributed legitimacy insult* occurs when group Y claims that group X unjustly legitimizes its own power and delegitimizes the power of group Y.

Potential Insult

An insult that is not intentionally produced and is not recognized by group Y is called a *potential insult*. Because neither group constructs this insult, at first glance it should not be considered an insult. However, it is treated as intergroup insult for two reasons: the impact on culture, and effects on a third party. First, if a potential insult is not recognized as an insult in a specific cultural context, it may still be perceived as an insult by another cultural group, or may later be considered an insult if sociocultural norms change. For example, the normative characteristics of a "culture of honor" among southern white males increases the likelihood of perception of insults that threaten their masculine reputation, increasing their readiness to engage in aggressive and dominant behavior.[25] The Western approach to Aboriginal people that treats them like children and fails to exhibit respect for their views can be considered as insult that not only constrains the relationship with them, but also plays a role in keeping Aboriginal peoples poor and politically disempowered.[26]

Second, the analysis of potential insult requires the analysis of the role of a third party in the dynamics of insult. The third party can confirm or denounce the insult produced by group X and reinforce or reduce the effect on group Y. While the third party is not central to the insult, it has a significant affect on its dynamics: it can effect a transformation between different types of insult. So, a potential insult can become attributed, fertile, or congruous depending on the sensitizing influence of the third party on group X, group Y, or both.

DYNAMICS OF INSULT

Transfer of Insult

Intergroup insult has complex dynamics. The more salient the in-group identity, the greater the likelihood that an insult to one in-group member or a small group within the in-group will be perceived as an insult to other in-group members or the entire in-group. This process is called a *transfer of insult* within the group—the perception that an insult targeted to some in-group members is an insult to the whole in-group. Transfer is more likely to occur if relations between the two groups are conflictual or if in-group members see differences between the groups as more significant than differences within the groups. This perception, called metacontrast, increases the awareness of intergroup differences in values, beliefs, and attitudes as well as similarities of members within the groups.[27] In this circumstance, any insult that targets an in-group member is perceived as an out-group attack on the entire in-group, and is felt by all in-group members. For example, transfer of insult occurs when the political and ideological leaders of a social group in conflict vigorously explain in their statements and publications why the actions of the out-group should be considered as offenses and treated as insults. The South Korean president, Lee Myung-bak, made a public statement that the emperor should apologize for Japan's harsh 1910–1945 colonial rule of the Korean Peninsula. This statement was perceived as a projection and legitimacy insult by the Japanese leadership, and it presented the statement to the general public as an insult to the whole of Japan. As a result, the Japanese government received full public support to employ harsh economic policies (reconsideration of an agreement with Seoul to engage in a so-called currency swap), and recalled the Japanese ambassador to South Korea.

Sensitizing

The process of transfer can be more effective if some in-group members enlighten other in-group members on why the out-group insult is important and how it impacts the in-group's image. In this situation, the members of group Y believe that they need to react to group X's insult to defend the identity of their group. This process can be called *sensitizing*: an increase of the motivation to protect the identity, self-esteem, and social position of group Y in the face of insult. This need to protect the image of group Y also depends on the salience of the identity of group Y and the history of conflict relations between groups X and Y. For example, the Russian Orthodox Church (ROC) presented Pussy Riot's "Punk Prayer" not only as blasphemy against the Orthodox religion, but also as an insult to the national identity of all Russian people. Numerous ROC statements appealed to the memories of a glorified war and invoked the patriotic feelings of Russian citizens. While the "Punk Prayer" did not express any overt connections to the history of Russia, the ROC creatively united the insult to the church with the insult to the heroism of the defenders of the motherland, connecting religious and national feelings and thus sensitizing all Russian citizens to this insult.

Learned Insult

Members of the in-group may also unintentionally influence the recognition of the actions of group X as an insult. A particular action of group X may not be perceived as insult by some members of group Y, but they can observe the reactions of other in-group members to it. Insulted in-group members can explain to other members of group Y why the words or actions of group X are insulting, thus imposing their perception of an insult on all members of group Y. Such an insult can be called a *learned insult*: in-group members "discover" the potency of a particular insult from other in-group members, and will subsequently treat it as an insult to the entire in-group. Within hours, Bouazizi's self-immolation became a learned insult for many unemployed young people in Tunisia and gave rise to protests around the country. Police attempts to settle the unrest only fueled violent reactions.

Generalization of Insult

A particular action of group X that is similar to an insulting act may also be perceived as an insult. The gesture of group X that is not intended as insulting and contains no insulting content, but is similar to a previous insult, is likely to be considered insulting by group Y. This process can be called *generalization of insult*: the actions and words of group X can be perceived as an insult based on their similarity to a previous insult. This process of generalization starts with a single action but gradually involves greater numbers of actions and words that can be labeled as insults because of their similarity. The meaning attributed to an insult becomes more general and multifaceted, including an increasing range of actions that differ more and more from the initial insult. *Generalized insult* can construct specific areas of meaning that reside on the social boundary between groups, and serve as tools for assessment of group X's actions and triggers for the reactions of group Y. For example, group X constructs an identity insult, targeting the self-esteem of group Y, by underestimating its overall level of education. Group Y then begins to see all words or actions of group X connected to the education of group Y as insulting, gradually seeing any action by group

X connected with cultural and social features of group Y as an insult. As a result, any time group X mentions cultural, educational, or social positions of group Y, the latter perceives this as intentional insult and responds with an aggressive reaction toward group X. The process of generalization of insult is evident in the disputes over islands between Japan and China and South Korea. All new actions connected with the disputed islands were perceived as new insults.

Conglomeration of Insult

The perception of insults also depends on their frequency. The more often an insult is repeated by group X, the more it is perceived as offensive and abusive by group Y. This process can be called *conglomeration of insult*: the impact of frequency on the perception of an insult's effects. If group X specifically targets group Y's identity, self-esteem, uniqueness, power position, or legitimacy and continues to construct similar insults over and over again, each new insult becomes more and more belligerent. The frequency of insults produced by the populations of western and southeastern Ukraine regarding the use of the red flag increased their perception as increasingly offensive and abusive, exemplifying the conglomeration of insult.

Delayed Insult

Some insults are not recognized as insults immediately, but are perceived as such after some period of time. This happens because an insult can be learned from other in-group members or a third party, or because of its inclusion in an expanding category of generalized insult. In both cases, the meaning of the insult develops over time, and the insulted party cannot respond to it immediately because the insult is not yet recognized. Nonetheless this insult will contribute to the conglomeration process: if the same insult or a similar one is repeated, it can generate a reaction more severe than would be provoked by a single insult. This insult can be called a *delayed insult*—the recognition of an insult some time after it was uttered. The conglomeration process can involve transferred and learned insults, resulting in the development of chosen trauma[28] that describes particular insults from the past as traumatic events still unmourned by the in-group. Conglomeration of insult is also central to mythic narratives[29] of suffering and unjust treatment that are used to justify present-day in-group perceptions and actions.

Diffusion and Reactivation

Some learned and generalized insults can become less offensive with time. Because learned insults arise from the imposition of meaning by other in-group members or a third party, they do not have a deep meaning for group Y, and their impact can gradually diminish. Similarly, because generalized insults are created through their inclusion in generalized areas of meaning, they have less potential energy and do not remain potent for very long. Such a process can be called *diffusion of insult*—a loss of the offensive effect of insult over time. However, in some situations, diffused insults can be reactivated and regain their potential. This process can be called *reactivation of insult*—the reappearance of a perception of offense long after the insult was perpetrated. Reactivation is often a product of public revalidation of past experiences. In the dispute between Japan and South Korea over islands known as Takeshima in Japan and Dokdo in Korea, both countries employ historic traumas and historic narratives of victimization. The traumatic experiences of World War II are central to the fight for power in Ukraine.

Through the dynamics of insult, the six forms of insult described above can be constructed separately or interwoven within other forms of insult. For example, insulting actions of group X aiming to increase self-esteem can also delegitimize group Y, thus connecting identity insult and legitimacy insult. Attributing a divergence insult to group X, group Y can also treat actions of group X as a projection insult. The leading type of insult can be identified based on the primary motivation of the groups X and Y that leads them to the construction of a particular insult.

The discussion on typology and dynamics of insult emphasizes the factors that produce insults and sheds light on the role of insults in conflict dynamics. In the case studies in the following chapters I will use this insult matrix and the conceptual framework elaborated above to analyze insults and the intergroup relations associated with them. The pervasiveness of insults as a perceived relational feature and an openly invoked frame of reference invites a careful examination of the cases and further study of insulting behavior as a concept and a process. The narratives discussed in the case studies represent attempts to reflect the existing debates and positions of the relevant actors themselves—they do not necessarily reflect the author's views. They are presented here in a simplified form, occasionally preserving historical inaccuracies embedded in the original respondents' narratives.

CHAPTER 2
Pussy Riot in Russia

On February 21, 2012, five young women entered the Cathedral of Christ the Savior in Moscow, shed their winter clothing at the altar, and began a performance of a "Punk Prayer," containing crude language directed toward Putin and Kirill I, the Moscow Patriarch of the Russian Orthodox Church (ROC). This 40-second performance, which normally would be treated as petty hooliganism, provoked an unusually harsh reaction by the government and the ROC, resulting in a two-year prison sentence for the young singers. One would expect that such a harsh verdict and the documented mistreatment of the women while they were in detention would provoke criticism and public protests against the government's actions. However, all polls showed that the majority of the Russian population supported the verdict and was satisfied with the government policy. Why did it happen? What are the reasons behind public support for the severe punishment for this short and silly performance? Analysis of insults delivered by the Pussy Riot, the government, and the ROC in this incident will reveal the deep roots of the current social conflict in Russia and help us better understand the dynamics of relations between government, the ROC, and the Russian public.

Vladimir Putin is now enjoying his third term as president of Russia, with a gap between his second and third terms mandated by the terms limits specified in the Russian constitution. During Dmitry Medvedev's presidency from 2008 to 2012, Putin served as prime minister, maintaining his position of power in a sequence of officeholders extending beyond Putin himself: "Changing the figure at the top—from Yeltsin to Putin, Putin to Medvedev, and now back to Putin again—became another of the means for keeping the system going as it created the illusion of change without actually changing the basic construction."[1] Therefore, Putin's election in 2012 was not a surprise. Despite mass protests against his reelection for the third term, Putin enjoys support from the majority of the population. In 2012, the percentage of the Russian population satisfied with his presidency ranged from 63 to 69 percent.[2] Only 32 percent of population saw his candidacy for a third term as unlawful, while around half of all Russian citizens saw his re-election as legitimate.[3] However, support for Putin has declined over the years: while in 2012 67 percent of the population had a positive assessment of Putin, this was a sharp decline from April 2008, when he had an 89 percent approval rating. Over the years, Russian citizens have also changed their opinion about Putin's personal qualities, seeing him as less decisive, energetic, intellectual, educated, responsible, and honest.[4]

To compensate for Putin's weakening popularity, state propaganda undertook to formulate a specific national identity of the Russian citizen: law-abiding, respectful to the state, and Orthodox. The resurgence of the Orthodox Church is not confined to Russia, but is an international phenomenon: "The Orthodox Churches in post-communist Eastern Europe have assumed increasingly prominent roles in shaping the new democracies, defining the boundaries of acceptable social norms, and influencing the electoral processes and party politics."[5] In 2012, two-thirds of the population believed that "the genuine Russian" should be Orthodox (69 percent) and respect the existing political regime (81 percent). Since 1989, the proportion of population who consider themselves Orthodox has increased more than fivefold, from 16 to 87 percent.[6] At the same time, only half of these people believe in God, and only 5 percent of Russians call themselves observant.[7] Only around 50 percent attended church at least once per year.[8] Thus, "being Orthodox" replaced "being a Soviet" in the consciousness of the Russian people, becoming a dominant feature of the social category "Russian." This model of the "ideal Russian" is a reflection of identity imposed by state propaganda: "People accept the structure that is given to them: 'To be Russian, it is important to be Orthodox.'"[9] This acceptance of Orthodox religion as a core of national identity is linked to submission to the state, suggesting a deep belief that the state defines society rather than vice versa.

The prevalence of the state over people is promoted by the close relationship between the Russian government and the ROC: "Political leaders, not only those from the radical right, rediscovered Orthodoxy as a legitimation element."[10] According to law, the Russian Federation is a secular state, without an established religion, where all religious organizations are equal before the law. However, the preamble to the 1997 federal law About the Freedom of Conscience and Religious Organizations recognizes the "special contribution" of Russian Orthodox Christianity to the country's history and to the establishment and development of its spirituality and culture.[11] In the last decade, the ROC has played an increasingly important role in politics, routinely consulting with government officials on policy. In July 2009, for example, Putin's political party, United Russia, and Patriarch Kirill announced an agreement allowing the ROC to review all draft legislation pending before the Duma. As a result, the ROC presented a package of proposals regarding the social and economic program of United Russia, extending Orthodox influence over Russian life.[12] On November 21, 2011, President Medvedev granted the Patriarch use of patriarchal chambers in the Faceted Palace within the Kremlin for meetings, receptions, and negotiations. The government also provides him with security guards and access to official vehicles, a privilege reserved mainly for state officials.[13] The ROC's leaders regularly visit neighboring countries on diplomatic missions, attending the inauguration of the newly elected president of Ukraine in February 2010, for example, and the foreign minister has praised the ROC for "playing a major role in bolstering Russia's international position."[14]

The interconnection between the government and the ROC is underscored by their respective leadership. At a meeting with representatives of the ROC in 2011, President Medvedev stressed the crucial role of Orthodox Christianity in the preservation of Russian traditional values and in countering doctrines that give rise to social strife, hostility, violence, and instability:

> Speaking about these 20 years from the perspective of my feelings as an Orthodox man, what happened is a miracle. Frankly speaking, I could not imagine 15 to 20 years ago that the recovery, the acquisition of faith for the vast majority of our people, would have such quick pace.... Today, thanks to our common activities and the efforts of the Holy Patriarch, the church fruitfully cooperates with government structures and social institutions.... We need to find enough will and energy to advance the values traditional to our state. It is especially important in a complex and quickly changing world, in the global informational space, that creates not only benefits but also very serious challenges. The church serves as the keeper of such everlasting values and immutable truths for our country.[15]

The president also noted that ideas different from mainstream Orthodox thinking are destructive for the country and may harm people. Thus, he posited Orthodox religion as a moral guide in defining good and evil, and united submission to the faith with the obedience to the state: "The Orthodox religion helps numerous people not only find themselves in life, but also understand very simple things. For example: what does it mean to be Russian, what is the mission of our people, what in a particular period made our people great and distinctive, and what in a particular time created many challenges for our people and our state, our Orthodox Church."[16]

President Putin also stressed the importance of collaboration between the government and the church. During a meeting with the religious leaders of the Russian Federation, Putin emphasized that "from the moment of the breakdown of the Soviet Union, neither the country nor any single person could lean morally on anything else besides religious values.... Today secularity should be based on a new regime of interrelations between the state and religious organizations—a regime of partnership, mutual help, and support."[17] He called the Orthodox religion a "state-building" religion and stressed that "we must inculcate ethnical norms in the consciousness of each our citizens."[18]

The ROC also issued public statements advocating the unity of church and state, as "one community" with "two autonomous powers."[19] The Patriarch's "Address at the Opening of the Eighteenth International Christmas Readings" emphasizes "the role that the ROC can play in strengthening the post-Soviet Russian state. Here, Patriarch Kirill functions almost explicitly as a political, rather than religious, authority figure."[20] Indeed his views on the political life of the country are conservative and support the power of the state over citizens. On March 18, 2010, Patriarch Kirill told students and faculty of Erevan State University in Armenia that political pluralism was "a toy" and "a passing fad." "It is not ours, not a church idea, political pluralism.... The values and traditions of the Christian religion are common values for all Russian people."[21]

The Russian people recognize the close relation between the ROC and the government. More than 50 percent of Russian citizens believe that the ROC has a significant influence on the state, and 49 percent think that the church collaborates with the Federal Security Service (FSB). Less than half of the population (48 percent) believes that only a return to Orthodox values can supply a basis for spiritual revival of Russia, and 14 percent believe that this interrelation between the state and church is too excessive. Only 30 percent of people think that the Patriarch is decent, and 23 percent that he is truthful.[22]

The ROC has tried to restore its positive image among the population and denied its close connection to the government, calling it as a myth.[23] Patriarch Kirill characterized the supposed relationship as a "pseudo-ideology, which is replacing Communist ideology. From this point arrives a conclusion: the church is dangerous for freedom; it will enslave your consciousness."[24] To destroy this myth, the Patriarch employed a *legitimacy insult*: he asserted that people blame the church for its close connection to the state because they support degraded goals. Thus, he delegitimized the opposition by connecting it to evil. In an interview he stressed, "It is a replacement of ideas. Our opponents are afraid, not of coalescence, but of the Christianization of our society. This [opposition] is the source of Devil's horns. The fear is that Orthodoxy, which was practically destroyed during the Soviet era, was able to return to the life of its people over the last 20 years."[25] The Patriarch not only moves the discussion from the collaboration of the ROC with the government to the process of increasing faith among the population, but posits that the opponents of a close relationship between the ROC and the state are enemies of Orthodoxy. He uses a metaphor of "horns" to emphasize the evil character of his adversaries.

The Patriarch furthered this legitimacy insult in another interview, stressing the moral prevalence of the church and the sinful character of all views that oppose the church's values.

> Today we live in a so-called era of postmodernity, when people insist not only on the right, but also on a necessity, to deny objective truth and, in relation to moral themes, common moral value.... And sin, which only yesterday was censured, today is introduced not only into the philosophy of the contemporary man, not only into practice, but also into law. In many countries, as we know, sinful manifestations of human passion are legalized. To resist this destruction of moral consensus in the society, the church must speak strongly and very persuasively. And as the church is gaining this power, it faces a huge organized opposition who defend the right of a person to sin.... The church will not stop showing that one choice is for good and another is for evil.[26]

In this statement, Patriarch emphasizes that the church needs power to oppose the growing tendency to legalize sins, and thus close relations between the church and state are crucial for the defense of truthful values and morality. He validates the close collaboration of the ROC and the government by means of the need to have the power to protect law and society and stresses that people who oppose this coalescence of the ROC and the government contest Orthodoxy, calling them supporters of evil goals. He delegitimizes their efforts to prevent further conjoining of faith and state institutions. Thus, a *legitimacy insult* is used to validate close collaboration between the church and the state, and disapprove of the sinful and evil intentions of the opposition.

For committed Orthodox Christians, who believe that the church connects people to God, this link between church and government seems a deep *identity insult*. The online media sensitized the public to this insult by printing stories alleging that the Patriarch enjoys luxuries that contravene the vow of poverty he took when he became a monk. These stories include selling cigarettes without paying the customs, spending 20 million rubles for the renovation of his apartments, and wearing a $30,000 Swiss watch, stories perceived as identity insults by church followers.

The watch, however, was more than a story. In 2009, the Patriarch was photographed wearing an expensive Breguet timepiece, and the photo was published on several websites, including the official site of the ROC. It provoked a negative reaction among the faithful, who perceived it as an insult to their religious faith and thus themselves. The following statements reflect this identity insult:

> To wear such watch, and at the same time to make speeches that renounce wealth and consumption, is not serious.
> Jesus Christ came to Jerusalem on a donkey and did not rent a gold carriage with white horses and camels and Roman legions as security forces. Jesus threw such people as Patriarch Kirill out from the Church.
> The new deception does not surprise any more.... Let them lie, if it does not contradict the religion that they worship.[27]

These statements, also insulting in their form, show that the public believes that the wealth of the church leader is in contradiction with Orthodox religious values and identity and offensive to the religious feelings of Orthodox believers.

Responding to this criticism, the Patriarch issued a statement that somebody intentionally added the watch to this photo, and that he did not wear such a watch even though he does own one: "Many people came and made gifts. And often I do not open boxes and do not know what is inside. And I found that I really have a Breguet watch, and that is why I never made any statements that the Patriarch does not have such a watch. Because yes, the box with such a watch, never worn, exists."[28] Following this statement, the real photo with the scandalous watch was edited on the ROC site. The watch was removed from the hand of the Patriarch, but, owing to amateurish editing, remained reflected in a tabletop.[29] When the public saw that the watch had "miraculously" vanished from his photos, the embarrassed Patriarch's press service had to acknowledge "a ridiculous mistake."[30] According to the official statement, "The photo, which provoked perplexity, was returned to its initial form. The edited photo has been removed from the cache-memory of the server for the site Patriarchia.ru. We apologize to all users of the site for the technical lapse."[31] The statement stressed that employees in the photoediting section of the patriarch's offices made the mistake and removed the watch from the photo without any special intent.

These events resulted in a new wave of identity insults on the Internet. For example, in one altered photo, one could see only the watch, without the Patriarch; a cartoon showed the Patriarch seeing only his watch in the mirror; another depicted Jesus asking the Patriarch, "What time is it now?" All of these satirical images aimed to strip the ROC of its positive identity and create a negative image of its leadership, thus creating *identity insults*.

Such scandals swirling around the Patriarch undermine the position of the ROC as a whole. Many Russians believe that the Patriarch is protected by the state and enjoys enormous support from the president. Moreover, for those with progressive views, this fusion of the church with a totalitarian regime is an identity insult. For these Russians it is disturbing to see the collaborative propagation of antiprogressive values, including limiting marriage to the union between a man and a woman and the reduction of women's rights. Many women also disagree with the conservative views of the ROC on the role of women in family and society. Pussy Riot became one expression of this disagreement.

Pussy Riot was formed in protest against President Putin's third-term presidency and the growing connection between the Orthodox Church and the government. The very purpose of the group was to perpetrate *identity* and *legitimacy insults*. The name of the group itself is insulting: it unites a degrading name for women's genitals with the idea of rebellion. In their statements members of the group oppose the debasing practices of the current regime, and offer themselves as a force for positive change, thus creating a negative identity for the government and a positive identity for their group. They create a *legitimacy insult*, citing high-level corruption, common poverty, and the loss of civil rights under Putin, calling Russia "a third-world dictatorship with all its nice and classy features: horrible economy based on natural resources, unbelievable levels of corruption, absence of independent courts, and a dysfunctional political system. And under Putin we are up for another decade of brutal sexism and conformism as official government policies."[32] They compare Putin's Russia to Libya under Gaddafi and North Korea under Kim Jong-un. In their statements regarding their goals, members of the group declared: "We realized that this country needs a militant, punk-feminist, street band that will rip through Moscow's streets and squares, mobilize public energy against the evil crooks of the Putinist junta and enrich the Russian cultural and political opposition with themes that are important to us: gender and LGBT rights, problems of masculine conformity, absence of a daring political messages on the musical and art scenes, and the domination of males in all areas of public discourse."[33]

Pussy Riot also aims to combat sexism against women: "Sexists have certain ideas about how a woman should behave, and Putin, by the way, also has a couple thoughts on how Russians should live. Fighting against all that—that's Pussy Riot."[34] The group believes that they are reviving the idea of unapologetic feminism in their fight against patriarchy, the blurred line between state and church, and male dominance. Yet they insist that there is much more work to be done on this front. Connecting themselves with feminist "Riot Grrrl" revolutionary movements and the musical tradition of bands like Le Tigre, Bikini Kill, L7, Sleater-Kinney, and Bratmobile, the women state, "We developed what they did in the 1990s, although in an absolutely different context and with an exaggerated political stance, which leads to all of our performances being illegal."[35]

Thus, in their statements, Pussy Riot created a *legitimacy insult*, positioning the Russian government as a third-world dictatorship. They delegitimized the current regime, pointing out that the power of Putin leads to corruption, absence of the rule of law, and human rights violations. They also called the current Russian government sexist, promoting men over women and revoking LGBT rights. They also positioned themselves as genuine defenders of human rights, especially the rights of women, and fighters against totalitarian regimes. Their legitimacy is based on a defense of gender and LGBT rights and rejection of male patriarchal dominance.

To *sensitize* the society, the group organized several public presentations. On January 20, 2012, Pussy Riot publicly performed their song "Putin Wet Himself / Revolt in Russia" in Red Square, Moscow's central square near the Kremlin. The song contained the following worlds:

> A column of insurgents moves toward the Kremlin
> Windows shatter in FSB offices
> The bitches piss themselves behind the red walls
> The Pussy Riot announces its abortion of the system
>
> Attack at dawn? I will gladly
> be whipped for our freedom and yours
> The Virgin in Majesty will teach us how to shout
> The feminist Mary Magdalene went to the demonstration
>
> Riot in Russia—from the charisma of protest
> Riot in Russia—Putin wet himself

Riot in Russia—we do exist
Riot in Russia—riot, riot

Get out in the street
and live on the Red Square
Show the liberty
of the wrath of the citizen

We are not satisfied with the culture of masculine hysteria
Gang leaders' management devours the brain
The Orthodox Church is the religion of the cruel penis
Patients get a prescription for conformity

The regime goes toward dream censorship
The time has come for a subversive clash
The pack of bitches from the sexist regime
will beg forgiveness from the feminist phalanx

Riot in Russia—from the charisma of protest
Riot in Russia—Putin wet himself
Riot in Russia—we do exist
Riot in Russia—riot, riot

Get out in the street
and live on the Red Square.
Show the liberty
of the wrath of the citizen.[36]

There are two major components of the legitimacy insult in Pussy Riot's statements: delegitimization of (*a*) totalitarianism and censorship by the current regime in Russia and (*b*) male dominance promoted by the church, which is strongly supported by the government. They use offensive words like "bitches," "gang," "pack," "piss/wet themselves," and "cruel penis" to reduce the adequacy of the government and of the ROC. According to the song, the two institutions have conglomerated into an illegitimate "sexist regime" that "devours the brain" and promotes "masculine hysteria." The women also increase their own validity by connecting Pussy Riot with the ideal of freedom and "charisma of protest" that leads to "abortion of the system."

The group became famous through their performance of the song "Punk Prayer" in a Russian Orthodox Cathedral in Moscow on February 21,

2012. They entered the Cathedral of Christ the Savior, shed their winter clothing at the altar and began a performance of "Punk Prayer." Desiring anonymity based on their anarchic aspirations, they wore bright-colored balaclavas that covered the whole head, leaving only the eyes exposed. The song included prayers to Virgin Mary to turn feminist and to rid Russia of President Putin, and also contained crude language directed toward both Putin and the Moscow patriarch Kirill I.

The song contained the following words:

> Virgin Mary, Mother of God, banish Putin, banish Putin,
> Virgin Mary, Mother of God, banish him, we pray thee!
> Congregations genuflect,
>
> Black robes brag gilt epaulettes,
> Freedom's phantom's gone to heaven,
> Gay Pride's chained and in detention.
> KGB's chief saint descends
> To guide the punks to prison vans.
>
> Don't upset His Saintship, ladies,
> Stick to making love and babies.
> Crap, crap, this godliness crap!
> Crap, crap, this holiness crap!
>
> Virgin Mary, Mother of God.
> Be a feminist, we pray thee,
> Be a feminist, we pray thee.
>
> Bless our festering bastard-boss.
> Let black cars parade the Cross.
> The Missionary's in class for cash.
> Meet him there, and pay his stash.
>
> Patriarch Gundy believes in Putin.
> Better believe in God, you vermin!
> Fight for rights, forget the rite—
> Join our protest, Holy Virgin.
>
> Virgin Mary, Mother of God, banish Putin, banish Putin,
> Virgin Mary, Mother of God, we pray thee, banish him![37]

The performance put the spotlight on the tight relationship between the church and the state. The lyrics again create a *legitimacy insult*, condemning the blending of the state and the ROC. They connect priestly black robes and militaristic gold epaulettes and associate black limousines as mafia symbols with a procession with the cross. Supporters of the church are criticized for these close relations; they "crawl to bow" and accept the denial of their freedom. The heads of the tandem government-church are depicted as "God blessed rotten leaders," collectively a regime that denies human rights, especially the rights of women and LGBT people, and prosecutes the opposition. The song also stresses that the Patriarch believes in Putin instead of God and calls Kirill "a bitch," offenses that aim to strip Putin and the ROC of their positive identity show their negative impact on the country. Pussy Riot emphasizes that they do not agree with the traditional limited role for women, "to give a birth and love," and proclaim their ability to challenge the existing situation. Thus members of Pussy Riot bring together all the previous *legitimacy insults* we have seen, denying the legitimacy of Putin and the ROC, and magnify the stance of Pussy Riot as the defender of freedoms and rights. The song denounces Putin's regime and its fusion with the ROC as invalid, thus creating a *legitimacy insult*. It portrays this regime as cruel, founded on militaristic values and mafia structures. Pussy Riot also posits the ROC as an illegitimate representative of the feelings and faith of Orthodox people, invoking the Virgin Mary to legitimize these claims. Thus, the *legitimacy insult* denies the power of the tandem of government and church.

The day after the performance at the cathedral, the group members stated in their interview with *Russky Reporter*: "Our attitude toward religion, and toward Orthodoxy in particular, is one of respect, and for this very reason we are distressed that the great and luminous Christian philosophy is being used so shabbily. We are very angry that something beautiful is being spoiled."[38] Thus they stress that the insult is not aimed at the Orthodox religion or feelings of believers, but rather at the immoral fusion of the ROC and the state, a union that diminishes the very idea of Christianity. In doing so, they reconfirm that the performance was a *legitimacy insult* rather than an *identity* one.

In the same day as the *Russky Reporter* interview, February 22, 2012, the Russian Orthodox Church began a criminal investigation of Pussy Riot, calling their actions blasphemous. The representatives of the ROC in this way created new *legitimacy insults*, forming a negative image of Pussy Riot. A spokesman called the song a "foolish, incompetent, and meaningless blasphemous action, which rested on folly or was created to show off.... I do not think that this action and ensuing discussions can hurt the church, but I think that they offend true believers.... Any time a person intentionally or unintentionally—and in this case it was organized deliberately and consciously—offends the feelings of other people, it harms both those who were offended and those who create the insult."[39] Another representative of the ROC stated:

> The religious illiteracy and insensibility of the current day are striking. I do not know what to tell people who ask with complete seriousness: what specifically did these girls do? For those who were raised as atheists, the actions of a punk group with an indecent name, which we today often and easily repeat, can be compared to an offense to state symbols, or abuse of the memorial to the heroes of World War II.... The church calls for principled assessment of this action in our society, including prosecution. If these female activists want to live in a lawful civic society—and, according to their words, it is their aim—they cannot do whatever they want. Freedom means reasonable self-restraint so as not to infringe on the freedoms of others. It looks like these "civic activists" do not understand these simple rules. We need to show them and their supporters that such actions cannot be performed.[40]

Patriarch Kirill condemned those who seek to "justify and downplay this sacrilege": "My heart breaks from bitterness that amongst these people there are those who call themselves Orthodox."[41]

These statements show that the ROC represented the actions of Pussy Riot as an identity insult rather than a legitimacy one and in turn, created *divergence insults*. To present the women as dissimilar to Russian society as a whole, to describe them as delinquent and inadequate, the ROC portrayed their action as both silly and as an intentional offense to sacral faith. The statements depicted the song and even the name of the group as "indecent." Stressing the aberrant nature of Pussy Riot's actions, the ROC representatives also portrayed the church as the defender of core Russian values of morality and sensibility. They employed the very value that was used by the women—liberty—and posited the punk group as violators of freedom and the ROC as its protector. Thus, a *divergence insult* created a firm social boundary between Pussy Riot and the rest of society, positing the delinquent rock group on one side and the ROC and Russian society on the other. The creation of a *divergence insult* to Pussy Riot and presentation of them as abnormal outsiders allowed the ROC to attribute to the rock group the intention to act out an identity insult against the entire Russian society. According to the ROC, these actions were unacceptable and should be punished. Additionally, ROC representatives tried to *sensitize* the public to the idea that Pussy Riot created an *identity insult* rather than a *legitimacy insult*. They explained to Orthodox believers that the group's action deeply hurt their faith, and they also enlightened nonreligious people about the harmful actions of the group, comparing their performance to an offense against the memory of war veterans.

The ROC was through these efforts able to transfer the insult to the public. Several conservative political groups announced that they would patrol churches to prevent Pussy Riot and their ilk from performing again, and some churchmen asked the government to make blasphemy a punishable crime. Public opinion polls show that almost half of respondents (46 percent) consider prison time up to seven years a fair punishment for the women's actions, and only 35 percent believe that this punishment is excessive.[42] People who see the possible sentence as extreme are generally younger (25–39 years old) and better educated and have a higher income. The majority of people who believe that the possible punishment is reasonable are most often retirees, inhabitants of small cities, and those with low income. Moreover, the majority of people who strongly condemn the group's action voted for Putin, while people who sympathize with the women supported alternative candidates.[43]

On March 3, 2012, members of Pussy Riot Maria Alyokhina (24, mother), Yekaterina Samutsevich (30, computer programmer), and Nadezhda Tolokonnikova (22, philosophy student and mother), were arrested for hooliganism. They were held without bail, with all appeals rejected, and put under 24-hour video surveillance, an illegal act in Russia. To protest their rights, the women went on a hunger strike. Throughout March, the members were threatened with losing parental rights, and their families received death threats.

Their arrest and subsequent abusive mistreatment in detention drew international attention to their cause. Multiple protests were held internationally on March 8 to mark solidarity with Pussy Riot. On April 5, Amnesty International called for the release of the group's members, characterizing them as prisoners of conscience because of the severity of the authoritarian response, and on April 11, the Russian rights ombudsman called for the release of the jailed women. Its head, Vladimir Lukin stated, "I hope the court makes a reasonable decision. We have spoken out against them being detained before their trial. Why are they in custody? Did they try to blow up the cathedral?"[44]

On June 4, a 3,000-page indictment was issued that called for five to seven years of prison for Pussy Riot members The women were given two working days to prepare for their trial, scheduled for July 9. Supporters of the group asserted that allegations of religious hatred belong to the Middle

Ages and the Inquisition, underlining that the trial was nothing but a witch hunt in which Pussy Riot would be the "poster girls" for the new Russian policy of crushing dissent.

The trial received heightened attention among the public. If in March 2012 only 50 percent of respondents had heard about Pussy Riot, by 2012 more than 80 percent of respondents reported that they were aware of the controversy surrounding this group. Three-fifths of respondents believed that the group's action was politically motivated; among them, 19 percent thought that women opposed Putin, and 20 percent thought they opposed participation of the church in politics. Only 23 percent of respondents believed that the performance of "Punk Prayer" was aimed against the church and the Orthodox faithful. Whereas in March, around half of respondents considered the seven-year sentence fair and 44 percent considered it excessive or illegal, in July only 33 percent judged sentence acceptable, and 58 percent thought it was too severe, or that no sentence should be imposed.[45] Thus the Russian public acknowledged the offensive character of "Punk Prayer," and many of them believed that the action was politically motivated. The majority of people considered that the punishment proposed for the women was inappropriate and looked like revenge by the church and the government. On July 30, the trial began, with the prosecutors demanding three years in a labor camp for all defendants. The defense reported abuse in detention, including lack of food, sleep, and medical attention. The defendants were placed in a wood and glass "cage," in which they were watched by a "rotating cast of guard dogs...lest the three women try to run away from the glass 'aquarium' in which they were locked during the trial."[46]

On August 2, Putin, making his first statement on the topic, said there was "nothing good" in Pussy Riot's church performance, but opined that they "should not be judged too harshly." He stressed, "I wouldn't really like to comment, but I think if the girls were, let's say, in Israel, and insulted something in Israel...it wouldn't be so easy for them to leave. If they desecrated some Muslim holy site, we wouldn't even have had time to detain them....Nonetheless, I don't think they should be judged too severely for this. But the final decision rests with the courts—I hope the court will deliver a correct, well-founded ruling."[47] His statement compared the incident to the likely result if two other Abrahamic religions—Judaism and Islam—had been insulted, and suggested that in both cases the punishment would have been very severe. Bringing the framework of major religions into the dialogue, Putin stressed the importance of a serious sentence but reduced the responsibility of the ROC and the government for a strict outcome.

Some believe Putin's statement led to harsher punishment for Pussy Riot. The prosecution depicted them as satanic hooligans. Prosecution witnesses, "injured parties," testified to having been "profoundly offended" by the group's outlandish actions. One witness called them "devil's pranks," while others claimed to be insulted by the performers' inappropriate attire (they were bare-armed) and provocative, high leg kicks in their choreography. One witness claimed to be offended by the way they crossed themselves: "It looked like a parody of christening." The candle-keeper of the cathedral said that "they basically spat in my face, in my soul, in my Lord's soul" and that she cries when she remembers seeing the group in the cathedral.[48] One of the prosecution's witnesses was a "witness of the clip": he wasn't in the cathedral during the performance, having only seen footage in a YouTube video. He stressed that watching the clip was extremely painful, like "hell being as real as the Moscow metro," and that Pussy Riot had "declared war on God, Christianity, and the government."

Thus, the prosecution tried to use an identity insult to the Orthodox believers as a main justification for the sentence. To attribute to the defendants this *identity insult*, the court employed a *divergence insult*, presenting the women as different from all Orthodox believers and as haters of their religion. The *divergence insult* stressed the social boundary between Pussy Riot and Russian society, depicting the group as offensive aliens who hated core Russian values. In public opinion polls conducted during the trial, 42 percent of respondents believed that the women were on trial because they offended religion and faith, while 29 percent believed that they had engaged in simple hooliganism. Only 17 percent thought that the women are on trial because they offended Putin. Respondents varied in their ideas about who initiated the arrest and subsequent trial: 35 percent believed that it was the Orthodox public, 27 percent believed it was the government or Putin himself, and 19 percent named the ROC as the initiator. Only 21 percent believed that the church should demand severe punishment, while 30 percent wanted the ROC to show mercy and request the release of the defendants, and 40 percent thought that the ROC should not be involved in the trial at all.[49] Thus, the Russian public acknowledged the offensive character of "Punk Prayer," and many people believed that the action was insulting to the Orthodox faithful and their feelings. However, the majority believed that the church should not request punishment for the women on trial.

All the defendants pled not guilty to charges of hooliganism based on religious hatred. Their performance was simply a form of political protest through art without a drop of hate, they claimed, designed to highlight the "fusion" of the KGB and the church. Nadezhda Tolokonnikova, one of the three women, said in a written statement that the main point of the performance was

> a protest against illegitimate elections and Patriarch Kirill's endorsement of President Putin. We are absolutely not happy with—and have been forced into living politically—by the use of coercive, strong-arm measures to handle social processes, a situation in which the most important political institutions are the disciplinary structures of the state—the security agencies, the army, the police, the special forces and the accompanying means of ensuring political stability: prisons, preventive detention, and mechanisms to closely control public behavior. Nor are we happy with the enforced civic passivity of the bulk of the population or the complete domination of executive structures over the legislature and judiciary. Moreover, we are genuinely angered by the fear-based and scandalously low standard of political culture, which is constantly and knowingly maintained by the state system and its accomplices. Look at what Patriarch Kirill has to say: "The Orthodox don't go to rallies."[50]

According to band member Katya Samutsevich, Putin should

> make use of the aesthetics of the Orthodox religion, historically associated with the heyday of Imperial Russia, where power came not from earthly manifestations such as democratic elections and civil society, but from God Himself.... Here, apparently, the authorities took advantage of a certain deficit of Orthodox aesthetics in Soviet times, when the Orthodox religion had the aura of a lost history, of something crushed and damaged by the Soviet totalitarian regime, and was thus an opposition culture. The authorities decided to appropriate this historical effect of loss and present their new political project to restore Russia's lost spiritual values, a project which has little to do with a genuine concern for preservation of Russian Orthodoxy's history and culture.[51]

In court she also stated, "The Patriarch spoke many times about the supernatural role of Vladimir Vladimirovich Putin in Russian history and called for the believers to vote for him and his party. He said that Orthodox Christians don't join protest rallies. This way he insulted many believers who have their own political opinions. We were perplexed by the Patriarch's statements and his instructions on how people should vote and how they should behave in political life."[52]

The third woman, Aloykhina, stated: "Speaking about Putin, we first of all mean not Vladimir Putin, but Putin as the system created by him. The vertical power structure, where all governing is carried out almost manually. And in this vertical power structure public opinion is completely disregarded."[53] In court she stated, "I am not afraid of your poorly concealed fraud of a verdict in this so-called court because it can deprive me of my freedom. No one will take my inner freedom away...I thought the church loves all its children, but it appears that the church only loves those who vote for Putin."[54]

In these statements the members of Pussy Riot stress that the blending of the ROC and the government offended their identity as Orthodox believers and as citizens of the country. Thus, they claim that the ROC and the Patriarch enacted an identity insult to all Russian society by proclaiming the divine power of Putin, presenting him as the savior of Russia. This insult was offensive to many believers because it denied the right of people to form their own political opinions, restricting genuine Orthodoxy to support for Putin. It is also offensive to citizens because it creates a regime of submission to and dominance by the state. The women of Pussy Riot declared that they aimed to decrease the legitimacy of a close interconnection between the state and the ROC. Thus, they carried out a *legitimacy insult*, stressing that the church does not support or love its devotees; instead it backs Putin and his totalitarian regime.

Denouncing this fusion of the ROC and the state, the women of Pussy Riot increase the legitimacy of those who fight for freedom, including themselves. They place the responsibility for the situation on the current regime and posit their performance as a civil act of opposition to the curtailment of human rights and freedoms. As Tolokonnikova states, "Who is to blame for the performance at the Cathedral of Christ the Saviour and for our being put on trial after the concert? The authoritarian political system is to blame. What Pussy Riot does is oppositional art or politics that draws upon the forms art has established. In any event, it is a form of civil action in circumstances where basic human rights, civil and political freedoms are suppressed by the corporate state system.... We've put on our political punk concerts because the Russian state system is dominated by rigidity, closeness and caste."[55] Samutsevich echoes these ideas: "In our performance we dared, without the Patriarch's blessing, to combine the visual image of Orthodox culture and protest culture, suggesting to smart people that Orthodox culture belongs not only to the Russian Orthodox Church, the Patriarch and Putin, that it might also take the side of civic rebellion and protest in Russia." Thus, in their statements, the women present their actions as a legitimacy insult, denouncing the current regime in Russia and increasing their legitimacy as responsible citizens and as Orthodox believers who want their country and church to become more humane and free.

On August 17, the verdict in the trail was announced. Having been found guilty, the convicted were sentenced to two years in labor camps. The court found no political motivation in Pussy Riot's actions and convicted them for religious hatred. As Judge Marina Syrova stated,

> The court determines the so-called "Punk Prayer," which the members of Pussy Riot performed this spring in the Cathedral of Christ the Savior, to be not only an insult to the feelings of believers, but by their action the defendants clearly showed their religious hatred and enmity to Christianity. This behavior does not correspond to the canons of the Orthodox Church independent of the place of their performance, whether in a cathedral or outside. Violation of the internal regulations of the Cathedral of Christ the Savior was only one of the means of demonstrating disrespect to society based on the motives of religious hatred and enmity and on the motives of hatred toward any social group. The actions of Tolokonnikova, Samutsevich, Alyokhina, and other unknown people humiliate and offend the feelings of a significant group of citizens, in this case based on their religious beliefs, provoking among them hatred and enmity, thus violating the constitutional foundations of the state.[56]

This court statement denies any political motives behind the performance. At the same time, it blurs the boundary between religious feelings and the state, positioning an insult to religion as an insult to the state. Thus, the court repudiates the *legitimacy insult* created by the group and posits it as an *identity insult* to religious and patriotic feelings.

In his statement after the verdict, Putin agreed with the punishment meted out. "It is right that they were arrested and that the court made this decision, because one must not abolish the norms of morality and ethics and destroy the country. What we would be left with?... I was not involved. They wanted this, they got it." Putin denied that the protest action was directed against him. "You know, based on expert testimony, everything that was connected with the president was specially put in later; in reality, they did not shout words [against the president] in the cathedral. I do not know if that is true or not. But if it is true, it means that it was (*a*) a means to attract attention and (*b*) a means of self-defense: to announce that they were not just hooligans and did not shit in the cathedral, but rather performed a political action."[57] In this statement Putin denies the political motivation of the Pussy Riot performance and, thus, rejects an assessment of their actions as a *legitimacy insult*. He positions "Punk Prayer" as an identity insult to all Russian people, stressing the offense to morality and ethics and using words like "hooliganism" and "shit." He also connects religion and the state, dissolving the boundary between intimidation of religious faith and threats to the country.

The church welcomed the verdict, calling the "Punk Prayer" performance "blasphemy and sacrilege, conscious and intended offence of a shrine, the manifestation of rough hatred towards millions of people and their feelings."[58] The ROC's official statement stressed,

> We do not agree with attempts to present this action as a prayer in nontraditional form. Unfortunately, these attempts have confused many people, including some members of the church, who were not aware that blasphemous and nasty words were pronounced at the altar of the Cathedral of Christ the Savior. Roistering in the cathedral was a continuation of deeply immoral public actions, performed earlier by the same people and their comrades, that remained unpunished. Blasphemy is a hard sin. Orthodox Christians should not participate in blasphemy, accept it, or support it directly or indirectly.
>
> The preservation of the foundations of the society is impossible without respect to the memory of people who died defending the motherland. Sacrilegious actions, committed in the cathedral devoted to the memory of Russian soldiers of 1812, are especially provocative during the celebration of 200 years of their heroism. The task of the state that respects its citizen is the prevention of offenses to believers' feelings, acts of blasphemy in religious shrines, and insults to cultural memorials. Religious and national feelings of the people were deeply offended by both the blasphemous actions and by the following claim of propaganda.[59]

Another representative of the ROC emphasized the threat to the whole society,

> I have a hope that the "criminal character" of the actions against the church sobers our society. If society shows indifference toward vandalism, terror will grow. The problem is that we completely lost the meaning of a "societal contract"—agreement between people that is not written in any law. For example, one should not curse in the presence of women and children, and showing disrespect to the memory of soldiers defending the country or to the symbols of our state should be prohibited. National and religious feelings are the most sensitive. Any offense against these feelings, even a minor one, hurts deeply the heart of the people. If we show intolerance to these behaviors, if vandals know that nobody in the society will support such public actions, if we stop calling the perpetrators "girls" and destroyers of crosses "boys," everything will end.[60]

The ROC's statements, lke the court verdict, dissolve the boundary between religion and state. Starting from the assessment of "Punk Prayer" as blasphemous against the Orthodox religion, the first statement unites religious feelings with national ones, involving national identity in the assessment of the situation. Next the statement recalls memories of war and invokes the patriotic feelings of Russian citizens. "Punk Prayer" did not express any connections to the history of Russia, but the ROC creatively unites the insult to the church with the insult to the heroism of the defenders of the motherland. The second statement echoes the previous one, connecting religious and national feelings and thus *transferring* the insult to all Russian citizens. It posits the actions of Pussy Riot as criminal behavior that is dangerous to the whole society and destroys its very foundations. Thus, according to both statements, Pussy Riot should be severely punished; every attempt to defend them is as anti-Christian (and anti-Russian).

Both the state and the ROC position the Pussy Riot performance as an identity insult not only to religious feelings of believers and the Orthodox religion, but also to the national and patriotic feelings of the citizens of the Russian Federation. They deny that Pussy Riot's actions had any political character and thus reject them as a *legitimacy insult*. They also *sensitize* the public to these actions as blasphemous and nonpatriotic and *transfer* the insult from religious believers to all citizens. This propaganda appeared to be effective and affected the public's view of the trial and verdict, as evidenced in public opinion polls conducted after the trial. These showed more negative perceptions of Pussy Riot after the trial than in the beginning, and an assessment of their actions as hooliganism and expressive of religious hatred rather than political action. After the trial, only 6 percent of respondents sympathized with the women, while 20 percent had a negative perceptions of them; 14 percent felt irritated and 17 percent enmity. More than 60 percent of Russian citizens believed that there should be criminal penalties for blasphemous actions.[61] Forty-four percent believed that the trial was fair, while 17 percent had doubts about its objectivity.[62] After the trial, 41 percent of respondents considered "Punk Prayer" an act of hooliganism, 29 percent a political action; 53 percent thought that the performers intended to offend Orthodox believers. Thirty-five percent believed that two-year sentence was adequate, 43 percent that it should be harsher, and only 14 percent that it was excessive.[63]

In spite of these numbers, Pussy Riot received support both within Russia and internationally. Despite a heavy police presence outside the courtroom, many protested the church's involvement in the trial and the harsh punishment for the women, chanting "Russia without Putin!" Opposition lawmaker Dmitry Gudkov told journalists that the trial was an example of political "repression" that risked a "civil war": "Today the regime has both openly and cynically committed a criminal act." Another opposition leader, Alexei Navalny, emphasized that the sentence was proof of the "destruction of the judicial system" and that anyone who failed to "stay quiet" also risked jail.[64] Madonna and the Red Hot Chili Peppers have publicly supported Pussy Riot, and Yoko Ono gave Pussy Riot the Lennon Ono Grant for Peace award. Paul McCartney wrote them an open letter, Bjork and Patti Smith dedicated songs to them. Peaches released a song called "Free Pussy Riot" and a video crammed with celebrity supporters.

In support of Pussy Riot, the Ukrainian group Femen cut down a cross. More crosses were cut down in towns and villages in Russia. The ROC considers these actions to be continuous insults to the very foundations of the Christian faith and Russian patriotic feelings rather than a protest against an unjust trial. According to the Church,

> Cutting down a cross is not an "ethical mistake." It is a challenge to existing culture, which is based on the cross—the victimhood of the Savior. Today, millions of people—believers and nonbelievers, Christians and agnostics—live according to moral principles that would not exist if 2,000 years ago there was no Golgotha. The destruction of the cross, for the sake of short-term popularity, is foolishness. But, unfortunately, it is also bigger and worse than foolishness.... Rejection of the Cross rejection of the meaning that created human culture and influences millions of people. Besides, this action is absurd because people who pretend that they fight for freedom destroy the cross created in memory of those who suffered in times with no freedom and gave their lives for our right to be free.[65]

Another ROC representative echoed these conclusions: "Those who commit such crimes are not initiators. It is beneficial to certain forces that aim to destabilize our society in different directions. They act in political and ethnic spheres, and now in a religious one. They try to create a complex gap and introduce opposition inside society. A religious factor is useful to employ to create destabilization, first in minds and then in the whole state and in political communities.... They [the women convicted] need mercy because they got into a very threatening game."[66] These statements posit cutting down of crosses as an identity insult to the Orthodox faith and a threat to the unity of the Russian state with the church.

CONCLUSION

The preceding analysis of insults created around the close connections between the ROC and the Russian government and around "Punk Prayer" as performed by Pussy Riot shows that the ROC and the state constantly use *legitimacy insults* to demolish the voices of opposition. The tandem of the ROC and the state denies the *legitimacy insults* of their opponents and posit them as *identity insults* to the faith and patriotic feelings of the masses. They dissolve the boundary between national and religious identity and posit the submission to the state as a religious responsibility of true believers. The political activities of the opposition are treated as blasphemy and offensive to the patriotic sentiments of masses.

To legitimize the collaboration of the ROC with the government, the church refers to the process of increasing faith among the population and the need for power to prevent the infiltration of sinful ideas into laws and society. It also delegitimizes opponents as enemies of Orthodoxy and as supporters of evil goals. Thus, the ROC presents political disagreement with overly close cooperation between the church and the government as an offense to the Orthodox faith.

Committed Orthodox Christians see the corruption of the ROC leadership as a deep *identity insult* to their faith. For progressive people, the fusion of the ROC with the government is also an identity insult because it imposes conservative values and views on Russian society, on sexual relations, and on the role of women. The actions of Pussy Riot started as a reaction to this *identity insult*; they created *legitimacy insults* as a way of expressing this opposition. They presented the Russian government as a Third World dictatorship, characterized by corruption and absence of the rule of law and human rights. They also stressed that the ROC-state tandem is sexist, promotes prevalence of men over women, and denies LGBT rights. Pussy Riot increased their legitimacy as opponents of the fusion of the ROC and the government, and as defenders of human rights, especially rights of women and LGBT persons. Pussy Riot also posited the ROC as illegitimate because it did represent the feelings and faith of all Orthodox people and validate their right to oppose official views of the ROC. Pussy Riot *sensitized* the society through public presentations.

The ROC presented the actions of Pussy Riot as an identity insult to the Orthodox faith, rather than a legitimacy insult, thus masking the political motivation of the women's actions. To portray their actions as an identity insult to the entire Russian society, the ROC created a *divergence insult* portraying "Punk Prayer" both as a delinquent action and as an intentional offense against sacral faith. It positioned the rock group as alien to Russian values and the church as defender of freedom and morality, establishing a social boundary between Pussy Riot and the rest of the society. Thus, as outsiders who offended society with an identity insult, the women deserved severe punishment. The ROC sensitized the Orthodox believers to an identity insult that deeply harmed their faith and *transferred* the *identity insult* to nonreligious people, comparing it with an offense to the memory of war veterans.

During the trial, the prosecution and the judge also used a *divergence insult* to strengthen the boundary between the defendants and the Russian society. They presented "Punk Prayer" as an identity insult to Orthodox believers and to the patriotic feelings of all Russian citizens as a justification for the harsh sentence. The court verdict denied any political motivation behind Pussy Riot's performance, repudiating the *legitimacy insult* created by the group. It stressed that the group created an identity insult not only to religious believers but also to all Russian patriots, thereby dissolving the boundary between the religion and the state. Similarly, Putin and Patriarch Kirill both rejected a view of "Punk Prayer: as a political action and a *legitimacy insult*. Instead, they positioned the actions of Pussy Riot as an identity insult, uniting religious feelings with national ones and blending religious identity with a national one. To achieve this purpose, they employed the memories of war and the heroism of the defenders of the motherland and appealed to the patriotic feelings of Russian citizens. Thus, they transferred an insult to the fusion of the ROC and the state into an insult to the sacral history and the very patriotic foundations of Russia as a state. This *transfer of insult* posited the actions of Pussy Riot as a criminal and treacherous to the whole of Russian society.

This dynamic of insults reveals the deep social conflict within Russian society, where opposition voices are suppressed by the authoritarian regime backed by the ROC. The danger within this situation becomes stronger as opponents to the fusion of government and church are presented as sinful, evil agents, haters of the Orthodox religion, and enemies of the Russian state. Preserving the stability of the existing regime, the government denies the political reasons behind protests. This shift of discourse from a political to a moral sphere impacts the perception of the opposition by the general public. While the protesters against the blending of the ROC and the government actually object to the growing primacy of the state over people, the majority of population in Russia now believes that the protestors aim to destroy Russian Orthodox society. Thus, support for the ideals of the opposition is diminished and collective actions are rare.

The resolution of this social conflict is complicated for many reasons.

One has to take into account the entrenched interests of the ruling elite and its desire to preserve the status quo, and the existence of more conservative sections of society (around 30 percent of voters) who are completely dependent on the state and fear change. The lack of a political alternative based on political organization (a party or movement), the absence of a new generation of leaders with broad public support, and the absence of an exit strategy (not just a method for dismantling the old system, but also a plan for building the new one) also make it easier for the authorities to keep the system going. Also missing now is another important political component that would get the "angry" sections of society up and moving: willingness to consolidate around a new strategy, be ready for an active political struggle and confrontation with the authorities, and readiness to make sacrifices in the name of the desired change.[67]

Yet more and more people in Russia become aware of the regime's consequences for Russian society and the freedoms of its citizens. In public opinion polls, only 33 percent of respondents say that "power should be concentrated in one pair of strong hands," while 59 percent of respondents take the view that "society should be built on the foundation of democratic freedom."[68] In the current situation of political repression and totalitarian pressure, it is critical to ensure that alternative voices will be heard and that all attempts by the government to portray opposition as unpatriotic will be revealed. Open discussions on the meaning of patriotism and loyalty to the state should be supported. Citizens need to accept that true patriotism means love of country and of its people, not submission to the government, and be ready to resist manipulations of popular opinion.

CHAPTER 3
Victory Day Violence in Ukraine

The red flag, representing the perished Soviet empire, was used during the celebration of Victory Day, commemorating the end of World War II, in some regions of independent Ukraine. Other regional Ukrainian administrations made the decision to rename Victory Day as the Day of Grief. Young people chanted "Shame" to old veterans, did not allow them to lay flowers, and pulled off their medals and other decorations. They also crushed a wreath held by the Russian consul general. Several months later, two groups of young people fried eggs and sausages on the Eternal Flame near the Tomb of Unknown Soldiers. Why did this aggression against old veterans occur in a country that significantly contributed to the fall of Nazi Germany? Why did young people feel no guilt for beating veterans or desecrating tombs? The analysis of the dynamic of insults constructed around the celebration of Victory Day will help reveal the roots of conflict in independent Ukraine.

Ukraine represents a clear case where conflicts over national identity have continued over the more than two decades since Ukraine achieved independence. The ethnic and regional divide between the southeast and west of the country is actively used by Ukrainian politicians:[1] "Since independence at the end of 1991, Ukraine has been divided between an anti-Russian, pro-European West and a more pro-Russian south and east. Ukrainian nationalism, anchored in the west of the country around Lviv (part of Austria-Hungary only a century ago and part of interwar Poland), is Western-looking, built against Russia as the significant rival, while the Eastern and Southern parts of the country see themselves as more organically linked to Russia."[2]

This divide stems from the history of Ukraine, which for a long time belonged to different empires and ideological systems. In September 1939, the Soviet Ukraine was enlarged by the Ribbentrop-Molotov Pact, which divided the territory of Poland between Germany and the Soviet Union. The Soviet Union also annexed Bessarabia and northern Bukovina (Western Ukraine) from Romania, augmenting its territory and control over non-Soviet people. Although the Paris Peace Treaties of 1947 recognized most of the territory incorporated into the Ukrainian Soviet Socialist Republic, the population of these Western territories considered the Soviet Union an alien occupying regime. When Nazi Germany and its allies invaded the Soviet Union in 1941, many Western Ukrainians initially regarded the Nazis as liberators. The Organization of Ukrainian Nationalists, Bandera faction (OUN-B) was committed to the establishment of a united, independent national state on Ukrainian ethnic territory, and accepted violence as a political tool against foreign, as well as Ukrainian, enemies of their cause. The Ukrainian Insurgent Army (UPA)—the military wing of OUN—engaged in a series of guerrilla conflicts during World War II against Nazi Germany, the Soviet Union, Czechoslovakia, and both underground and Communist Poland. Activists in the national movement in Western Ukraine hoped that the German occupation would foster the development of an independent state of Ukraine. Nazis provided some assurances to these ends, as they were seeking support based on anti-Soviet, anti-Ukrainian, anti-Polish, and anti-Jewish sentiments. Together, they formed the Ukrainian auxiliary police and the Ukrainian SS division, the 14th Waffen Grenadier Division of the SS Galicia (1st Ukrainian), which played a substantial role in the killing and ethnic cleansing of the Polish and Jewish population as well of communists and their supporters in regions of Volhynia and Galicia. However, the German army soon changed its policies and brutally extinguished most activities of the Ukrainian national movement. In some western regions of Ukraine, the Ukrainian Insurgent Army survived underground and continued its resistance against the Soviet authorities well into the 1950s, though many Ukrainian civilians were murdered by both sides in this conflict.

Most Ukrainians in the east and south fully resisted the Nazi occupation by organizing underground resistance and partisan movements. A significant subset of Ukrainians fought against Nazi Germany in the Red Army under the leadership of Joseph Stalin. Of the estimated 11 million Soviet troops who fell in battle against the Nazis, about 25 percent (2.7 million) were ethnic Ukrainians. Total civilian losses during the war and German occupation in Ukraine are estimated at seven million, including over a million Jews. These sacrifices and resistance to Nazi occupation contributed to Ukraine becoming a founding member of the United Nations in 1945.

Currently, Ukraine is divided completely by differences in moral values, ethnic identity, and perception of history.[3] Cultural differences are antagonistic, regionally fixed, and rest on the historic character of the Western and Southeastern regions. These regions were parts of different states for centuries, developed within fundamentally different state structures and empires, have different histories, and represent different experiences. This distinction of backgrounds resulted in significant differences in geopolitical vectors of development and assessments of history. Despite a common perception that Ukraine is moving toward Europe, the society embodies multiple trajectories.

The elites in this society tend not to produce compromises, shared decisions, or common visions. Instead, the ruling class reinforces differences and uses ethnic and regional identities to elide class divisions and redirect attention away from economic issues. Black-and-white thinking and the search for an enemy are easily manipulated by those who capitalize on differences for their political purposes. Different views and beliefs are presented as enmity, threat, and exploitation. The mass media contribute to the problem through scandals, playing up conflicts and ignoring opportunities for compromise. Controversies over Victory Day have recently emerged in the Ukraine, further polarizing this society. Considering the national reverence for Ukraine's efforts during World War II—also called the Great Patriotic War of 1941–1945—this conflict elicits deeply entrenched feelings among citizens.

Historic interpretations of World War II are contested and differ between the Western and Southeastern regions of Ukraine. According to the narrative popular in the east and south, people in the 1930s perceived Stalin's regime ambiguously. Some people in west Ukraine collaborated with the Nazis to bolster their hopes of independence. Some committed violent crimes against Poles, Jews, and communists. This history of OUN/UPA cannot be accorded to the whole of Ukrainian society; many Ukrainians do not justify their actions and support their celebrations. The majority of people see the Great Patriotic War as something they can be proud of, and perceive the red flag as a flag of glory and victory. According to the narrative popular in the west of Ukraine, Russia dictates the writing of Ukrainian history, especially as it relates to the history of World War II. As the UPA is the only movement that fought against both Stalin and Hitler, its adherents see the red flag as the foul flag of totalitarianism.

Therefore, the interpretations surrounding World War II in the Ukraine are contrary and conflicting. On one hand, the population of Western Ukraine considers OUN-UPA and Bandera's struggle as an anti-Soviet, anti-totalitarian fight rather than collaboration with Germans. Conversely, the population of Southeastern Ukraine glorifies the victories of the Red Army and a Soviet power that liberated the world from Nazism. Moreover, the Soviet narrative that dominated historic interpretations of these events from 1940 to the 1990s depicted the OUN-UPA as traitors and fascists who collaborated with the Nazis and were responsible for the mass killing of fellow citizens. In the wake of the Orange Revolution of 2004, President Victor Yushchenko, who was supported by the population of Western Ukraine, came to power. He tried to alter the dominant Soviet narrative, promoting a perception of OUN-UPA as national heroes and freedom fighters. Yet there was no evolution or gradual process of altering the values of the Soviet period. His feverish actions to promote OUN/UPA and Bandera diminished the idea of creating a history of Ukraine that is separate from Soviet history. President Victor Yanukovich, who replaced Yushchenko, was supported by a majority of voters in Southeastern Ukraine in opposition to the Ukrainian nationalism of Yushchenko. Many experts stress that his government created conflicts over history and language, reintroducing Soviet narratives, norms, and values as a challenge to Ukrainian independence.

THE FIGHT WITH VETERANS

The events of spring 2011 represent a vivid example of the role of insults in the conflict over history in Ukraine. On April 21, Verhovna Rada (the parliament of Ukraine) passed the law On Commemorating the Victory in the Great Patriotic War of 1941–45, which supported the use of a replica of the red flag of victory in the Great Patriotic War. According to this law, replicas of the red flag should be used during the celebrations of Victory Day observed by state officials, local officials, and other organizations. The law also specifies the use of red flags on buildings and flagstaffs together with the state flag of Ukraine. This resolution became law after decisions by several southeastern regions of Ukraine, including Zaporozhe, Lugansk, and Crimea, to use replicas of the Soviet red flag during celebrations of Victory Day.

The authors of this law argued that use of the red flag helps reestablish a balance of ideologies in the country and gives an opportunity to supporters of the Soviet army to celebrate its great achievements. According to them, the law promoted respect for the values connected with the Soviet victory over German Nazism. They stressed that the red flag is the symbol of victory and should be an essential part of the celebration of Victory Day. For example, the decision to use the red flag in Crimea was based on "the vital significance of the victory of the Soviet people in the Great Patriotic War, the main battle of World War II, as well as willingness to preserve the memory about real heroes who fought for freedom and independence of the Soviet motherland under the red flags."[4] Supporters also stated that their decision was based on public opinion in Ukraine: according to sociological group Rating, in April 2011 55 percent of respondents had positive opinion about the use of the red flag, and around 30 percent were opposed.[5]

The opposition perceived decisions to display the flag by local and state parliaments as intended to increase the loyalty of the voters, who brought the Yanukovich Party of Regions into power. According to the opposition, the red flag law was a shameless manipulation of the Ukrainian public and a glorification of totalitarian ideology. Thus the opposition treated the law as an attempt by the government to improve its image among population. Opposition leaders condemned the government's actions, calling these officials "radicals of specific political sort" who promoted "red flag hysteria."[6] A strong reaction to the red flag law was observed among the population of Western Ukraine and the pro-Ukrainian movements, which immediately claimed that the government wanted to impose a pro-Soviet ideology on the whole of Ukraine.

The adoption of red flag laws by regional governments and at the state level was not originally intended as an insult; rather, the decision was made to increase support among a constituency in the midst of deteriorating economic conditions. The red flag was a token paid to the older generation of voters for their support of regional parties. So the insult was not intentional, but it was perceived as such by the opposition and the population in the west. Why did it happen? First of all, the opposition saw the red flag law as alien to the values of Ukrainian independence. For them, the Soviet Union represented an aggressive invader that had transformed Western Ukraine into a colony of Russia, a totalitarian regime that repressed fighters for Ukrainian independence. They perceived Soviet symbols as a representation of the values of Russian imperial nationalism, and a counterweight to their anti-Soviet and antitotalitarian values. The opposition also believes that the government created conflicts over history and language by introducing the red flag law as a challenge to Ukrainian independence. Yanukovich introduced these ideas of the Soviet past and a Russian model alien to the Ukrainian people, one that diminishes the values that they fought for during the Orange Revolution and enjoyed during Yushchenko's rule. They believe that pro-Soviet and pro-Russian forces are taking over Ukraine, threatening its very independence and imposing outworn, evil values. This feeling of being subjected to the imposition of alien values and ideological systems results in an *attributed divergence insult*.

This construction of a divergence insult is evident in the following statement: "The Ukrainian government, current Russian government, and Russian nationalists treat World War II as a geopolitical conflict that was won by the 'Russian people—winners' and the state. Certainly, these ideas are not stated openly, but are reflected in the rhetoric of the state propaganda that uses nationalistic, state-based categories. And the red flag, actually, is turning into an imperial white, black, and gold one."[7] This statement connects the use of the red flag with totalitarian and nationalistic values and condemns the Russian and Ukrainian governments and pro-Russian nationalists for reviving this ideology in Ukraine. They see it as an imperialistic attempt to control the development of independent Ukraine and return to its colonial and totalitarian past.

Second, the population of Western Ukraine believes that the west-east divide rests on core ideological differences. In the west, citizens support Ukrainian independence and democracy based on a deep historic heritage, national consciousness, connection with European history, the Magdeburg law,[8] and the Ukrainian national movement. In the south and east, citizens support postcolonial pro-Russian and pro-Soviet ideals, extending back to colonization during the Romanov dynasty and again during the Soviet period; here, people have a Russian identity and embrace a more positive view of the Soviet legacy. The population of Western Ukraine does not want to be associated with this pro-Soviet ideology and the continuation of a colonial regime, supported by Great Russian imperialist nationalism and embodying a Russian identity that rests on the violence of, and welfare provided by, the state, leading ultimately toward a totalitarian regime and forced assimilation.[9] Hence, they perceive the red flag law as part of this alien ideology and constructed an *attributed divergence insult*.

The following extracts are examples of the perceptions of these events as an attributed divergence insult:

> Myth number one is that the red flag is a symbol of victory. On the contrary, under this flag, the Soviets started a bloody war on September 1, 1939. This fact is hidden by those who want to enforce upon Ukrainians Stalin's interpretation of World War II history. Many Ukrainians do not really know who started the war. It was Joseph Stalin and Adolf Hitler![10]
>
> Neither the Ukrainian government nor the president needed to have been great statesmen to understand the provocative and subversive character of this suggestion. Even if they watched only Russian TV and used no other sources of information, they would certainly have known that the Soviet flag is absolutely unacceptable for a significant

portion of the Ukrainian population, primarily in the western but also in the central part of the country. They should certainly have known that for millions of Ukrainians the Red Flag is first and foremost the symbol of occupation, of terror and genocide, Gulag and Holodomor, Russification, and national humiliation."[11]

These statements posit the red flag as a symbol of a totalitarian violent regime similar to the Nazi state and show ideological opposition between values promoted by these regimes and values of the many people in Ukraine, especially in its western regions. They stress similarities between the totalitarianism of Hitler and Stalin and create a strong impermeable boundary between the ideologies of these regimes and ideas of the progressive Ukrainian population. They perceive the red flag law as a threat to this social boundary and defend an essential distinction between two sets of social values.

This divergence insult provoked actions that were intentionally insulting and aimed at the creation of a strong social boundary separating off the regions that accepted the red flag law and protection of the values of Ukrainian independence. The local administrations of the western regions immediately made the decision to ban the use of the red flag. They stated that the symbols of a nonexistent state were prohibited because of the repression of the Ukrainian people under Soviet rule. The representative of the party Svoboda in the city council of Lutsk, Svyatoslav Borutsky, stated: "Repressions resulted in millions of victims were conducted under the red flag. This was the main reason to prohibit the use of the symbols of a nonexistent state."[12] The city council decided to ban the use of any Soviet symbols on the state and communal buildings of Lutsk as well as the use of Soviet flags and symbols during public meetings. Moreover, some regional western administrations decided to rename Victory Day the Day of Grief and invite veterans of the UPA into local schools to describe the heroic fights of the UPA against both Soviet and Nazi regimes.

The ban on the red flag in western regions, the promotion of the heroic memory of OUN-UPA among schoolchildren, and the positioning of the Soviet Union as an evil and brutal regime similar to Nazi Germany were specifically planned as a response to the attributed divergence insults and aimed at the restoration of social boundaries and prevention of the imposition of totalitarian and imperial Russian values. In this dynamic, the actions and words of both sides were increasingly perceived as offensive based on their similarity with previous insults through the process of *generalization of insult*. All statements, actions, and decisions that were connected with the celebration of Victory Day became progressively offensive and insulting for the participants in these events. The political and ideological leaders representing the populations of Western and Southeastern Ukraine used their statements and publications to illuminate the offenses committed by the other group. They explained why values and ideals of the other side are wrong and malevolent and why it is important to preserve social boundaries between these groups. They also justified their responses by reference to the offensive actions of the other side, thus *transferring insult* to in-group members. The meaning of the insult became deeper and more intricate by including diverse verbal statements and actions of both sides. The whole semantic area of interpretation of the victory in World War II and the connotation of the red flag became extremely sensitive and potentially insulting. The more often these insults were repeated, the more offensive and abusive they became, thus increasing the *conglomeration of insult*.

In these insults, representatives of Western Ukraine also delegitimized the pro-Soviet ideology and feelings of pride among Red Army veterans. At the same time, these actions legitimized views of the UPA as a freedom movement that fought against both Hitler's and Stalin's totalitarian regimes. This *legitimacy* insult rests on the employment of internationally recognized assessments of World War II and the evaluation of the various Ukrainian regions as evil or good. Thus, it associates the pro-Soviet population of the southeast with the evil side of Nazi ideology and Stalinism, while connecting Western Ukraine with the side of glorious victory over totalitarianism and communism. As a response to *divergence insults* attributed to Ukrainian government and pro-Soviet groups, the insulted side—Western Ukraine—constructed a *legitimacy insult*. This dynamic was also influenced by the process of *sensitizing*, when representatives of Western Ukraine tried to justify their actions in the eyes of a third party—the European Union.

Communists and veterans of the Red Army immediately recognized this *legitimacy insult* as an offense. Thus, while the dynamic of the insult started with attributed insults, it was transferred into a *congruous* insult. Communists and veterans protested the delegitimization of their ideals and the legitimization of the values of Ukrainian nationalists by producing a *relative* insult. In this insult, they positioned their in-group as one that has the rights and capacities to define the meaning of Victory Day and denied the rights of the population of Western Ukraine. The people's deputy from the Communist Party, Alexander Golub, stated that he understood why people in Western Ukraine wanted to establish a Day of Grief instead of a Day of Victory. "This is because they are descendants of people who fought together with fascist Germany and lost in this war. Thus, for them it is grief and mourning. I understand them very well."[13] He also said that "the normal people" are proud of the great victory and the Soviet Red Army. Communists and Red Army veterans in L'viv[14] (the major city in the west of Ukraine) lodged a protest against the "imposition of nationalistic ideology, the rehabilitation of OUN-UPA, and attempts to decrease the world-renowned significance of the victory of the Soviet people in the Great Patriotic War."[15] Thus, this *relative insult* created the relative deprivation of the rights of the population of Western Ukraine to define the connotations of Victory Day.

The statements made by the people's deputy and by the participants in the mass protest in L'viv also show that the supporters of the red flag recognized the processes of legitimization and delegitimization as well as relative deprivation, and tried to defend their legitimacy and rights. They, in turn, connected Ukrainian nationalists with Nazism, stressing the history of collaboration of Ukrainian nationalists with fascists during World War II. This connection with Nazis delegitimizes the representative of Western Ukraine. At the same time, these statements legitimize pro-Soviet groups by emphasizing international recognition of the Soviet victory. This *legitimacy* insult was produced intentionally and was recognized by Western Ukrainians. Both the people's deputy and participants in the mass protest constructed the *congruous legitimacy insult*, aiming to reverse the insult inflicted by the other side.

The use of the phrases "descendants of people who fought together with fascist Germany" and "rehabilitation of OUN-UPA...and attempts to decrease the world-renowned significance of the victory of the Soviet people in the Great Patriotic War" reveals the tendency to use internationally recognized values, as with the *legitimacy insult* created by Western Ukraine. Boosting the legitimacy of the red flag law rests on referring to global recognition of the Great Victory, and the attempt to decrease the legitimacy of the population of Western Ukraine rests on connecting them with Nazi and fascist movements. This insult has a much broader connotation, delegitimizing the whole group and its narrative while advancing the narrative of the in-group.

The verbal insults were later reenacted when a group of World War II veterans and representatives of NGOs came from the Southern and Eastern regions of Ukraine to L'viv to celebrate May 9—Victory Day. The organizers of this action were told that the main aim of this visit was to support Red Army veterans in L'viv and to honor the memory of Soviet solders that died on the territory of Western Ukraine fighting the Nazi occupation. They brought with them red flags and flowers that they planned to lay at the Tomb of the Unknown Soldier on the Hill of Glory. They recognized that the majority of the population of L'viv has different, and even opposing, views on Victory Day and the meaning of the red flag. But for these groups it was important not only to confirm the legitimacy of their views but also to delegitimize the other side by decreasing positive social acceptance of the ideas of Ukrainian nationalism. People from Eastern and Southern Ukraine came to L'viv to restore their positive validity provided by the social identity of people who had fought and won in World War II. This claim for legitimacy rested on opposition to Western Ukrainian nationalists who lost in this war and were condemned by the Soviet government for their collaboration with the Nazis.

The visiting group also actively *transferred insult* to the representatives of the local population who sympathized with the Red Army or the idea of the Great Victory. Many local people joined this group. There were many veterans who came to honor the memory of lost friends, members of families of killed solders, and people who wanted to thank defenders of their land by laying flowers to the Eternal Flame. This process also involved *sensitizing* because the reaction of third party—the Russian Federation—was considered essential in the developing situation. Russia was finally involved in the dynamics of insult when the Russian consul general, Oleg Astakhov, decided to honor the memory of Soviet solders on the Hill of Glory. A group of Russian diplomats under the leadership of the Consul General joined in a procession with a wreath, which they also intended to lay at the tomb.

Thus, the next round of the *legitimacy insult* involved a growing number of social groups. If the first congruous *legitimacy insult* was constructed between pro-Soviet representatives of Southeastern Ukraine and Ukrainian nationalists from Western Ukraine, the next *legitimacy insult* brought two new social groups to the pro-Soviet side: the Red Army veterans from L'viv and representatives of the Russian government in Western Ukraine. The next round of *legitimacy insult* created a divide within the population of Western Ukraine: Soviet veterans in L'viv were offended by the actions of their local administration and saw them as unjust delegitimization of their ideals. They decided to join the visitors from the southeast to increase the validity of their beliefs and memory of their friends who died in the fight against fascists. The participation of the Russian consulate brought an international dimension into the conflict. The representatives of the Russian government aimed to relegitimize the Soviet victory in the Great Patriotic War that was essential for the national identity of the current Russian Federation. Thus, the new round of *legitimacy insult* brought the Russian dimension into the ideological divide in Ukraine.

Ukrainian nationalists who believed that the independence of Ukraine was a result of their nationalist struggle saw these actions as delegitimization of their efforts and ideals. The recognition of this *legitimacy insult* is evident in the commentary on the Russians' behavior: "The Russian intent to deepen the Ukrainian divide has become an obsession, as well as efforts to discredit any strong anti-Soviet, pro-European Ukrainian identity as rabidly anti-Russian, xenophobic, and crypto-fascist. These intents may perfectly resonate with the Party of Regions' desire to marginalize the political opposition by a complex two-fold strategy. One aspect was mentioned already: re-Sovietization and Russification of Ukraine as a way to weaken Ukrainian identity and undermine the power-base of the Orange opponents."[16] This statement emphasizes the attempts of Russia and pro-Russian groups in Ukraine to delegitimize Western Ukraine by associating it with fascism and xenophobia. At the same time, the statement delegitimizes opponents by connecting them to Soviet and Russian nationalistic ideology. Thus, this insult was also a congruous legitimacy insult.

In addition, the visit of representatives from other regions of Ukraine and participation of the government representatives from the Russian Federation developed a *relative* insult. Ukrainian nationalists identified this action as a relative deprivation of their rights that was unacceptable. According to one of the leaders of the Western ultra-right-wing party Svoboda, "If Svoboda did not stand against these actions, we would allow the humiliation of the Ukrainian people as red flags were placed on the administration building, brought to the streets of L'viv. We did not permit it."[17] Nationalists claimed that people from Eastern Ukraine had no right to come to L'viv, celebrate their holiday, and support Stalinist ideas. Thus, the Ukrainian nationalists saw the visit of veterans and people from the southeast as an intended demonstration of their supremacy over other groups and treated their actions as a *relative insult*. The following excerpt supports this vision of insult: "One may find some disturbing analogies between Russian supremacists waving red flags in Western Ukrainian cities and Ulster unionists marching with their flags through the Catholic quarters to celebrate the 1688 historical victory and symbolic dominance of the colonizers over the aborigines."[18] This statement makes a comparison with another conflict over power, that in Northern Ireland, and invokes colonial experience. It associates the Russian Federation and pro-Russian, pro-Soviet groups in Ukraine with colonizers and Western Ukraine with the colonized population. This comparison not only uses the idea of colonization to legitimize Ukrainian nationalism and delegitimize Russian imperial ideology but also calls for the restoration of the rights of Ukrainian nationalists.

This combination of *relative* and *legitimacy insults* was strong enough to provoke open violence. Ukrainian nationalists from the party Svoboda attacked both groups—visitors from the southeast of Ukraine and local veterans. Several hundred young people representing Svoboda came to the memorial. They chanted "Shame" to veterans, did not allow them to lay flowers, and removed their medals and other decorations. A group of protestors broke through a police cordon outside the Hill of Glory and tried to prevent the unfolding of the red flag. They also crushed the wreath held by the Russian consul general. These actions aimed to show who has the right to control L'viv and what specific actions are allowed and not allowed. So this insult was carried out as a *relative insult*.

The deputy of the city council Andrei Homistkiy, a member of Svoboda who led the group, stated: "Representatives of the city intend to check if there any provokers with red flags."[19] Another leader of the party claimed: "All Ukraine saw that it was a planned provocation.... Svoboda did everything possible to prevent these events. We protested against the red flag law. We were writing, speaking, and warning about the possibility of a visit of paramilitary people with guns.... We were saying that it was not right to permit this scenario.... These bloody Bolsheviks flags are clear provocation."[20] The L'viv Regional Council issued a statement to the Ukrainian people: "[On] May 9 in L'viv [occurred] a cynical provocation. Existing power openly showed that they were working [according to] the Kremlin script written by the FSB. They work on sharpening of social contradictions and divisions of Ukraine."[21] Thus, relative insult aimed to show the supremacy of Ukrainian nationalists in Western Ukraine and to justify their violent actions based on their exclusive right "to the town." They claimed that they had to defend their rights and position in their own region.

These aggressive actions, including the beating of veterans and destruction of memorial wreaths, were perceived as *legitimacy insults* by pro-Soviet supporters and representatives of the Russian Federation. One of the leaders of the Communist Party of Ukraine stated: "This nationalistic abscess should be removed. It cannot be cured, it is too late.... All pro-fascist and Nazi parties should be prohibited—immediately! Try instigators of these actions in courts, and close the regional governments of L'vov, Ternopol', and Ivano-Frankovsk. And if that is not done, organize an all-Ukrainian referendum and make a decision about separation of Nazi Galichina from Ukraine. Because it disgraces all of us! It offends the whole country! Because of these fools our fathers and grandfathers, who went through the war, now feel themselves to be outlaws! It should not be forgiven!"[22] Many Ukrainian observers also criticized Svoboda's actions. "It became a negative tradition for L'vov when veterans of the war and citizens were trying to lay a wreath on the tombs of Soviet soldiers, to honor their memory, and became victims of violence and humiliation.... The events in L'vov demonstrated once more that the problem of neo-Nazism in Ukraine is growing."[23] These statements are attempts to delegitimize Ukrainian nationalists and reconfirm the exclusive position of pro-Soviet groups in Ukraine. They claim that pro-Soviet forces have the authority to dismiss the administrations of the western regions, put representatives of the party Svoboda on trial, and carve out and discard sections of the country.

The Russian Foreign Ministry immediately reacted to the nationalists' actions by condemning the new insult, now raised to the international level between Russia and Ukraine: "The actions by extremist forces resulted in the humiliation of the veterans and citizens who were celebrating the day of the victory over fascism."[24] The Russian council in L'viv stressed that "in civilized society, in which we believe we live, such acts should not be permitted."[25] Commentators in Russia recognized the legitimacy insult and responded with a congruous legitimacy insult in the mass media. The following statements are examples of the construction of the insult. One partisan asserted, "Finally the real face of the neo-Bandera group is revealed. Everyone, even supporters of 'independence,' now understand that we can no longer be tolerant of these hooligans. Those who can tear the Victory Flag off and throw smoke bombs at veterans should face the might of state power."[26] Another Russian commentator echoed these ideas" "There is still no policy in Kiev that can bring the deeply anti-Russian ego of these people into a normal human state." These statements instigate the use of law against the nationalists and suggest that the government of Ukraine should use all of its authority to punish pro-fascist groups.

FRYING EGGS ON THE ETERNAL FLAME

The *generalization of insult* involved another series of incidents connected with the history of World War II. On December 16, 2011, Anna Sin'kova and her friend, a young representative of the group Bratstvo (Fraternity), tried to fry eggs and sausages on the Eternal Flame near the Tomb of Unknown Soldiers in Kiev, the capital of Ukraine.[27] The women called their action political—a protest against the symbols of a totalitarian regime.[28] They were arrested and put on trial. Sin'kova did not accept her guilt and received a suspended three-year prison sentence, which would be enforced if she violated the conditions of her probation. Her friend was released without penalty because she repented and accepted responsibility for her offensive actions.

To support Sin'kova, who was in prison, three young activists from the Svoboda party repeated her protest. They simulated the cooking of scrambled eggs in a pan over the Eternal Flame near the Tomb of Unknown Soldiers and then ate them in the nearest park. Their actions were recorded on a video that was posted on the Internet. They were subsequently arrested and put on trial. On January 6, 2012, they were convicted and received three years in prison, again a suspended sentence, with a probation period of two years.

These protestors intended to diminish the value and achievements of the Red Army, thus creating an *identity insult*. They also emphasized the differences between their views and the official narrative of the victory of the Soviet army. By insulting the symbol of the Great Victory they wanted to show disagreement with the ideas of totalitarianism. Thus, they constructed a *divergence insult*, protesting against the imposition of Soviet history. The actions of these young people were perceived as insulting by the majority of the population. They saw these offensive actions as an *identity insult* to the memory of people who gave their life in the fight against fascism. As of this writing, the prosecutor's office is planning to appeal to change the decision of the court, asking for a stricter verdict. As the prosecutor stated, "We will not allow them to defame the memory of our predecessors—soldiers who died defending our motherland."[29]

CONCLUSION

The conflict that started with the issuance of the law supporting the use of old symbols resulted in violence against old veterans. Analysis of the case study shows the complex dynamics of insults, from the construction of attributed insults to the gradual development of congruous insults. The major type of insult constructed by both sides in this conflict is a *divergence insult*. It was strengthened by the development of *legitimacy* and *relative* insults. These insults were gradually *transferred* to other in-group members and even some members of the out-group. The more often these insults were repeated, the more offensive and abusive they became, thus increasing the *conglomeration of insults*.

The use of *divergence insults* helped both sides to reinforce the social boundary between them and prevent the imposition of alien values, beliefs, and traditions. Representatives of Western Ukraine positioned the red flag as a symbol of the values of a totalitarian regime and Russian imperial nationalism, as distinguished from their anti-Soviet and antitotalitarian values. They saw a need to defend Ukrainian independence from the imposition of alien values and the ideology of the pro-Soviet and pro-Russian forces. Similarly, representatives of Eastern Ukraine saw the promotion of UPA and Ukrainian nationalism as an imposition of both Nazi and pro-Western ideology and wanted to separate themselves from these ideas. These divergence insults stressed the erroneous and malicious values and ideals of the other side and emphasized the importance of preserving the social boundary between the groups.

To fortify these divergence insults, both sides employed *legitimacy insults*. Representatives of Western Ukraine delegitimized the victory of the Red Army and pro-Soviet ideology and praised the UPA as a freedom movement against totalitarian regimes. Representatives of Eastern Ukraine delegitimized Ukrainian nationalists, connecting them with Nazism, and legitimized pro-Soviet groups by emphasizing international recognition of the Soviet victory. These *congruous legitimacy insults* employed international approaches to the assessment of the World War II, delegitimizing the whole out-group and its narrative while advancing the narrative of the in-group.

Relative insults helped enforce the *divergence* and *legitimacy insults*. Representatives of Eastern Ukraine positioned themselves as the only group that has the right and capacity to define the meaning of Victory Day, and denied the right of the population of Western Ukraine to delineate its connotations. The visit of representatives from other regions of Ukraine to L'viv developed into a relative insult, perceived by Ukrainian nationalists as a deprivation of their rights. The violent actions of the young Ukrainian nationalists who demonstrated their right to control L'viv also were planned as a *relative insult*. In addition, representatives of Svoboda justified their violent actions through the need to defend their rights and position in their own region. Both groups actively *transferred insult* to a growing number of social groups and created a divide within the population of Western Ukraine.

The particular types of insult that came into play are indicative of the roots of the conflict in Ukraine and provide insights into its dynamics.

The conflict over Victory Day started with an attributed *divergence* insult. The opposition and Western Ukraine treated the red flag law as an imposition of totalitarian values on the whole of Ukraine and a threat to the social boundary between pro-European and pro-Soviet parts of the country. The use of a *divergence insult* in this emergent conflict emphasized a strong need to preserve the ideological and value divide between two parts of the country and nonacceptance of the Soviet version of history by the majority of the Western Ukrainian population. This was a situation of unstable coexistence in which any attempt to infiltrate through the social boundary provokes a strong negative reaction and all attempts to impose ideas on the other side are vigorously rejected. Actions like the red flag law are triggers that initiate the exchange of offenses.

The attempts to infringe on the social and ideological distance between Western and Southeastern Ukraine provoked *legitimacy* insults by both sides and thus are congruous insults. In their attempts to preserve the social boundary and prevent imposition of alien values, both sides started the process of legitimization of their ideals and delegitimization of those belonging to the other side. This process was based on the involvement of internationally accepted values. Thus, the population of Western Ukraine used the dichotomy of totalitarianism versus freedom: Stalin and Hitler were associated with the totalitarian side, while Ukrainian nationalists were presented as fighters for freedom. Their *legitimacy insult* aimed to delegitimize the red flag and pro-Soviet values and legitimize the fight of Ukrainian nationalists. The population of Southeastern Ukraine used the dichotomy of threat of fascism versus Soviet victory: the Ukrainian nationalist movement was blamed for collaboration with Nazis and the Soviet army was presented as the victor over the Nazi regime and a liberator of Europe. This *legitimacy insult* aimed to delegitimize Ukrainian nationalists and legitimize the red flag and Soviet legacy. Both sides were redefining the social boundary, trying to associate the insulted side with Nazis and thus reduce its social and ideological validity.

The use of a *legitimacy insult* brought the conflict to a new level. Offenses were no longer used to emphasize differences and preserve the boundary between groups. Instead, the sides were attacking each other's validity by linking the out-group to fascist and totalitarian ideologies. Praising the values of the in-group and associating it with fighters for freedom accompanied these abuses. This level of conflict invokes meta-frames, positioning both sides within widely accepted dichotomies of good and evil. Thus, the conflict highlights a moral dimension that requires such conflict resolution practices as acknowledgment and identity negotiation. Both sides should acknowledge the legitimacy of the other side and its claims, treating historic narrative as a deep belief in a particular state of intergroup relations, rather than as truth. Such efforts at resolution could be carried out during specially organized workshops on identity negotiation.

The use of *divergence insults* was also supported by the development of *relative insults*. Both groups tried to deny certain rights to the out-group and emphasize their own privileged position. They emphasized their inclusive rights to control a specific territory or group, make decisions, and define the connotations of historic events and holidays. *Relative insult* also rejects the rights of the out-group to make particular decisions or actions, thus bringing the normative dimension to the conflict. A relative insult defines what the out-group can do and what it cannot do because of its subordinate position. In this conflict, the representatives of the southeast constructed a relative insult and came to L'viv to demonstrate their rights to glorify their ideals. The representatives of Western Ukraine constructed a *relative insult* by denying the right of pro-Soviet groups to celebrate Victory Day in L'viv. The interaction of the two *relative insults* resulted in violent actions committed by the most radical representatives of the west.

The use of these insults and violence define the nature of the conflict as well as an approach to its resolution. To resolve this conflict, a third party should conduct a negotiation of the issues that were emphasized in the specific legitimacy and relative insult. Can veterans from other regions honor the memory of their friends by laying flowers on their tombs? Can they use the red flag, which is permissible according to the law passed by the national government but prohibited by the local administration? Can representatives of a local population resist mass demonstrations by people from other regions? These and many other issues should be negotiated as legal issues without invoking their ideological underpinnings.

The side in the conflict that committed violent acts does not want to accept its responsibility. When representatives of the radical party Svoboda showed ferocity toward the veterans, they justified their actions as a response to a *relative insult* and highlighted the need to defend their rights and positions. They claimed that well-orchestrated incitements by visitors from the southeast targeted their most essential values and deep beliefs and could not go unanswered. Thus, according to representatives of Svoboda, responsibility for violence should be ascribed to the pro-Soviet groups as provokers.

Through processes of *generalization and conglomeration*, the conflict became wider and more complicated because it included more and more diverse actions and issues. Starting from an interpretation of the victory in World War II and the connotation of the red flag, the conflict was transformed into a fight for control over specific territory and indeed the whole country. It included third parties, the European Union and Russia. The latter became involved in the dynamics of conflict when the Russian consul general decided to lay a memorial wreath on the Hill of Glory and was violently stopped by Ukrainian nationalists.

The dynamic of insult shows the transformation of the conflict from the preservation of a social boundary to legitimization and the definitions of rights of both groups and involving international third parties. The constructed insult reveals the core issues of the conflict and provides ideas for its resolution. The use of an *attributed divergence* insult illuminates the deep need for the divergence of two systems of values and beliefs within the country and protection of their ideological sovereignty. Attempts to infiltrate the existing social boundary and impose the ideology of one group on the other lead to processes of legitimization and delegitimization, evident in the *legitimacy insult*. The analysis of *legitimacy insults* shows that both groups use international views on fascism and totalitarianism as a reference frame for the legitimacy of their group's values. Thus, interpretation of the history of the middle of twentieth century is a core issue in the conflict between Ukrainian regions. It also creates the foundation for a *relative insult* that involves definitions of the right to action in all territories, control over Ukraine, and a capacity to define the meaning of history and particular holidays. The use of *relative insults* reveals that both sides deny the rights of the out-group and perceive it as subordinate to the in-group.

The absence of deep roots of violence in the construction of these insults indicates that the conflict has not become protracted and hostile, and that violent actions will not be essential to its dynamics. As Kuzio mentions, "Ukraine's regional divisions grew under both Presidents Yushchenko and Yanukovych [Yanukovich] but the country is unlikely to sink into civil war and inter-ethnic conflict because ethnic or religious hatreds do not run deep in the country."[30] Thus, the role of a third party could be limited to negotiation, mediation, and diplomacy.

The resolution of such a conflict with international dimensions requires a complex intervention by the third party. Thus, to reduce this conflict it is important to preserve the existing status quo and not violate the impermeable boundary between two groups. The attempts to develop a common identity based on a common vision of history will be perceived as an imposition of an alien ideology. Their divergent historic narratives do not prevent the two sides from collaboration in other areas and peaceful coexistence within the national boundary of Ukraine.

CHAPTER 4
Murder and Release

A convicted murderer who used an ax to strike an Armenian colleague 16 times in his sleep was released from custody to the cheers of the public and hailed as a national hero. The killer's quick pardon by Azerbaijan's president sparked outrage in Armenia and worldwide, yet the Azerbaijani public saw him as a victim and a symbol of their victory in the Nagorno-Karabakh conflict. What are reasons behind such overwhelming support for the murderer among the Azerbaijani public, and why did the Azerbaijani government consider the release of this murderer a foreign policy success? How did a perpetrator become a victim and the symbol of a nation? The following analysis of insults sheds light on these issues and the Nagorno-Karabakh conflict as a whole.

NAGORNO-KARABAKH CONFLICT

The conflict over Nagorno-Karabakh took over 25,000 lives; close to 600,000 people were displaced, and even after the ceasefire of 1994, the conflict continued to claim lives. This mostly mountainous and forested region lies in the middle of the South Caucasus and has an area of 4,400 square kilometers. The roots of the conflict between Armenia and Azerbaijan over this region lie in the administrative division of the South Caucasus. Following the tensions between two new Soviet republics in the early 1920s, the Nagorno-Karabakh Autonomous Oblast (region) was created within the Azerbaijani SSR on July 7, 1923. The Armenians, who perceived the granting of Karabakh to Azerbaijan as unfair and illegitimate, contested this decision, while those in Azerbaijan hailed it. Both countries employed historical evidence, documents, and maps to reinforce their position.[1]

In 1988, following the Gorbachev perestroika ideas of democratization and reformation, Karabakh Armenians saw a fresh opportunity to re-establish the jurisdiction of Armenia over the region. The local authorities in Nagorno-Karabakh cast votes for the unification of the region with neighboring Soviet Armenia, and around 80,000 people signed a petition to Moscow to support unification. The result of grass-roots mobilization against Soviet territorial divisions of the old leadership, the national movement to unite the region led to a sharp reaction in Azerbaijan, which strongly opposed a sovereign Nagorno-Karabakh. Marches through Armenian towns ensued, provoking tensions between the two ethnic groups, Azeris and Armenians. In 1989, the unification of Nagorno-Karabakh with Armenia was unilaterally proclaimed by the Armenian Supreme Soviet and the National Council of Nagorno-Karabakh. However, the Soviet government in Moscow rejected the Armenians' demands and returned the region to Azerbaijani administration. In 1991, Azerbaijan claimed direct control over the area and abolished the Nagorno-Karabakh Autonomous Oblast. In response, the Armenian population in the Nagorno-Karabakh region organized a referendum to establish an independent state. The Armenian majority in the region (76 percent), and the Azeri boycott of the referendum guaranteed passage. The failing Soviet government was powerless to negotiate a solution and, in November 1991, started the withdrawal of the 11,000 Soviet troops stationed in the region. Following the proclamation of independence by both states, the same year a full-scale war between Azerbaijan and Nagorno-Karabakh, supported by Armenia, began. The conflict was fueled by Armenian-Azerbaijani clashes, persecution, and ethnic pogroms in Sumgait and Kirovabad in 1988–1989, Baku in January 1990, and Khojali in February 1992, all of which killed thousands.

On March 24, 1992, in Helsinki, the Conference for Security and Cooperation in Europe (CSCE) worked on a draft ceasefire agreement and a resolution of the conflict. The delegate from Belarus proposed the idea of a "Minsk Conference" as the venue for discussion of the ethnic warfare. The planned event was called off because of an upsurge in fighting, but the name "Minsk Process" became the official title of the Karabakh peace process. The first CSCE negotiations took place in Rome and eventually led to the peace conference in Key West, Florida, in 2001.

Simultaneously, in collaboration with Russia, the Minsk Group started to negotiate a ceasefire. On July 27, 1994, three military chiefs representing Armenia, Nagorno-Karabakh, and Azerbaijan signed the ceasefire, which created the Lachin corridor that links Armenia proper to

Nagorno-Karabakh.[2] In December 1994, the CSCE was transformed into the Organization for Security and Cooperation in Europe (OSCE), which deployed its first-ever peacekeeping force to the Nagorno-Karabakh conflict zone.

The ceasefire document confirmed the intention of all sides to build on the immediate postwar truce and move towards a lasting peace. While Armenian and Azerbaijani sides had a common interest in finishing the fighting, their ultimate goals were very different. Armenia was interested in the creation of a new "security zone" around Nagorno-Karabakh and consolidation of its forces in this zone. It strongly supported peacekeeping forces in the region that could keep the ceasefire boundary stable and fixed. Azerbaijan saw the ceasefire line as dividing its own territory and treated it as a temporary solution. Thus, the Azerbaijani government opposed the deployment of a Russian peacekeeping force in 1994 as well as any action that would reinforce the OSCE monitoring mandate.

The roots of this violent war are multifaceted. First, it emerged from a desire to change the national territorial boundaries. Second, as the region was established during Soviet times, the conflict is a backlash against the collapsed regime, allowing fresh opportunities for autonomy.[3] Third, ethnic groups are expressing autonomy through secessionist and sovereignty claims,[4] which are in turn fueling ethnic fears and hatred.[5] Fourth, ideological manipulations and employment of historic narratives lead to ethnic mobilization and confrontation.[6] Last, the competition between popular-nationalist movements on both sides[7] helps influence ethnic conflict and secessionist ideology. However, scholars agree that the main issue that caused the war and the following "frozen" conflict was the status of the disputed territory of Nagorno-Karabakh. Since the ceasefire, the Karabakh Armenians have been in full control of the territory and the surrounding regions and have insisted that Karabakh should be recognized either as independent or unified with Armenia. They insist that independence was achieved based on the principle of self-determination and cannot be negotiated. The Azerbaijani side treats the conflict through the lenses of state sovereignty and Azerbaijan's territorial integrity. They position the region as an integral part of Azerbaijan and demand the return of all occupied territories.

Nagorno-Karabakh is often described as a "frozen conflict," but tensions between both sides are not easing in any way. The war displaced a large number of Azerbaijan's people, who lost their homes and livelihoods and still experience feelings of trauma and loss. A few dozen young soldiers die each year on the 110-mile-long Line of Contact that divides Armenian and Azerbaijani forces. Many observers see the situation as inherently dangerous and cite a tired peace process, an atmosphere of mistrust between the parties, a fragile ceasefire, and a lack of leverage on the part of the mediators:[8] "The reasons why the conflict over Nagorno-Karabakh remains unresolved despite the existence of a serious and well-tested negotiation process stem mainly from local dynamics and the calculations of local actors, rather than the conduct of the international mediators and the format of the negotiations."[9]

Governments of both countries continuously exacerbate the conflict in their speeches. Azerbaijani president Ilham Aliyev stresses that he wants peace but that Azerbaijan should be ready for war. The official Azerbaijani document states that "Baku [Azerbaijan's capital] would agree to no more than autonomy for Nagorno-Karabakh within the framework of territorial integrity of Azerbaijan, and in case the ongoing peace negotiations would not lead to this result, Azerbaijan would use force and start a second Karabakh war."[10] Based on the massive export of Caspian oil, Azerbaijan increased its military budget from $160 million in 2004 to $300 million in 2005 and $600 million in 2006. Similarly, Armenian president Serzh Sargsyan emphasizes his peaceful intentions but highlights the need to prepare for a fight. In a speech to Armenian soldiers, the president, wearing camouflage fatigues, said, "I have no doubt that if the time comes, we will not only do again what we did in 1992–94, but will go even further and solve the issue once and for all; the issue will be closed for good."[11] Thus, "Elites in power have equally used the conflicts as a resource, as a political instrument of reinforcing their position vis-à-vis competitors."[12]

Both nations in fact support continuous fighting around Nagorno-Karabakh. Azerbaijani people see their country as a wealthy, self-confident nation that is uninclined to make compromises with the Armenians. Armenians treat the secession of Nagorno-Karabakh in the framework of the sovereignty achieved by Kosovo and South Sudan.[13] The war memorials, ceremonies, and military exercises organized by the Karabakh Armenians as a part of daily life in Nagorno-Karabakh aim to transmit the message "No return to the past, no compromise."[14] The narratives of the imminent great victory of Armenia or the tragedy of Armenian occupation of Azerbaijani land are actively promoted by the state-controlled television and mass media in both Armenia and Azerbaijan. Both societies still hold "black-and-white attitudes of the late 1980s and early 1990s, which cast the other side as the enemy."[15]

The teaching of history in both countries also contributes to hostile attitudes helps justify each side's claims. An Armenian textbook describes Nagorno-Karabakh as an essential Armenian land: "The land of Artsakh, the central and largest part of which was better known throughout the

20th century as 'Nagorno-Karabakh' or 'Mountainous Karabakh,' is one of three ancient provinces of Armenia located in the eastern end of the Armenian Plateau.... Artsakh is important for Armenia's history and civilization in many ways.... The fact that Nagorno-Karabakh autonomous region was created within the borders of Azerbaijan was a hostile act against Armenians committed by Stalin under the pressure of Turkey."[16] By contrast, Azerbaijani textbooks emphasize that "Karabakh is one of the ancient regions of Azerbaijan. The name of this inseparable part of Azerbaijan consists of two different Azerbaijani words: 'gara' (black) and 'bag' (garden). Armenians are newcomers who appeared on the Caucasus due to mass migration from neighboring Turkey and Iran as a result of Russian-Turkish and Russian-Persian wars in the 19th century. The creation of the Armenian Nagorno-Karabakh autonomous region by Russian communists was a result of Armenians' strong ties with Moscow and the continuation of its old imperial politics of 'divide and rule.'"[17] Thus, history textbooks in both countries glorify their ancestors who brought Nagorno-Karabakh to prosperity, extending the national narrative into the distant past. Stories of victimhood depict another ethnic group as an enemy and justify claims to Nagorno-Karabakh region.[18] According to the historic narrative in Armenia, Nagorno-Karabakh was liberated by the Armenian military force and could not be returned to Azerbaijan; the historic narrative in Azerbaijan describes Nagorno-Karabakh and seven adjacent regions as occupied by Armenian military forces and stresses the necessity of liberation of these regions by Azerbaijan.

Let us look more specifically into the official position and public attitudes in Azerbaijan. Azerbaijani attitudes toward the Nagorno-Karabakh conflict have developed against the backdrop of a long history of rooted hostility and mistrust between the two peoples. The current regime, led by President Ilham Aliyev, promotes the narrative of a "country at war" and suppresses any opposition, violating basic rights and civil liberties.[19] "Like its citizens, the government values stability above all else, and will go to great lengths to prevent the population considering alternatives to its rule."[20] Social life is characterized by feelings of deprivation, apathy and fear,[21] and mistrust of others.[22] The narrative of historical injustices done to Azerbaijan by the Armenians dominates official and public discourse. The Azerbaijani people believe that they were victimized—not only by the Armenians but also by Russians, who continuously supported Armenia. In addition, they believe that the current situation in Nagorno-Karabakh is a reflection of the war of the Christian world against the Muslim world. This Azerbaijani idea of victimhood is developed in opposition to the Armenian victim discourse, depicting Armenians as a "particular/specific community" bent on territorial claims and a mission to occupy the lands of other nations that belonged to Armenia in different periods of history. Azerbaijani leaders refer to "Greater Armenia" as a myth of an Armenian golden age. They believe that Russia backs the territorial claims of Armenia and provides political support. Another cruel intention attributed to Armenians rests on a religious division between Christians and Muslims. According to the Azerbaijani side, "The Armenians are defending Christianity against the Muslim threat in the region." Thus, Azerbaijanis define themselves as the "victims in the Caucasus not only because they are Muslims, but also because they are Turks. In this context, it is believed that there is a worldwide hostility against the Turks and the Nagorno-Karabakh conflict is seen as proof of this. Azerbaijanis argue that the great powers are trying to weaken Turkey and Azerbaijan through this conflict."[23] This perception of Armenians strongly impacts Azerbaijani views on the Nagorno-Karabakh conflict. People in Azerbaijan see Armenians as cruel aggressors and occupiers who are trying to manipulate the opinions of third parties. But they hold on to "an expectation that Western powers will recognize the injustices done to the Azerbaijanis and act accordingly during the peace process."[24] Public opinion in Azerbaijan is strongly influenced by the government and rests on rigid negative stereotypes of Armenians as the principal enemies of Azerbaijan, and on ideas of victimization and injustice.

THE MURDER

During a NATO-sponsored Partnership-for-Peace English Language Training course held at the Zrinyi Miklos National Defense University in Budapest, Ramil Safarov, an Azeri army lieutenant, walked into the bedroom of a sleeping Armenian soldier, Gurgen Margaryan and struck him 16 times with an ax, partially decapitating him. He also attempted to kill another Armenian officer but was stopped by fellow students. What was the main motivation for this brutal attack?

During the night of the murder, on February 18, 2004, Safarov was alone in his room because his roommate—a Ukrainian officer—had returned home to attend the funeral of one of his relatives. That morning, Safarov bought an ax, a knife, and a sharpening stone, hid them under his bed, and then spent the night hours sharpening the ax. He waited until 5:00 a.m., then ventured into the Armenian quarters. As he explained during interrogation, "According to my knowledge this is the time, when sleep is the deepest, when they do not wake up for small noise, and I also had to be sure [of] the place where the person that I wanted to kill was sleeping, because his roommate is of Hungarian citizenship. I didn't want to hurt him, because he is really nice guy."[25] Safarov's plan was to kill two Armenian soldiers. As Gurgen Margaryan's room was closest and he might possibly alert others, he would be the first victim. Safarov entered the room and switched on the light. Safarov hit Margaryan on the forehead with the flat side of the ax and then chopped Margaryan's neck, almost severing his head as Balazs, the Hungarian roommate of the murdered officer, ran to wake up other students and called security. Safarov then lit a cigarette and smoked, tossing the smoked cigarette on Margaryan's body.

When he was asked why he threw the cigarette on the corpse, Safarov answered: "Since I hate them so much and I prepared for revenge for so long, it was a relief for me. As long as I didn't care about him it didn't mean whether I threw the cigarette onto the ground, or on his bed or into his eyes."[26] As the representative of the Budapest police acknowledged, "We suspect Ramil S. of having committed murder with unusual cruelty...the number of wounds...the victim's head was practically severed from his body."[27] After finishing his cigarette, Safarov went out to the hall to look for the other Armenian officer, but he didn't know exactly where his room was. Two rooms were locked and Safarov began hitting a closed door with his ax, shouting in Russian, "Come out, wherever you hide, I will find you." Other residents emerged from their rooms and calmed him down until police arrived.

During his first interrogation after the killing, Safarov said that the roots of his actions lay in the Nagorno-Karabakh conflict. He cited the violence of Armenian soldiers who murdered innocent Azerbaijani civilians: "The very tragedy that I was talking about happened on February 26, 1992. At that time Armenian soldiers attacked the Karabki Hodzani area, where were only civil citizens, particularly children and women and old people and around 8,000 people were killed. This is my blood.... Armenians occupied my place of birth for 1 year in 1993, August 25. This is memorable as it happened on the date of my birth. I don't know how many people were killed at that time, but even though it's [a] huge number. That was the time when I lost part of my close relatives as well."[28] He said that these violent events influenced his decision to become a soldier and that his only motivation was to "fight against Armenians and to kill as many as possible in the fight."[29] Describing his service in the army, he said, "I have not killed any other Armenian, just injured soldiers to get them to hospital.... I felt sorry that I haven't killed any Armenians."[30]

Describing his motivation, Safarov said that Armenian officers had "walked close to me they...mumbled something in Armenian and laughed at me. That was the time when I decided that I [would] kill these two persons, the Armenians, I [would] cut their head off. The reason for this is that Armenians kill Azerbaijanis in the same way...because of that laugh at me the feeling of animosity became bigger and bigger and that's why I decided that day in the morning that I will kill both of them."[31] Safarov presented the killing as revenge, stressing retaliation as his main motive. As he stated, "Since he is an Armenian his mother would cry as much as our mother cried when they lost their child."[32] Balazs, the Hungarian roommate of the murdered officer, later said that Safarov "left with such an expression on his face as if he had completed something important well enough."[33]

Safarov presented the main motivation for the murder as a *projection insult*. He invoked the autocracies committed by Armenian solders against Azerbaijani civilians, women, and children, stressing that his relatives were among people who were violently killed. He further emphasized that all Azerbaijani people who were killed in this conflict are his relatives by blood and soul. He also believed that this brutal violence was unprovoked and Azerbaijani people were innocent in this war. Accordingly, Azerbaijani people have a right to retaliation, so that the relatives of murdered Armenian soldiers should feel the loss and mourning that Azerbaijanis have felt. Moreover, the killing of Armenian solders was not only justified by their brutality, but also honorable and obligatory for Azerbaijani soldiers. Disappointed by his inability to kill Armenian soldiers during the war, Safarov felt that he had failed in his duty to contribute to retribution. The very presence of Armenian soldiers in close proximity was insulting to Safarov, and he perceived all their jokes and conversations as specifically targeting him and insulting him. He saw the murder of a fellow student not as a criminal act, but as a logical act of retaliation. He rationally planned this killing, insulted the dead by throwing a cigarette on the body, and prepared to commit a second killing. Thoughts that murdering a sleeping human being is a brutal, immoral crime never crossed his mind. It was a symbolic act of retaliation, organic to his life and his hatred. Thus, Safarov's explanation of his actions was presented as a *projection insult*.

The initial reaction of Armenian officials was to portray Safarov as a representative of the Azerbaijani government, claiming that the crime was a direct consequence of a policy of aggression, hatred, and animosity towards the people of Armenia. In an official statement, the Ministry of Foreign Affairs of Armenia asserted that "this crime is the logical consequence of the anti-Armenian hysteria that has been left unrefined by the Azeri authorities over the years and of the warmongering militarist propaganda of recent months, which consistently infects all of Azeri society.

It is evident... that such state policy has crossed the bounds and officials, representing Azerbaijan abroad, can commit cold-blooded murder."[34]

In his speech at the 497th meeting of the Permanent Council of the Organization for Security and Cooperation in Europe (OSCE) Armenian ambassador J. Tabibian emphasized that the murder was "committed in cold blood, deliberate and premeditated, according to the accused's own admission.... Fanning the flames of hatred, state sponsored and propagated Armenophobia in and by Azerbaijan provides a pretext, a reason, a motivation, better yet, a license to those who are inclined to operate outside the law, thinking they are doing national duty."[35] The spokesperson for the Armenian Ministry of Foreign Affairs, Hamlet Gasparian, also stressed the connection between the murder and official narratives in Azerbaijan. "Such an act is the logical consequence of the warmongering statements of the Azeri government, old and new, and of the anti-Armenian hysteria that has been left unrefined by the Azeri authorities over the years. The horrifying act and the way the crime was executed reminds one of the anti-Armenian pogroms in Sumgayit, in Kirovabad in 1988 and in Baku in 1990 much before the Nagorno-Karabakh War started."[36]

These three statements stress that the murder is a direct consequence of the anti-Armenian narratives of hate promoted by the Azerbaijani government. According to Armenian officials, these narratives not only justify aggressive actions against Armenian people but give license to kill. This atmosphere of hatred leads to deliberate, premeditated, and brutal actions by Azerbaijani people, including the murder of Gurgen Margaryan. The statements also deny the claims that Armenian violence during the war in Nagorno-Karabakh provoked Safarov to murder. They indicate that the war was a result of violent crimes committed by Azerbaijani people against an Armenian minority before the war began. According to statements, the Azerbaijani leadership represents the Armenian people in a hostile light, denying their positive identity and rights to retaliation. The Azerbaijani official narrative attributes aggressive intentions to Armenians and depicts them as brutal and amoral, dehumanizing and devaluating them. Thus, these statements present the murder as an *identity insult* and create the *transfer* of insult, presenting it as an offensive action of Azerbaijani people against all Armenian people.

In response to Armenian statements, Azerbaijani mass media and officials strengthened the idea of a *projection insult* as a motivation for murder. The Azerbaijani Defense Ministry stressed that Safarov's actions were a direct consequence of his suffering from Armenian violence, and thus his mental state must be considered. The statement pointed out that many of Safarov's relatives were killed by Armenians during the war. Members of his family had to flee an Armenian-occupied region and as internally displaced persons (IDP) "were living in a Baku hostel in deplorable conditions."[37] Thus, officials in Baku represented Safarov as a victim of Armenian brutality. The following week, at a specially organized press conference, the Karabakh War Veterans' organization stated that it "did not rule out that the Armenian officer had made insulting remarks in his relations with Safarov, which brought about the incident in the end."[38] The Azerbaijani mass media further developed the idea of a *projection insult*, stressing that Safarov was systematically and purposefully offended by Margaryan and another Armenian officer. On February 25, Azerbaijani Space TV reported, "It turned out that a week before the incident, the killed man and another Armenian officer insulted Safarov in a dormitory. The tension was defused through the intervention of other officers. However, as Safarov did not produce a strong reaction, the Armenian officers regarded this as his cowardice and cruelly insulted him. When they learned that Safarov was from the currently occupied Cabrayil District, the Armenian officers started insulting him in a crueler way and exasperated him."[39] In reporting this news, Azerbaijani agencies cited "unofficial sources" in Budapest.

Two days later, on February 27, the Azerbaijani ombudsman added more detail about the insulting behavior of Armenian officers: "Not only did he [the Armenian officer] play a tape with the voices of suffering Azerbaijani women and girls, but he also cleaned his shoes with an Azerbaijani flag in front of Ramil [Safarov]. At that moment Ramil defended his national honor and responded immediately and correctly to this. I think that the world community should accept this."[40] While these claims were not supported by any witnesses during the trial, they created a strong sense of the murder as a *projection insult*. The idea that the killing was an organic part of the current conflict and a symbolic retaliation for all Azerbaijani sufferings was repeatedly stressed in official statements and comments. For example, the political analyst Gaderli stated that "there is a growing expectation that somehow, someday this must come to an end. Many people think that something needs to be done in response to Armenia. So whatever Armenia has done, for good or for bad, should somehow be retaliated."[41]

Along with stressing the suffering of Safarov and the provocative behavior of Armenian soldiers, officials and mass media created the perception of the murder as a heroic act. The newspapers supported Safarov's actions, calling him "a hero for the entire Muslim world."[42] According to the Baku-based political analyst Zardusht Alizadeh, "It's not only the Armenian soldiers and officers who are occupying our land that Azerbaijanis consider their enemy. It's not only the 'Armenian terrorists' who were killed in the fighting. Because of a very skillfully constructed propaganda campaign, it's all Armenians who are considered the enemy. That's why a man who killed an Armenian in his sleep is automatically categorized as a hero."[43] The presentation of the murder as heroism was based on both the idea of general insult to the Azerbaijani people and descriptions of specific insults to Safarov.

This presentation of a *projection insult* by officials *sensitizes* Azerbaijani public creating the perception of Safarov as the victim and Margaryan as the taunting aggressor. Many Azerbaijanis believe that Margaryan had urinated on the Azerbaijani flag or used it to polish his shoes. They also assume that the Armenian officer had provoked the attack and was not asleep at the time of murder. The statements of people interviewed by Radio Free Europe on the streets of Baku illustrate this belief: "I think he was a hero, because he protected the honor and dignity of the Azerbaijani people"; "Safarov did the right thing by killing Margar[y]an."[44]

Thus, Azerbaijani officials and mass media projected the brutality of murder onto Armenian side. They justified Safarov's aggressiveness, which was provoked by the violent actions of Armenians and insulting behavior by Armenian officers. Azerbaijani officials reduced Safarov's responsibility for committing murder by ascribing provocative intentions to Armenians. They portrayed Armenian officers as typical representatives of aggressive and brutal Armenian people and justified Safarov's behavior as a natural reaction to this insult. Thus, this *projection insult* eradicated the negative features of Azerbaijani murderer by imposing them on Armenians as an out-group.

The murder trial began in November 2004. In April 2006 Safarov was found guilty of both the murder of Margaryan and the intended murder of the other Armenian officer and was sentenced to life in prison in Hungary. This decision was actively protested by the Azerbaijani Union of Liberation Movements, which sent appeals to the government and law-enforcement institutions of Hungary and heads of international organizations residing in Baku. The chairman of the Supreme Executive Council of the Union, Tahmasib Novruzov, stressed that the sentence of Safarov did not take into account his sufferings during childhood.[45] Azerbaijani officials also considered this sentence an *identity insult* to all Azerbaijani people. Ali Akhmedov, a member of the Azeri presidential party stressed: "Both Karabakh and Ramil became victims of saboteurs."[46]

THE RELEASE

On August 31, 2012, Hungary extradited Ramil Safarov back to his native Azerbaijan. The decision was made based on an agreement between the

Azerbaijan and Hungarian governments and the assurances from the Azerbaijani government that his sentence would be enforced. Some experts in Hungary connect this decision with the negotiation of the natural gas contracts between Hungary and Azerbaijan and plans for energy supplies through and from the Caucasus.[47] Others suggest that the decision might be linked to a debt sale of Hungarian bonds or some other bilateral economic deal.[48] But Azerbaijan's ambassador to Budapest denied that the Azerbaijani oil fund had any such investment plans. Officials in Budapest also rejected this information: "The state oil fund... is not considering any investment into debt obligations or other financial tools in Hungary."[49]

Commenting on the extradition, Vilayet Guliyev, Azerbaijani ambassador to Hungary, said that "this [did] not happen suddenly. We had been working on this for many months. The extradition process from beginning to end was done by order of the Azerbaijani president and implemented by the embassy."[50] Zahid Oruj, a member of the Azerbaijani Parliamentary Committee for Defense and Security, confirmed that the Azerbaijani embassy in Budapest was specifically opened with the aim to release Safarov. He stated that "at that time, i.e. when the incident happened with Ramil Safarov, in Hungary there was no embassy of Azerbaijan. Now I can report that the main purpose of the establishment of the Azerbaijani Embassy in Hungary was to ensure the legal protection of Ramil Safarov. Azerbaijan in a short time was able to bring its relations with Hungary to the highest level. Along with this, the release of Ramil Safarov on the one hand was thanks to the efforts of Azerbaijan, on the other hand thanks to his personal behavior."[51]

Safarov arrived in Baku on a special flight of Azerbaijan Airlines and was immediately pardoned by the president of Azerbaijan, Ilham Aliyev. The "Order of the President of the Republic of Azerbaijan on the pardoning of R. S. Safarov," issued on August 31, 2012, stated: "Guided by paragraph 22, Article 109 of the Constitution of the Republic of Azerbaijan, I hereby order: 1. Ramil Sahib Safarov, a citizen of the Republic of Azerbaijan, who was born in 1977, and was sentenced to life by the decision of the Budapest Capital Court of Hungary dated April 13, 2006, shall be pardoned. 2. This order shall take effect from the day of its issuance. Ilham Aliyev, President of the Republic of Azerbaijan."[52] Not only did the Azerbaijani government not try to downplay the event, it made every effort to publicize its decision and actions even in the face of mounting international criticism. Materials immediately were made available in English to publish on official websites. The embarrassed Hungarian government emphasized that it was not involved in the decision to pardon Safarov and released a letter signed by Vilayat Zahirov, the deputy minister of justice in Azerbaijan, in which Azerbaijani government guaranteed that any "sentenced person" would "serve the remaining part of their prison sentences in the Republic of Azerbaijan."[53]

Safarov also was given a hero's welcome, promoted to the rank of major, and given a flat and all the pay he had lost since his arrest eight years ago. Explaining the release, Azerbaijan sent a note to the Hungarian government, which stated that the "procedure for transfer and pardon of Safarov was made in accordance with Azerbaijani and international law."[54] Azerbaijani Foreign Ministry spokesman Elman Abdullayev said that the country's constitution gives the president of Azerbaijan exclusive right to pardon. He stressed agreement and cooperation with Hungary: "Azerbaijan has been working in this direction for some time and we greatly appreciate the cooperation of Hungary in this matter."[55] He also added that Safarov's situation should be reconsidered based on Armenian violence in the Nagorno-Karabakh conflict and Safarov should be treated as a victim who witnessed ethnic cleansing by Armenia against the Azerbaijani population.[56] Zahid Oruj, a member of the Azerbaijani Parliamentary Committee for Defense and Security, confirmed that "Safarov became a kind of symbol. His release will raise the moral and psychological mood of the society. This is because the people of Azerbaijan, due to the imprisonment of the Azerbaijani officer in Hungary, experienced a certain complex and anxiety. Azerbaijan, achieving the release of Safarov, thus demonstrated its strength as a nation.... Safarov's action is not an ordinary criminal case. Figuratively speaking, the verdict was passed not against Ramil Safarov, but against the Karabakh war."[57]

These statements tried to establish the legitimacy of Azerbaijani actions based on several foundations: domestic and international law, the agreement by Hungary, psychological conditions of the prisoner, and a *projection insult* as a motivation for murder. The legitimization process encapsulated this *projection insult*, emphasizing the cruelty of Armenians in Nagorno-Karabakh and the (alleged) offensive behavior of the Armenian officer at the NATO school. Therefore, the decision to release Safarov was placed in the framework of the Nagorno-Karabakh war to present Azerbaijani sufferings as justification for the murder. According to these statements, it had a symbolic meaning for the whole Azerbaijani nation as an indication of victory in the Nagorno-Karabakh conflict.

The release of Safarov provoked strong protests worldwide. As Thomas de Waal stressed, "Leaving him [Safarov] a free man without public comment would have been bad enough. The Azerbaijani government went much further than that, treating Safarov as a hero.... From the political perspective, to call the Azerbaijani government's actions a mistake is an understatement."[58] Maja Kocijancic, spokeswoman for the high representative of the Union for Foreign Affairs and Security Policy, Catherine Ashton, stressed that the decision of the Azerbaijani government did not meet the terms of the agreement between Hungary and Azerbaijan: "According to what we know now, on the basis of the information gathered, it would appear that certain conditions and commitments that were agreed between Hungary and Azerbaijan on the transfer of Ramil Safarov have not been met and in that respect we will continue or we will try to be in touch with the Azeri side to hear the explanation why this has happened and why the behavior that is endangering the fragile situation the region is continuing."[59] The European Parliament reacted by passing a resolution describing the decision to release Ramil Safarov as "a gesture which could contribute to further escalation of the tensions" between Azerbaijan and Armenia. Representatives of the European Union considered the actions of the Azerbaijani state "a violation of the diplomatic assurances given to the Hungarian authorities."[60] Similar protests were expressed by the leadership of many European countries, including Russia.

The administration of the US president Barack Obama also expressed its concerns. Tommy Vietor, a spokesman for the US National Security Council, said: "President Obama is deeply concerned by today's announcement that the President of Azerbaijan has pardoned Ramil Safarov following his return from Hungary. We are communicating to Azerbaijani authorities our disappointment about the decision to pardon Safarov. This action is contrary to ongoing efforts to reduce regional tensions and promote reconciliation.... The United States is also requesting an explanation from Hungary regarding its decision to transfer Safarov to Azerbaijan."[61]

Despite international protests, Azerbaijani people celebrated Safarov's return home as a national holiday. The deputy chairman and executive secretary of the ruling New Azerbaijan Party, Ali Akhmedov, presented the release as a triumph of determination, courage, and justice.

> Both Karabakh, and Ramil became victims of saboteurs. The first is occupied by the enemy, while the other for so many years was imprisoned. Ramil was released, next is the liberation of Karabakh. Please God, the day will come, when President, Supreme Commander Ilham Aliyev announces the liberation of Karabakh. All believe and wait for it. One injustice has been relegated to history, the other, I believe, will also be eliminated.... Azerbaijani people and the state are known worldwide for their love of peace, they treat with respect all peoples, religions and cultures. In world history no cases of Azerbaijan's violence, injustice against any country have been recorded. Azerbaijan has the right to expect from the other the same treatment and is very glad that Hungary was able to assess all of this.[62]

The head of the Department on Work with Law Enforcement Agencies of the Azerbaijani presidential administration, Fuad Alasgarov, established a direct connection between the murder in Budapest and the Nagorno-Karabakh war: "Ramil Safarov, a native of the Jabrail region occupied by the Armenians, is an IDP. He lost a lot of close friends, and these tragedies took place before his eyes, ran into his childhood memories. One can imagine the emotional state of a person who lived through all these tragedies as a child, as a result of permanent provocations against him by the Armenian officers, insults to the flag and the people of Azerbaijan at NATO exercises in which he participated as an officer of the Azerbaijani army."[63] A statement by a member of the Azerbaijani delegation to the Parliamentary Assembly of the Council of Europe (PACE), Rafael Huseynov, echoed the presentation of the murder in the framework of the Nagorno-Karabakh conflict: "This problem is directly related to the aggression of Armenia against Azerbaijan, occupation of 20 per cent of Azerbaijan with nearly one million people who became refugees and internally displaced immigrants, the loss of thousands of lives, people maimed for life and to the aggressive policy of Armenia, which has continued for over 20 years. Discussing Safarov's issue, we also need to discuss the details of this conflict. Every time opening this discussion, you will allow us to once again draw attention to this problem."[64] The statement of the deputy executive secretary of the New Azerbaijan Party, Mubariz Gurbanli, also stresses that the murder should be considered a response to Armenian brutality: "The act committed by Safarov at that time, was forced. Insult by the Armenian to our people, wounding our national feelings forced him to take this step."[65]

These statements created a strong parallel between Safarov's imprisonment and the occupation of Nagorno-Karabakh, describing them as similar tragedies and traumas for Azerbaijani people. Both situations presented the victimization of Azerbaijanis by Armenians, as well as injustice that was done to Azerbaijanis. Thus, the murder of an Armenian officer was a direct consequence of the occupation of Nagorno-Karabakh by Armenians. The release of Safarov was positioned as a symbolic event that would lead to the liberation of Nagorno-Karabakh. Blaming Armenians for the violence, the statements posited Azerbaijani people as peace-loving and tolerant. They stressed that the international community should adopt this view on the conflict and support the Azerbaijani side because it has been victimized by Armenia. Thus, denying responsibility for murder and projecting aggressiveness and violence on Armenian side, the statements reinforced the *projection insult* that was used during the trial.

The Armenian government and public responded to Safarov's release with active protests. The president of Armenia, Serzh Sargsyan, immediately invited heads of diplomatic missions of the UN member states and heads of the offices of the international organizations accredited in Armenia for a special meeting. In his statement he said: "I have nothing to say about Azerbaijan—just plainly nothing. That country speaks about itself with the actions it takes, and I am not the one to explain those steps.... With their joint actions the authorities of Hungary and Azerbaijan have opened the door for the recurrence of such crimes. With this decision they convey a clear message to the butchers. The slaughterers hereafter are well aware of impunity they can enjoy for the murder driven by ethnic or religious hatred. I cannot tolerate that. The republic of Armenia cannot tolerate that. The Armenian nation will never forgive that."[66]

The same critical descriptions of Azerbaijan and resentment by Safarov's release were repeated in the speech of Armenian foreign minister Edward Nalbandian at the General Debate of the 67th Session of the UN General Assembly. He emphasized that international organizations have been "alerted about flagrant cases of xenophobia, racism, intolerance and violations of human rights in Azerbaijan, alerted on the policy of hatred against Armenians.... The latest such case is the Azeri government's release and glorification of the murderer Safarov, who had slaughtered with an ax an Armenian officer in his sleep, during a NATO program in Budapest simply because he was an Armenian. The Azerbaijani leadership made him a symbol of national pride and an example to follow by youth."[67] He also connected the murder and release with the Nagorno-Karabakh conflict, stressing that the actions of the Azerbaijani government "seriously undermined" the negotiation process and that "Armenia and the international community are speaking in one language regarding the Nagorno-Karabakh issue."

These statements produced both *identity* and *legitimacy* insults, creating a negative image of the Azerbaijani people and government and delegitimizing their actions. Azerbaijan was presented as a society driven by ethnic and religious hatred, characterized by intolerance and xenophobia, that violated human rights and supported brutal killings. According to the Armenian president, the release of the murderer continued an Azerbaijani policy of hate—it was not an unexpected surprise. The pardon and glorification of Safarov were presented as unlawful actions that destroyed the legitimacy of Azerbaijani government. Like Azerbaijani officials, representatives of the Armenian government also used the Nagorno-Karabakh conflict as the frame for the release. However, they delegitimized the Azerbaijani government, asserting that its actions undermined the negotiation process and bolster the Armenian government, which was supported by the international community. Thus, this dual *identity* and *legitimacy insult* allowed

Armenia to present the release as an unlawful act by the aggressive and bigoted Azerbaijani government.

While emphasizing that the actions of the Azerbaijani government were predictable because of the hostile nature of Azerbaijani society, the Armenian government also stressed the flaw the Hungarian decision. The repatriation and subsequent pardon of Safarov sparked a diplomatic conflict between Armenia and Hungary. At a special meeting with ambassadors and representatives of international organizations, Armenian president Serzh Sargsyan announced that Yerevan was suspending diplomatic relations and all official contacts with Budapest. Explaining this decision he stressed: "With these joint actions, Hungary's and Azerbaijan's authorities have cleared the way for a repeat of such crimes."[68] The Speaker of the Armenian National Assembly, Hovik Abrahamyan, canceled his visit to Hungary and turned down the invitation of his Hungarian counterpart to pay an official visit to Bucharest in late September.

On September 1, hundreds of people protested outside the Hungarian consulate in Yerevan, burning the Hungarian flag and throwing eggs, tomatoes, and coins. Groups of Armenians also protested outside Hungarian embassies in other world capitals, burning Hungarian flags and distributing flyers with insulting statements and rhetorical questions about Hungary, for example, "Hungary—have you gone mad?"[69] President Sargsyan appealed to Armenians, asking them not to burn the flag of Hungary: "I would like to address our society, specifically the youth, and ask them not to burn the flag of Hungary because the flag of Hungary is not the flag of Hungary's party in power. Hungary's flag is not the symbol of Hungary's prime minister. We have had very good relations with the Hungarians for hundreds of years. And the inhuman act by one person, or one party, one government should not be grounds for us to become enemies with the Hungarians."[70] Thus, the Armenian president one more time stressed that the Hungarian government made the wrong decision, but the people of Hungary should not be held responsible for it. He also positioned Armenia as tolerant, a democratic country that condemns violence.

The statements of Armenian officials provoked a new waive of reactions from Azerbaijan. The director of the Center for Strategic Studies under the president of Azerbaijan, Farhad Mammadov, noted that "holding...a meeting of the Security Council of Armenia and a five-minute nervous speech of President Serzh Sargsyan at the meeting with the ambassadors of UN member states have demonstrated that Sargsyan actually admitted his untenability. By his actions and statements he showed that Armenia is not able to oppose the active foreign policy of Azerbaijan.... The return of Ramil Safarov is a signal for Armenia, as this country has no leverage because of its weakness and vulnerability." Speaking about the diplomatic conflict between Armenia and Hungary, he stated: "I think Hungary is not particularly upset by the fact of freezing diplomatic relations with Armenia. However, the Hungarian authorities and the public will feel the brunt of propaganda of Armenians at [the] global level, because the most absurd and dirty accusations will fall to Hungary. Admittedly, the Armenians do it best. I think that Hungary should raise the level of threat of terrorist attack, as the EU visa-free space is home to over half a million Armenians, potentially ready to commit a terrorist attack." He went further, connecting the current president of Armenia with terrorism: "It should be recalled that the existence of a politician in the face of Serzh Sargsyan as the president of Armenia is the most prominent example of impunity for the killing of hundreds of Azerbaijanis by Armenian thugs led by Serzh Sargsyan during the ethnic cleansing in Nagorno-Karabakh."[71]

Other statements echoed the positioning of the Armenian president as a propagator of terrorist ideology. Azerbaijani Foreign Ministry spokesman Elman Abdullayev said: "As for the Armenian side, Sargsyan's hysterical statements, who is one of the leaders of the group that committed the Khojaly genocide with cruelty, are nothing like [sic] show and populism."[72] Political Analysis and Information Provision Department head Elnur Aslanov also emphasized: "It is important to stress that despite everything, Azerbaijan is not against Armenians, [but against] the Armenianism ideology in the form that justifies ethnic cleansing and killing of civilians, women and children, rather than the Armenians."[73]

These responses of Azerbaijani officials furthered the *projection insult* and brought it to a new level, connecting it with a *relative insult*. Azerbaijani officials described Armenians and their current president as aggressive brutal slaughterers, terrorists who executed mass killings of Azerbaijani people and continued to threaten them and other countries. They stressed that Hungary may be under imminent threat by Armenian terrorists who fight for their immoral cause. Thus, Azerbaijani officials denied that the decision to release Safarov was a legal error and ascribed all responsibility for the ongoing conflict to the Armenian side. They also created a *relative insult* through the denial of the right of Armenia to condemn Azerbaijani actions. They asserted that the Armenian president cannot influence international perceptions and call for condemnation because of his involvement in ethnic cleansing, stressing that he and the country he leads have no leverage in the international community. Presenting the speech of the Armenian president as "nervous" and "hysterical," Azerbaijani officials furthered the *relative insult*, stripping him of reasonableness, intelligence, and influence. The statements also emphasized that vulnerable and weak Armenia cannot oppose actions by Azerbaijan in the international arena. Thus, Azerbaijani officials created a *relative insult* and brought the *projection insult* to a new level, blaming the leadership of Armenia for the development of the conflict and characterizing the Armenian president and Armenian society as aggressive terrorists. This blending of *relative* and *projection insults* allowed Azerbaijani officials to posit Armenia as weak, without influence, while emphasizing the triumph of Azerbaijani foreign policy.

CONCLUSION

The preceding analysis of the insults employed by both sides of the conflict reveals the specificity of relations between Azerbaijan and Armenia. The Armenian side used *identity insults* to create a negative image of Azerbaijani society as cruel, barbaric, xenophobic, and full of anti-Armenian hysteria. The Azerbaijani side employed *projection* and *relative insults* to deny its responsibility for the development of the conflict and presented its actions as provoked by the brutal aggressiveness of Armenians, who lack international leverage. Both sides used *legitimacy insult* to position themselves as the rightful side in the conflict and presented the other side as illegitimate and undeserving of the trust of the international community.

In all his statements, Safarov presented a *projection insult* as the main motivation for the murder. He stressed that the killings of innocent Azerbaijani people by Armenian solders was unprovoked brutality and that it justified retaliation. He saw the murder as an honorable and obligatory action, which would help relatives of murdered Azerbaijani people feel better. Placing his interaction with Armenian soldiers in Budapest in the context of the Nagorno-Karabakh conflict, he saw all their actions as insulting and provoking. Thus, he committed the murder as a symbolic act of retaliation, justified by a *projection insult*.

Azerbaijani officials and mass media strengthened this projection of responsibility for the cruel murder onto the Armenian side as a needed defense provoked by the cruelty of Armenians in Nagorno-Karabakh and the insulting behavior of Armenian officers. They countered the negative image of the Azerbaijani murderer by redirecting it onto the Armenian people. Azerbaijani officials presented the imprisoning of Safarov in parallel with Azerbaijani sufferings in the Nagorno-Karabakh conflict and legitimized the decision to release Safarov as a symbolic act of victory in the war. *Projection insult* helped Azerbaijani leadership to posit Azerbaijan as peace-loving, tolerant, and victimized by the brutality of Armenians. The presentation of the current Armenian president as a violent, ruthless slaughterer and terrorist who represents Armenian society deepened this *projection insult*, explaining all Azerbaijani actions as justified by the continuous threat to their society. Therefore, this insult was employed to diminish the responsibility of Safarov, avoid the critics of the Azerbaijani government's decision to release him, and ascribe provocative and threatening actions to the Armenian side.

The Armenian side used an *identity* insult to present the killing and the release of the murderer as an example of the policy of aggression and animosity towards the people of Armenia. According to Armenian officials, hostile representations of the Armenian people created a culture of hate to justify aggressive actions against them, including violent crimes and ethnic cleansing both before and during the war. Azerbaijan society was positioned as driven by ethnic and religious hatred, violating human rights and supporting brutal retaliations and killings.

Both sides strengthened these insults by connecting them with a *legitimacy insult*. The Azerbaijani side denied the legitimacy of the Armenian government because of its involvement and support of ethnic cleansing and brutal policies in Nagorno-Karabakh. Azerbaijan officials used the label of terrorism, a red flag for the international community, to condemn and delegitimize Armenian society. The presentation of Azerbaijanis as the subjects of Armenian terrorism positioned the Azerbaijani people as moral and suffering victims and the Armenians as vicious and hostile, thus legitimizing actions of the Azerbaijani government. The release of Safarov despite Armenia's protests was presented as a symbol of Armenian weakness in comparison with a just Azerbaijan, which enjoyed support by the international community, thus creating the *relative* insult.

The Armenian side also used a *legitimacy insult* to reinforce an *identity insult* and bolster the negative image of Azerbaijani people and government. Like the Azerbaijani officials who used terrorism as a legitimacy frame, the Armenian side employed the value of the success of the negotiation process. It delegitimized the actions of the Azerbaijani government as ruining the negotiation process and legitimized the Armenian government, claiming support by the international community. This *legitimacy insult* helped Armenia present the release as an unlawful action by an aggressive and bigoted Azerbaijani government that destroyed the fragile possibility for peaceful resolution of the Nagorno-Karabakh conflict.

Analysis of these differences and similarities in the use of insult deepens our understanding of the conflict's dynamics. The main distinctions between Armenia and Azerbaijan are in the respective prevalent use of *identity* or *projection* and *relative* insults and in framing *legitimacy* insults in terms of terrorism or success of the peace process. Thus, the Azerbaijani side denied all responsibility for the ongoing conflict, imposed it on Armenia, and undermined peace negotiations, justifying its position by presenting Armenia as a terrorist state that could not participate in real negotiations. These framings helped the Azerbaijani government to continuously use the state of war and external threats to impose its control within the country as well as avoid a peaceful agreement that could determine the status of Nagorno-Karabakh. Azerbaijan also prevented informal contacts across the conflict lines and delegitimized ongoing projects by nongovernmental activists and middle-level officials from Armenia and Azerbaijan to promote dialogue. The policies of the Armenian side aimed to demonstrate to the international community a willingness to come to an agreement in the Nagorno-Karabakh conflict that would confirm its independence as well as highlight the continuous impediments to the peace process thrown up by a bigoted and aggressive Azerbaijani society.

The analysis of the dynamic of insults shows that the international community should pay "more attention to the dangers of a new Armenian-Azerbaijani conflict over Nagorno-Karabakh. The conflict is not 'frozen,' as it is frequently described.... This slide can be halted, but the time to start working harder on diplomacy is now."[74] Current efforts by international organizations on the level of formal diplomacy have resulted in little progress toward a peaceful settlement of the conflict. Activities at the middle and grass-roots level, however, may allow the expression of alternative voices and the transformation of both societies. "If ordinary connections are to be maintained between increasingly estranged societies, people who engage in these activities need proactive support from outsiders."[75] Analysis of the insults used in this case provides insights that are critical in designing particular third-party interventions that might decrease the impact of identity, projection, and legitimacy insults used by both sides in the conflict.

CHAPTER 5

Islands between Two Countries

The president of Korean paid his first-ever visit to a small, rocky island inhabited only by a few police officers and promised to defend it to death. Japan recalled its ambassador to South Korea and the Japanese Foreign Ministry refused entry to a South Korean diplomat delivering an official letter, barring the doors of the Ministry of Foreign Affairs building. Japanese, Chinese, and South Korean activists swam to contested islands to demonstrate their respective nation's ownership, some of the participants drowning along the way. A Chinese naval vessel directed a weapons-guiding radar lock on an escort vessel of the Japanese Maritime Self-Defense Force. Numerous protests sparked in China, while thousands of people gathered at Japanese consulates, overturning Japanese cars and throwing fish against the walls.

All these events represent disputes between Japan, China, and Korea over two small groups of islands. Why are these neighboring countries aggressively demonstrating their power, engaging in diplomatic tit-for-tat, and contesting control over uninhabited rocks? Why do Japan, China, and Korea continuously claim these islands, using different interpretations of history and law? The following analysis will revel the reasons behind these island disputes and show how insults became central to the dynamics of these conflicts.

Japanese relations with both China and Korea have a long history of contention, with numerous battles and incidents of ethnic violence. The two most recent wars between China and Japan occurred over control of specific territories. The first Sino-Japanese War (August 1, 1894, to April 17, 1895) involved fighting between the Chinese Qing dynasty and the

Japanese Meiji dynasty over control of Korea. A modernized Japan overcame Chinese forces, which were also—unsuccessfully—trying to modernize. The Japanese victory had two immediate effects. First, it shifted the center of regional power dynamics in the Pacific from China to Japan, and second, it left China humiliated in the international community, leading to internal revolutions and the subsequent establishment of the Republic of China in 1911.

Another defining event for Sino-Japanese relations occurred on September 18, 1931, when Japanese military personnel exploded a bomb near a railroad owned by Japan's South Manchurian Railway. The Japanese government then used the incident as an excuse to invade the province of Manchuria in northern China. This day is still remembered as a national humiliation by most Chinese. When the truth behind the Makuden (Manchurian) Incident was exposed to the international community in 1933, Japan was forced to withdraw from membership in the League of Nations.[1]

Another day of national humiliation for the Chinese was the beginning of the second Sino-Japanese War (July 7, 1937, to September 2, 1945), which became a front in the Pacific theater in World War II. It started when Japanese military stationed in China (as permitted by the Boxer Protocol of 1931) conducted training maneuvers in the vicinity of the Marco Polo Bridge near Beijing without notifying the Chinese government, as Japan had agreed to do. Thinking they were under attack, the Chinese military fired several shots. While intergovernmental negotiations were held to organize a search for Japanese soldier who went missing during the brief exchange of fire, a renegade segment of the Japanese army took over the Marco Polo Bridge for a short period. When additional forces arrived, the Chinese were able to reclaim the bridge, but the incident served as the incitement for the full-scale invasion of China by Japan. This invasion is characterized by mass slaughter, including the Nanking Massacre, when some 250,000 to 300,000 people, including women and children, were killed.[2]

Since the 1950s Sino-Japanese relations have gone through their ups and downs. Japanese officials have issued formal apologies for war crimes committed during World War II, and in 1972 People's Republic of China (PRC) and Japan established a diplomatic relationship.[3] Yet increased cooperation between the two countries has been troubled by controversies over Japanese history textbooks, Japanese commemorations of soldiers who died in the second Sino-Japanese War, and anti-Japanese demonstrations in China.

Similarly, the history of interactions between Japan and Korea includes Japanese invasions and control over Korea. Exploiting the unstable situation in Korea at the end of nineteenth century, Japan determined to exert its influence. Using gunboat diplomacy, Japan imposed a harsh treaty, signed on February 26, 1876, that allowed Japan to intervene in Korean politics.[4] On October 8, 1895, Empress Myeongseong (Queen Min) of Korea was assassinated by Japanese agents because she was seen as an obstacle to their expansionist policies.[5] After winning the Russo-Japanese War, Japan stationed troops throughout the Korean Peninsula and forced Korea to sign the Elusa Protectorate Treaty of 1905, which created the legal foundation for turning Korea into a Japanese protectorate.[6] Although the Korean imperial family's status was "heightened" so as to make them Japanese nobility, Emperor Gojong of Korea protested the, sending a secret envoy to the Hague Conference on World Peace. In retaliation, in 1907 Japan forced the emperor to abdicate. As a result of the new Japan-Korea Treaty of 1907, Korea turned over internal administration to Japan and pledged to obey the local Japanese government. Finally, in the Japan-Korea Treaty of 1910 Japan completely annexed Korea.[7] During the 35-year Japanese occupation, Koreans were arrested for political reasons (in 1912 alone there were more than 52,000 arrests) and 20,000 Korean laborers were transferred to Japan to sustain industrial production, especially mining operations. More than 75,000 Korean cultural artifacts were relocated to Japan during the occupation.[8]

After its defeat in World War II, Japan lost control of Korea. On September 9, 1945, the Japanese governor-general of Korea surrendered to the United States in Seoul, effectively ending the tenure of the Japanese administration. Despite the passage of time, the occupation has left a deep trauma among the Korean population. Korean workers who returned in 1945 demanded the payment of wages for work performed in Japan, and the Japanese refusal caused popular outrage.[9] When Korea demanded the return of cultural articles, only a portion were repatriated, and many still remain in the Tokyo National Museum and in private collections. The relationship between the two countries has remained fraught with conflict.

In 1965, the Treaty on Basic Relations normalized Japanese-Korean diplomatic relations. In accordance with this treaty, Japan provided $800 million to Korea in compensation for the 35 years of occupation ($500 million in loans and $300 in grants). South Korea, in turn, agreed to demand no more compensation at the levels of government to government and individual to government.[10] Still, some issues connected with the occupation remain unresolved, including the denial of Japanese responsibility for Koreans forced to perform as "comfort women," and the historical records of the occupation in Japanese textbooks and official Japanese statements. For example, in 2007 Japanese cabinet official Shimomura Hakubun admitted the existence of comfort women but claimed that the system existed because many Korean parents sold their daughters off.[11] Similarly, on March 27, 2010, during the centennial anniversary of the Japanese annexation of Korea, the minister of government revitalization, Edano Yukio, claimed that the Japanese occupation of Korea and China was inevitable, as the latter two countries were unable to modernize, suggesting that the Japanese brought advancement to both during the occupation. Thus, the relations of Japan with Korea and China are still influenced by unmourned traumas, unresolved disputes about wars and occupations, and a slow process of reconciliation.[12] "The dilemma of Japanese flattery (*omoneri*) of China versus Japanese national contempt (*anadori*) for China is as great an influence on Sino-Japanese relations as the changing national calculation of political and economic interest."[13]

THE JAPANESE-CHINESE DISPUTE OVER ISLANDS

The dispute between China and Japan involves the Senkaku Islands, known as Diaoyu in Chinese, an uninhabited outcropping of five islands and three large rock pieces that lie in the middle of rich fishing grounds and potentially richer oil and gas deposits. The islands have been at the center of disputes for centuries. On January 14, 1895, the Japanese government annexed the Senkaku Islands to Okinawa, claiming that China had not previously controlled them. One year later, the islands were leased to Japanese investor Tetsushiro Koga, who built plants to process bonito fish and albatross feathers, employing 280 workers. His son continued the business until 1932, when Zenji Koga purchased four of the five Senkaku islands. Eight years later Koga abandoned the business, leaving the islands uninhabited once more. In 1945, following the Japanese surrender to the Allies at the end of World War II, the United States occupied the islands.

In 1969, the UN Economic Commission for Asia and the Pacific released a report stating that oil reserves had been located in the vicinity of the islands. Two years later, based on an agreement between Japan and the United States concerning the Ryukyu Islands and the Daito Islands, Okinawa—and along with it, the Senkaku Islands—were returned to Japanese control. Immediately, both the Chinese government and the Taiwanese government declared ownership. These claims were supported by anti-Japanese protests in China and Taiwan. In 1972, the Kurihara family from Saitama Prefecture of Japan purchased the islands from the Koga family, perpetuating ownership of the island by private citizens of Japan. In 1978, a nationalist Japanese group, Nihonseinensha, built a lighthouse in Uotsuri, one of the islands. In the same year, a fleet of 100 Chinese fishing boats sailed close by. However, the Japan-China Peace and Friendship Treaty, signed in 1978, mitigated the growing conflict. According to the treaty, the dispute over the islands was in effect shelved, to be resolved at a future time, and "all disputes shall be settled by peaceful means without resorting to the use or threat of force."[14] Chinese leader Deng Xiaoping underlined that the dispute should be resolved through the wisdom of the coming generations.[15]

During the next 30 years, tensions over islands flared several times. In 1996, the Japanese group Nihonseinensha built a new lighthouse on another Senkaku island. In protest, activists from Hong Kong dove into waters near the islands; one of them drowned. A few days later, tens of thousands of Chinese gathered to mourn the activist's death and protest the Japanese claims to the islands. In 2004, Mainland Chinese activists occupied one of the disputed islands and were removed by the order of the Japanese prime minister. One year later, 50 Taiwanese fishing boats staged protests around the islands, claiming harassment by Japanese patrols.

In 2010, a Chinese fishing boat collided with a Japanese Coast Guard patrol boat, leading to the arrest of the fishing boat captain. China repeatedly requested the release of the skipper, but the Japanese government kept him in captivity for an additional 10 days. In protest of the incident, Chinese non-governmental fisherman groups held protests outside the Japanese embassy in Beijing demanding the withdrawal of Japan from the islands and organizing marches outside of the Japanese consulate in Shanghai. Other protests were also held in nine cities throughout Mainland China. A private Japanese school in Tianjin, China, was vandalized, and other Japanese schools were shut down for a week. Protesters also gathered outside the Japanese consulate in Hong Kong, burning Japanese flags and chanting aggressive slogans. In Taiwan, protesters threw fish at the building housing the Japanese Interchange Association and burned Japanese flags to voice their anger. When a giant panda on loan from China died in a Japanese zoo after being sedated to collect semen for artificial insemination, China sent investigators, evoking conspiracy theories connecting the panda's death to the boat captain's arrest.[16] China canceled all high-level diplomatic relations with Japan.[17] The Chinese assistant minister of foreign affairs claimed that China had been insulted when the Japanese dubbed the Chinese reaction to events on the islands "hysterical."[18] In response, large-scale anti-Chinese protests occurred in seven cities in Japan, including Tokyo. When the fishing crew members were released, China treated the release as a diplomatic victory over the Japanese government.[19]

While many of statements and actions by China and Japan in the past were offensive, the present analysis of insult will concentrate on the events of 2012–2013. On April 16, 2012, Tokyo's right-wing nationalist governor Shintaro Ishihara stated that he and six other nationalists would consider purchasing the Senkaku Islands. He stressed that Japan wanted to take control over the disputed territory and that no other country had any right to claim it: "Tokyo has decided to buy them. Tokyo will defend the Senkaku Islands.... Why would any country have a problem with that?"[20] Stressing the importance of Japanese ownership, he stated that he could build a dock on the islands. In response, China warned that it would take "all necessary steps" to protect the islands. Liu Weimin, a foreign ministry spokesman, said: "Any unilateral action taken by Japan on the Diaoyu and nearby islands is illegal and invalid, and cannot change the reality of China's ownership.... We do not wish statements in Japan to encroach on China's sovereignty and harm China-Japan ties. I believe they not only damage the overall state of China-Japan relations, but also harm Japan's international image."[21]

Certain leaders in Japan warned against radical moves that could harm Sino-Japanese relations. On June 6, 2012, the Japanese ambassador to China, Uichiro Niwa, declared, "If Mr. Ishihara's plans are acted upon, then it will result in an extremely grave crisis in relations between Japan and China.... We cannot allow decades of past efforts to be brought to nothing."[22] However, the foreign minister, Koichiro Gemba, as well as many right-wing politicians, disowned Niwa's statements. Portraying the sale of one of the islands as strictly an internal issue, Gemba said: "The change of ownership is a domestic matter that does not concern the international community."[23] The chief cabinet secretary, Osamu Fujimura, stressed that Niwa's statements reflected the ambassador's personal position and not the government's official stance.[24] Ishihara also strongly criticized the ambassador, suggesting that Niwa needed to learn more about the history of his own country before making such comments, and questioning his ability to serve his country's interests: "He is not qualified to be Japan's ambassador to anywhere."[25] Niwa apologized for his comments in a letter to Gemba, stating, "I am extremely sorry. I will not make comments like this."[26]

Japanese statements like Gemba's posited the purchase of the islands as a strictly internal issue, stressing Japan's rights to the islands and therefore weakening the foundations of claims by other countries (meaning China). They created a *legitimacy insult* confirming the lawfulness of ownership by

Japan and rejecting any rights claimed by China. All alternative views on this issue were strongly condemned: Ambassador Niwa was presented as a person who was disloyal to his country, did not know and respect its history, and could not protect its interests. Depicting the ambassador in this light, government officials and nationalists created a *divergence insult* that positioned him as outside mainstream ideology. They established a social boundary between loyal patriots of the country and those who take into consideration the interests of other countries. This *divergence insult* also emphasized the homogeneity of belief in exclusivity of Japan's ownership. It helped strengthen the *legitimacy insult* by contributing to the legitimization of Japan's rights and the delegitimization of Chinese claims.

China's reaction to this *legitimacy insult* included not only reaffirmation of its rights over the islands and denial of any Japanese claims, but also raising questions about the adequacy of Japanese foreign policy. Thus, China also created a *legitimacy insult*, presenting Chinese ownership of the islands as real and beyond question and Japanese attempts to purchase islands as illegal. In addition, China brought the *legitimacy insult* to a new level, presenting Japanese actions in the international arena as incompetent and harmful for its image.

A month later, Japanese prime minister Yoshihiko Noda declared that Japan would consider buying the islands from the private owners. Japan's chief cabinet secretary, Osamu Fujimura, confirmed the legal foundation for these actions: "It is clear that the Senkaku islands are inherently Japanese territory from a historical point of view and in terms of international law."[27] In response, China's Foreign Ministry spokesperson Liu Weimin underlined that China would take necessary measures to protect its sovereignty and that its land and sovereignty were not up for sale: "No one will ever be permitted to buy and sell China's sacred territory.... China will continue to take necessary measures to firmly uphold its sovereignty over the Diaoyu islands and its affiliated islands."[28] The position of the Chinese government was supported by numerous Chinese protesters who waived placards that read "Return the Daiyou Islands," "Japan must confess to its crimes," and "Smash Japanese Imperialism."

These statements not only strengthened the *legitimacy insults* created by both parties but also added new dimensions into the processes of legitimization and delegitimization. Japan used the criteria of historic truth and international law to support the legality of buying the islands and to counter China's interpretations of history and the applicable law. The reference to international law raised the *legitimacy insult* to the level of international relations and positions of both countries. China employed the idea of a sacred land as core to its national identity and invoked victimization by a brutal, imperialistic Japan. The idea of victimization helped to create a parallel between the violence of Japanese invaders during previous wars and current Japanese intentions to take over the islands. Doing so placed the dispute within a framework of the history of Japanese invasions and imperialistic ambitions. Thus, both China and Japan brought their *legitimacy insults* to new levels, introducing new criteria for judgments on the legality of their actions: history, international law, national integrity, and victimization. The issue of the islands was captured by the contentious history of Sino-Japanese relations, *reactivating* previous insults to, and humiliations of, the Chinese people by Japanese invaders.

In July 2012, three Chinese patrol boats entered the waters around the islands. China stated that the boats were carrying out a "fishery protection mission."[29] To promote Chinese ownership, activists sailed from Hong Kong and landed on the disputed islands. Some fled before being captured, while others were deported by Japan. The Japanese government condemned these Chinese actions. In support of the government, Japanese activists also landed on the islands. Ten nationalists swam ashore from a flotilla that carried about 150 people close to the islands and raised the Japanese flag. One of the politicians on the flotilla, Kenichi Kojima, stated: "I want to show the international community that these islands are ours. It is Japan's future at stake."[30] This foray was treated as an illegal action in breach of Chinese sovereignty by the Chinese Ministry of Foreign Affairs. The Foreign Ministry spokesman Qin Gan said: "Any unilateral action taken by Japan on the Diaoyu Islands is illegal and invalid."[31] New protests flared, and thousands of people gathered at Japanese consulates, overturning Japanese cars and shouting slogans denouncing Japan's claims to the islands. Japanese vice foreign minister Kenichiro Sasae responded that the anti-Japanese protests in China were "unacceptable" and regrettable.[32]

These actions by Chinese and Japanese activists were aimed at demonstrating their rights over islands as well as their power to control the territory. The rhetoric of power also became evident in the statements of government officials. A diplomatic and security advisor to Japanese prime minister Noda said: "We need to consider various uses of constabulary forces, including the Self-Defense Force."[33] Representatives of mass media and academics saw the logic of attitude. Jeffrey Kingston, director of Asian studies at Temple University's Tokyo campus, said: "On a rational basis, both sides have a lot to lose if this escalates. On the other hand, both have something to lose if they don't appear strong and assertive."[34]

These actions and statements demonstrated the transformation of a *legitimacy insult* into a *power insult*: the validity of claims to sole ownership of the islands was supported by the demonstration of power. The landings on the islands by activists, sailing of official boats in the island waters, and aggressive protests were meant to display the supremacy of one's own side and to impose control over the islands. Statements by officials, the mass media, and academics confirmed that legitimization of rights of ownership must be supported by strong evidence of power and dominance over the other side.

To reduce the growing tensions and prevent the conflict that might mount if the Japanese nationalist faction led by Tokyo governor Ishihara bought the islands, the Japanese government took the initiative purchase them. In August and September, Japan issued several statements justifying its plans for the acquisition. There can be no doubt, Prime Minister Noda states, that the Senkaku Islands are an integral part of Japan. In a speech to the UN he reiterated his position and his unwillingness to compromise on the issue: "So far as the Senkaku islands are concerned, they are an integral part of our territory in the light of history and of international law."[35] In another statement, Noda underlined the legality of the purchase. A "part of the Senkaku islands that was held by a private citizen was transferred to governmental possession in order to ensure the stable management of it.... It is not a new acquisition. It was held under the private ownership of a Japanese citizen and was a transfer of ownership within Japanese law."[36] He also stressed that while Japanese actions were legal and justified, China refused to accept reality: "We have explained this to China at length. But it seems that China has yet to understand that and, because of that lack of understanding, there has been an attack or acts of violence and destruction against Japanese citizens and property there."[37]

Japan's plans to purchase the privately held portion of the islands rendered China furious. China's new president, Xi Jinping, said: "Japan should rein in its behavior, not utter any words and prevent any acts that undermine China's sovereignty and territorial integrity."[38] Chinese Foreign Ministry spokesperson Hong Lei explained that his government was watching the situation: "The Chinese government is monitoring developments closely and will take necessary measures to defend its national territorial sovereignty."[39]

Despite these warning from China, on September 10, 2012, Japan purchased the Senkaku Islands for 2.05 billion yen ($26 million). Japan's chief cabinet secretary, Osamu Fujimura, underlined that the government had historic and international legal grounds to buy the islands and that the issue was a strictly domestic one: "The acquisition and possession of the Senkaku Islands is a case in which the ownership of land under Japan's sovereign territory will be transferred from the previous owner to the Government. I believe that this matter is therefore not something that should raise any kinds of issues for other countries or regions."[40] He also stressed that Japan had bought the islands to promote their stable and peaceful management, underscoring that "the Government in no way desires the circumstances related to the Senkaku Islands to negatively impact the broader aspects of Japan-China relations. From the perspective that it is important to avoid misunderstanding and any unforeseen situation arising between Japan and China, to date both Governments have been engaged in a process of close communication through diplomatic channels to respond to any concerns that China has had."[41] Fujimura also underlined that the government would not build on the islands, countering Governor Ishihara's statements about building a dock.

In response, the Chinese Foreign Ministry declared that Japan's unilateral move to purchase and nationalize the islands was "totally illegal and invalid": "This constitutes a gross violation of China's sovereignty over its own territory and is highly offensive to the 1.3 billion Chinese people. It seriously tramples on historical facts and international jurisprudence. The Chinese government and people express firm opposition to and strong protest against the Japanese move."[42] To address the claims about historic Japanese ownership, the statement underlined that "the Diaoyu Island and its affiliated islands have been China's sacred territory since ancient times. This is supported by historical facts and jurisprudential evidence."[43] To support this assertion, the statement provided an extensive review of the history of Chinese ownership over the islands since the Ming dynasty. The statement also denied the validity of the Japanese presentation of international law: "According to international law, the Diaoyu Island and its affiliated islands have already been returned to China. Facts are facts, and history is not to be reversed. Japan's position on the issue of the Diaoyu Island is an outright denial of the outcomes of the victory of the World Anti-Fascist War and constitutes a grave challenge to the post-war international order."[44] Like Japan, China blamed the other side for increasing tensions between two countries: "The Chinese government has always attached importance to developing relations with Japan.... Yet, to ensure sound and stable development of China-Japan relations, the Japanese side needs to work together and move in the same direction with China. The 'purchase' of the Diaoyu Island by the Japanese government runs counter to the goal of upholding the larger interest of China-Japan relations."[45]

While the Japanese government tried to mitigate the conflict by purchasing the islands rather than have them become the property of right-wing nationalists, in justifying this action it created a *legitimacy insult* to China. The Japanese government utilized historic evidence as well as international and domestic law to present the issue as a completely external one and to deny any possible grounds for China to intervene. Thus, it validated its rights to make exclusive decisions on ownership of the islands and delegitimized all Chinese claims to the territory. To further legitimize its position, Japan employed a *projection insult* blaming China for the increasing tensions. The Japanese government presented itself as a country that worked toward peace and cooperation in the region and had openly explained the situation in the islands to China. Despite the positive and peaceful intentions of Japan, China preferred to stoke tensions and was solely responsible for the growing hostility. The depiction of China as aggressive and inadequate increased Japan's legitimacy and devalued Chinese claims. Thus, the *legitimacy insult* was strengthened by the creation of a *projection insult*.

The purchase of the islands by the Japanese government and its justification was perceived by China as a *legitimacy insult*. In response, it created a new *legitimacy insult* aiming to invalidate all claims and statements made by Japan. The delegitimization of Japanese actions involved a general assessment of them as illegal, as well as complete refutation of all justifications for the purchase of the islands by the Japanese government. The official Chinese statement presented its version of history, which depicted the islands as the sacred territory of China since ancient times. It also questioned the validity of the transfer of the islands from the United States to Japan in the framework of international law. Finally, it employed the discourse of pos-war reconciliation and justice, positing Japanese actions as a recurrence of its aggressive, imperialistic policies. Bringing up the memory of humiliation and invasions during World War II led to the *reactivation* of insult—the reappearance of offenses in the previous actions. This reactivation of insult increased the potency of the *legitimacy insult*. Thus, China validated its exclusive rights over the islands and delegitimized their purchase by the Japanese government. This *legitimacy insult*, like the Japanese one, was reinforced by accusing Japan of initiating the conflict and aggressively invading Chinese territory. At the same time, the statement stressed that China had done its best to maintain peace in the region and tried to preserve positive relations with Japan. Thus, China also created a *projection insult*, ascribing responsibility for the conflict to Japan and denying its own provocative actions. This projection insult helped delegitimize Japanese actions and present Japan as an aggressive invader.

Chinese vice president Xi Jinping called the purchase by Japan "a farce." Citing the Cairo Declaration and the Potsdam Proclamation, he stressed that "Japan should rein in its behavior, not utter any words and prevent any acts that undermine China's sovereignty and territorial integrity."[46] Chinese Foreign Ministry spokesperson Qin Gang stated that China was disappointed with and opposed Noda's "obstinacy" regarding his "wrongful position" in the dispute.[47] In other statements, Chinese officials accused Japan of stealing the islands and underlined that Japan must stop all activities that violated Chinese territorial sovereignty, claiming that Japan should correct its mistakes and return to the route of negotiation.[48] Chinese Foreign Minister Yang Jiechi stressed: "The moves taken by Japan are totally illegal and invalid. They can in no way change the historical fact that Japan stole Diaoyu and its affiliated islands from China and the fact that China has territorial sovereignty over them."[49]

Japanese deputy ambassador to the UN Kazuo Kodama rejected the Chinese arguments: "There is no doubt that the Senkaku islands are clearly an inherent territory of Japan based on historical facts and international law."[50] He added that China and Taiwan started asserting claims to the islands only in the 1970s, when valuable natural resources were discovered. The position paper on the Japan-China relations surrounding the islands released by the Japanese government stated that the Senkaku Islands were an "inherent part" of Japan and that purchase of the islands from private ownership was aimed at normalizing bilateral relations with China: "In light of such maritime activities by China, former Tokyo Governor Shintaro Ishihara announced last April his plan to purchase the Senkaku Islands and develop a variety of facilities on them . . . in an effort to minimize any negative impact on the bilateral relations, the Government of Japan decided to purchase the islands and transferred the ownership of the islands from a private citizen to itself under domestic civil law."[51] Stressing that the decision to purchase the island was final, Japan stated that it would do its best to resolve issues peacefully: "Japan's basic position that the Senkaku Islands belong to Japan is unshakable. Japan actually exercises valid control over the islands. . . . Japan is committed to continue dealing with the current situation in a calm manner from a broad perspective. . . . Japan, as a peace-loving nation, has consistently made great contributions to peace and prosperity of Asia after World War II."[52] It also blamed China for escalating the conflict and for violent actions against Japanese citizens.

The months following the purchase of the islands brought more tension. On September 14, 2012, six Chinese patrol vessels sailed in the waters around the islands. According to the Japanese Coast Guard, one vessel communicated through radio: "Daiyou is China's territory. This ship is carrying out lawful operations. We urge you to leave the waters immediately."[53] The Chinese Foreign Ministry confirmed the incident: "These law enforcement and patrol activities are aimed to demonstrate China's jurisdiction over the Diaoyu Islands and its affiliated islets, and ensure the country's maritime interests."[54] Japan's chief cabinet secretary, Osamu Fujimura, said these violations of territorial waters by six vessels at one time were "unprecedented" and "extremely regrettable," adding: "We strongly protest the intrusion by the latest Chinese vessels. We are taking all possible measures to be ready for any development."[55] Japan's foreign minister, Koichiro Gemba, condemned Chinese actions and called for nonescalation: "We lodged a strong protest and also we made a strong case that the Chinese side should leave from the territorial waters around the Senkaku islands.... I'd like to underscore that we should never let the situation escalate and we have strong hopes for the Chinese to respond in an appropriate and calm manner."[56]

On December 13, 2012, a Chinese State Oceanic Administration aircraft flew over the islands. On January 30, 2013, a Chinese naval vessel directed a weapons-guiding radar lock on an escort vessel of the Japanese Maritime Self-Defense Force. On February 4, Chinese vessels intruded into Japanese waters for 14 hours. These actions were perceived by the Japanese government as a dangerous provocation and unilateral escalation of the conflict by China: "China continues to take provocative actions, attempting to change the existing order through coercion and intimidation."[57] Beijing refuted these claims, calling them a "deliberate fabrication" and "malicious speculation," accusing Japan of endangering Chinese vessels. Luo Yuan, deputy secretary-general of the Academy of Military Sciences, pointed out to Hong Kong's *Wen Wei Po* that the radar incident was "yet another lie concocted in Japan" with "ulterior motives of deliberately aggravating tensions between China and Japan."[58] A spokesperson for the legislature's chief advisory body, Lu Xinhua, claimed that if patrol boats or planes operating close to one another clashed, Japan would "be held solely responsible for all consequences" regardless of intention.[59]

China was furious at the purchase of the islands. Chinese officials presented Japan's actions as illegal on numerous grounds: history, law, and the concept of international sovereignty. To delegitimize the purchase, Chinese officials depicted it as theft, accusing Japan of foul actions. They validated their position by presenting the islands as the sovereign territory of China that could not be bought by any other country. This *legitimacy insult* sought to convince Japan to reverse its decision and increase international support for the Chinese position. However, when this tactic did not work, China demonstrated its jurisdiction over the islands by several actions meant to prove Japan's inability to control the situation. Chinese patrol vessel sailed in the island waters, Chinese aircraft flew over the islands, and a weapons-guiding radar lock demonstrated China's power and support its rights over the territory. These actions created a *power insult* by emphasizing the prevalence of China in the disputed territory and demonstrated Japan's inability to stop these activities. The *power insult* also sought to force Japan to annul the purchase of the islands and resume negotiations over them. By frequently sailing patrol ships and flying aircraft near the islands, the Chinese *generalized* the insult, increasing its impact on the other side and provoking greater antagonistic reactions by Japan. To support this *power insult*, China also used a *projection insult*, denying its own actions and presenting them as pure fabrications by Japan. Chinese officials called Japanese officials liars who wanted to escalate the situation and put all responsibility for escalation of the conflict on China. They emphasized that Japan was solely responsible for all tensions over the islands and should mitigate the conflict by returning them to China.

To support its decision to buy the islands, Japan also responded with a *legitimacy insult*. The frequency of previous similar *legitimacy insults* created the *conglomeration* of insults, increasing their potency and widening their scope. As with previous *legitimacy insults*, Japan employed historic evidence and international law to validate its claim that the purchase of the islands is an exclusively internal matter. However, this new insult included a novel dimension: the Japanese government stressed that the purchase was the best solution in light of the intentions of right-wing nationalists to acquire this territory. The latter could provoke a conflict in the region, and therefore the Japanese government's decision was based on its concern for stability and peace. Thus, Japan legitimized its decision not only based on historic and legal grounds but also on the grounds of preservation of peace in the region. It also delegitimized China's claims for the islands, stressing that Chinese interest appeared only after the discovery of possible oil and gas reserves near the islands. The delegitimization process also included the presentation of China as a noncollaborative and provocative agent. The later depiction also became a foundation for a *projection insult*. In numerous statements, Japan presented Chinese actions as unprovoked aggression and an illegal use of force. Japan blamed China for exacerbating the conflict and intruding into sovereign Japanese territory. At the same time, Japan stressed its peace-loving nature and its sincere wish to preserve peace. Thus, this *projection insult* helped intensify the legitimacy insult and strengthen the validation of the Japanese decision to take over the islands.

THE JAPANESE-KOREAN DISPUTE OVER ISLANDS

The dispute between Japan and Korea involves two tiny rocky islets surrounded by 33 smaller isles, known as Takeshima ("bamboo island") in Japan and Dokdo ("rock island") in Korea. These islands were annexed by

Japan from South Korea in 1905, five years before the Japanese occupation of the Korean Peninsula. On April 24, 1939, the islands were put under the jurisdiction of Goka Village on Oki Island, Shimane Prefecture. In 1940, imperial Japan transferred the islands under military jurisdiction, naming the islets Maizaru Naval Station. After Japan's defeat in the Pacific War in 1945, the islands were controlled by the US military. In September 1947, the Supreme Commander for the Allied Powers (SCAP) established the islands as an aerial bombing range. After the signing of the San Francisco Peace Treaty in 1952, Japanese Foreign Ministry resolution Number 34 designated the island as a bombing range, stating that "these rocks would be designated as a facility by the Japanese Government."[60] One year later, following several bombing incidents that involved Korean ships, the US military removed the islands from the list for area practice.

In 1953, a Korean volunteer coast guard ship established patrols to watch over the islands. Several Japanese patrol vessels sailed within close distance of the islands and several times landed on the islands, erecting a Japanese territorial marker on its shore. Korean coast guard ships responded with gunfire, sinking a Japanese ship on July 12. The Japanese government protests received no reaction from Korea. In 1954, the Koreans constructed a concrete lighthouse, a building, and a helicopter landing pad on the East Islet and, in 1982, designated the islands as "Natural Monument No. 336." In February 1996, responding to South Korean plans to build a wharf on the islands, Japanese foreign minister Yukihiko Ikeda publicly claimed them as Japan's territory.[61]

On April 17, 2006, Japanese Coast Guard vessels were sent for a survey mission to the Dokdo Islands. Japanese vice foreign minister Shotaro Yachi said that a proposal to use Korean names for geographical features on the seabed had been submitted for review at the approaching international oceanographic meeting and "the aim of this survey [was] to collect necessary data so that we can submit an alternative proposal." "Surveys like this are also conducted by other countries. We should handle this calmly under international law," said Shinzo Abe, the chief cabinet secretary and spokesman for the Japanese government.[62] However, the Korean government, through its minister of foreign affairs and trade, Ban Ki Moon, stated that stern measures would be considered should the survey mission go ahead, assert that "if the Japanese government pushes ahead with the survey, we will deal with it sternly according to the relevant international and local laws," adding that Japan should cancel its plans or take full responsibility for any physical clashes.[63] The Japanese government responded that it was acting within the confines of international law. Abe declared that such surveys were routine in the international realm and must be evaluated under international law.

A week later, Korean president Roh Moo-hyun vowed to deal more sternly with Japanese claims over the islands: "the government of South Korea will completely review its countermeasures against Japan's claim to Dokdo."[64] He added that Japan's claim to the islands was similar to its actions during the "imperial war of aggression" and Japanese dealing with its former colony, Korea: "Dokdo is a symbol in correcting the wrong history of Japan's aggression and enhancing Korea's sovereignty."[65] He also stressed that Japan's glorification of its history of aggression promoted a distorted interpretation of history that could harm a cooperative relationship between Korea and Japan in the future, as well as peace in East Asia.

Japan's survey of the islands sent the message to Korea that Japan considered the ownership a continuing issue. Despite protests of the Korean government, Japan continued with the survey to show its rights to sail near the islands under international law. As a foundation for this action, the Japanese used discussion of geographic names on the international level. This action created a *legitimacy insult* that underscored claims to this territory and invalidated the current ownership of Korea. To strengthen the insult, Japan involved the dimension of international law and presented the survey as a usual practice that should be tolerated by Korea if it values international standards. In response, Korea also created a *legitimacy insult*, stressing the legality of Korean ownership and the unlawful nature of Japanese actions. To increase the intensity of the insult, Korea brought in the framework of the history of Japanese aggression, comparing the current survey with aggression by imperial Japan. This framework helped increase the validity of Korean ownership that resulted from regaining its sovereignty after the Japanese invasion. It also presented the rights of Korea to the islands as a symbolic correction for all the wrongdoings of Japan. Appealing to the idea of Korean victimhood resulting from aggressive Japanese actions, the Korean government created the *reactivation* of insult. Thus, both countries used *legitimacy insults* to support their rights to the islands and utilized internationally accepted dimensions to sustain their claims: Japan referred to international law, while Korea invoked the victory over imperial Japan and sovereignty of Korea.

On August 10, 2012, Korean president Lee Myung-bak visited the disputed islands, becoming the first sitting South Korean president to do so.[66] President Lee arrived by helicopter from the nearby island of Ulleungdo, staying 70 minutes and speaking to police guards there. He stated in his speech: "Dokdo is truly our territory, and it's worth defending with our lives."[67] Reaction to the president's visit in Korea was ambiguous. Lee's ruling party declared the move to be a meaningful one in defense of Korea's territory, while Korea's opposition parties declared that he had simply pulled a publicity stunt to divert criticism away from his administration's political woes.

In response, Japan issued statements lodging strong protests against Lee's action. Japanese PM Yoshihiko Noda declared: "Today the South Korean President Lee Myung-bak visited Takeshima. It is contrary to our nation's stance that Takeshima is historically—and under international law—an integral part of our national territory and is completely unacceptable... So for this visit to come at this time is extremely regrettable. I believe it is necessary for the Japanese government to take a resolute stance on this matter."[68] He claimed that the Korean action was regrettable at a time when he and Lee had been pushing for a "positive future between Japan and South Korea."[69] The Japanese foreign minister, Koichiro Gemba, questioned the reasons behind Lee's visit to these rocky islands and called it unacceptable. He declared that he had gotten "no word" from Seoul, adding, "It didn't seem yesterday like the South Korean foreign ministry had a full grasp of the situation either."[70] He underlined that Japan would consider taking the case to the Court of International Justice (ICJ) despite the fact that Korea had previously refused Japan's attempts to defer the issue to international courts in 1954 and 1962.[71] Tokyo also responded to the visit by summoning Shin Kak-soo, the South Korean ambassador to Japan, in protest, and recalling its own ambassador to Seoul, Masatoshi Muto.[72]

On the day after the visit, South Korea's national soccer team defeated the Japanese in the bronze-medal match at the London Games. After the final whistle, a South Korean player raised a sign that declared "Dokdo is our territory." Both the International Olympic Committee and FIFA barred him from the medal ceremony and withheld his award pending an investigation of the incident. However, the Korean government exempted this player from compulsory military service and included him in the country's World Cup team.[73]

The Korean government supported Korea's legal ownership of the island with an unprecedented move: the first-ever visit by a Korean president to the islands. Considering that this is a tiny island with a small number of police officers there, a 70-minute visit was highly symbolic. It aimed to create a *power insult* to Japan, emphasizing that Korea had full control over islands and would defend them in any circumstances. The insult also presented Japan as having no force to challenge the existing ownership. This *power insult* was repeated on an individual level when a soccer player demonstratively stressed the Korean rights to the islands at an international competition. This *power insult* was heightened by the victory of the Korean national team over Japan, and drew a parallel between soccer and dominance over the islands. The insult became even stronger when, despite condemnation of this behavior by international sports organizations, the Korean government rewarded the player. This reward was intended to increase the validity of the Korean position and presented Japanese claims as having no lawful foundation, thus creating a new *legitimacy insult*.

As expected, Japan was furious at these actions: Japanese officials called this visit unacceptable. They created *a legitimacy insult*, stressing that Japan has full rights to the islands based on historic evidence and international law. In addition, they validated Japanese claims by creating a *projection insult*: Japan was depicted as having nonviolent intentions to keep peace in the region and use international law as a basis for conflict resolution, while the Korean action was presented as extremely provocative and as ruining the cooperation between the two countries. Thus, this *legitimacy insult* was strengthened by a *projection insult* that involved a new dimension of peace and cooperation in the region, legitimizing Japan as a country concerned about stability, and delegitimizing Korea as an inflammatory and conflictual agent of international relations. To support the inclusion of this dimension in the *legitimacy insult* and stress differences in foreign policy between Japan and Korea, Japan recalled its ambassador to Korea. This action created a *power insult* designed to reinforce the *legitimacy insult* and demonstrate Japan's intention to impose control over its relations with Korea.

On August 22, 2012, the South Korean president, Lee Myung-bak, made a statement that before coming to Korea for a planned visit, the Japanese emperor should apologize more clearly for Japan's harsh 1910–1945 colonial rule of the Korean Peninsula. The Japanese Parliament issued a resolution condemning South Korea's "illegal occupation" and calling on Lee to retract his remark and apologize to the emperor. The language of the resolution was offensive to South Korea, calling Lee's statement "quite irreverent."[74] Japanese foreign minister Gemba also characterized South Korean presence on the disputed islands as an "illegal occupation," referring to historical documents showing Japan's sovereignty over Takeshima since the middle of the seventeenth century.[75] Japanese prime minister Noda sent a letter to the Korean president condemning his remarks regarding the Japanese emperor, a letter soon published online.[76] The South Korean government returned the critical letter to Lee. South Korean Foreign Ministry spokesperson Cho Tai-young stated that the letter "included contents that we cannot tolerate.... It's only natural to send such a letter back."[77] However, the Japanese Foreign Ministry refused entry of the South Korean diplomat delivering the letter and would not open its diplomatic doors to him. Japan's Osamu Fujimura said that it was "inconceivable for [a] letter between nations' leaders to be sent back."[78] According to

South Korean officials, the letter was later mailed to Tokyo. Noda underlined that Tokyo accepted the letter's return, preferring not to "tarnish the dignity of Japanese diplomacy," advising the Koreans to cool their jets.[79] Tsuyoshi Yamaguchi, Japan's senior vice foreign minister, said, "I'm sorry, but they're behaving like kids in a scuffle."[80]

The Korean government continued to use the frame of an aggressive imperialistic Japan and Korean victimhood to validate Korean ownership. The Korean president reactivated this insult by demanding further apologies from the Japanese emperor. This *legitimacy insult* provoked a strong reaction in Japan that strengthened its own legitimacy insult, calling the Korean presence on the island an "illegal occupation." They also questioned the relevance of the Korean president's remarks regarding Japanese emperor. These two *legitimacy insults* provoked a set of *power insults* when both countries were sending and returning to each other the official letter. The sequences of these actions created *generalization* of insults, when each new insult was built on the previous one. These *power insults* stressed each country's own strength and control over the situation and downplayed the power of the other side.

On August 24, Noda went live on TV, stating, "There is not the slightest doubt that Takeshima is our nation's territory," and emphasizing that he would do everything to defend national interests.[81] He vowed to take the issue to the ICJ, stressing that the proper path was to settle this issue in accordance with law and judicial processes. Noda also stated that that no one could benefit from agitating domestic opinion in either country, referring to the Korean president's visit to the islands as intensification of tensions: "To defend our national interests, I will say what needs to be said, and do what needs to be done.... But it doesn't serve any country's interest to whip up domestic opinion and needlessly escalate the situation."[82] In response, the South Korean government claimed in the document that the islands were part of the sovereign territory of Korea.[83]

The conflict over the islands also impacted economic relations between Japan and Korea: Japan decided to hold the extension of the agreement with Seoul for a so-called currency swap, which would expire in October. It was originally adopted after the 2008 financial crisis to bail out South Korea, which at the time was running out of foreign currency. The Japanese finance minister, Jun Azumi, said the decision would depend on South Korean responses to Japan's outrage over Lee's demands for the emperor's apology: "Things have reached the point where the Japanese people may not be able to accept the argument that political relations and economic relations are separate."[84]

In the beginning of September 2012, the Japanese Foreign Ministry placed a newspaper advertisement insisting that "it is time to realize. The Takeshima issue is basic knowledge," advocating Japanese sovereignty, and questioning Korean claims to the islands. "Korea claims it began administering Dokdo before Japan, but the descriptions in its reference materials are ambiguous, while there is no clear evidence to support its claim."[85] The message was placed in 70 Japanese newspapers for a week, including nationwide dailies and regional papers. Korean foreign minister Kim Sung-hwan described the ad as "historically regressive," adding, "Inevitably you wonder what they may have to do with the upcoming elections in Japan." Moreover, Kim said Seoul was to run counter-ads, saying, "We're preparing to explain to the Japanese people why Dokdo belongs to Korea from a historic, geographic and legal perspective."[86]

Unable to change the ownership of the islands diplomatically, Japan brought the issue to the international court. This move created a new *power insult* demonstrating that Japan would use any actions or measures to ensure that the islands remained Japanese territory. Japan also demonstrated its power on the level of economic relations, reconsidering financial assistance to Korea. All these repeating power insults on different levels—diplomatic, economic, and international—created the *conglomeration* of insult, increasing their potency and producing multifaceted effects. To increase the support for its position among the Japanese public, the government launched a massive information campaign in newspapers, stressing the lawful and genuine foundations for its ownership of the islands and presenting the Korean evidence as ambiguous and vague. Thus, the Japanese government *sensitized* the public to these insults. This *legitimacy insult* helped create overwhelming support among Japanese citizens for the policy, and strengthened the power insults created in the conflict.

Korea reacted by refusing to participate in a process conducted by the ICJ, a move that defeated the Japanese application. This refusal stressed the power of Korea and its control over the islands, as the ICJ proceedings must include both sides—the case could not proceed without Korean participation. This *power insult* helped Korea confirm its ownership over the islands and reaffirm its position regarding the illegality of the Japanese claims. Korea also utilized a *projection insult*, presenting Japanese claims as arising from the political situation in Japan and as the source of the conflict in the region, while Korea was depicted as aiming for stability and cooperation. The Korean government further strengthened a *legitimacy insult*, presenting the lawful foundations for its ownership—historic, geographic, and legal—at the level of domestic and international mass media.

CONCLUSION

In their fight over ownership of the islands, China and Japan employed several insults. The core type of insult was a *legitimacy insult*, used by both sides during all stages of the conflict. To strengthen this legitimacy insult, Japan utilized a *divergence insult*, aiming to increase internal support for its action, and both countries developed *power* and *projection* insults, aiming to demonstrate their force but attribute all responsibility for growing tensions to the other side. In the dynamic of this conflict, the *legitimacy insult* became more complex, including new dimensions and frameworks of interpretation.

During the entire conflict, Japan used *legitimacy insults*, positing the purchase of the islands as a completely internal issue of the country, legitimizing its exclusive rights of ownership, and delegitimizing Chinese claims for this territory. In the beginning of the dispute, when the purchase of the islands were only considered, Japan employed a *divergence insult* to increase in-group support for this action and diminish all criticism as a demonstration of disloyalty to the country. Creating a social boundary between faithful compatriots and opponents, the Japanese government increased the perception of the issue as a domestic matter that should not be a concern for any other country. Reacting to the Chinese government's protests, Japan then increased the complexity of the *legitimacy insult*, utilizing the dimensions of historic truth and international law and lifting the conflict to the level of international relations.

China reacted to Japanese intentions to buy the islands with a *legitimacy insult*, reaffirmation of its rights over the islands, and invalidation of Japanese claims to the territory. To further delegitimize Japanese attempts to purchase the islands, China presented them as illegal and questioned the adequacy of Japanese foreign policy. As the conflict evolved, China employed more specific criteria accepted by the international community, including national sovereignty and victimization by imperialist aggressors. The idea of victimization helped create a parallel between the violence of imperialistic Japan and current Japanese intentions to take over the islands. The issue of the islands was introduced as an integral part of a contentious history of Sino-Japanese conflicts, *reactivating* previous insults and humiliations of Chinese people by Japanese invaders.

As the conflict further evolved, both sides created *power insults* to support the legitimacy of their claims by demonstration of their power. The supremacy of each side was validated through landing on the islands by activist from both countries, sailing of official boats in the islands waters, and violent protests on the streets.

The purchase of the islands brought the conflict to a new stage; however, the *legitimacy insult* continued to dominate relations between Japan and China. In justification of its action, the Japanese government validated its rights to make exclusive decisions on ownership of the islands based on the historic evidence and international and domestic law and delegitimized all Chinese claims to this territory. This new insult also involved a novel dimension: presentation of the purchase of the islands as an act of preserving peace, a move that would prevent right-wing nationalists from acquiring the territory. To strengthen this insult, Japan employed a *projection insult* further legitimizing its position as a country that waged peace and promoted cooperation in the region, and castigating China for increasing tensions. In numerous statements, Japan blamed China for exacerbating the conflict and intruding into sovereign Japanese territory.

Perceiving the purchase of the islands by the Japanese government as a *legitimacy insult*, China created a new *legitimacy insult* assessing Japanese action as an illegal and underhand move, as a mistake, and as theft, based on the Chinese interpretation of history and international law. It also created a *reactivation* of insult, utilizing the discourse of postwar reconciliation and justice and depicting Japanese actions as a reappearance of imperialistic intentions. This *legitimacy insult*, similar to the Japanese one, was reinforced by a *projection insult* that presented Japan as the initiator of the conflict and an aggressive invader, while China was depicted as the victim that wanted to maintain peace in the region. When this *legitimacy insult* failed to reach its goal of convincing Japan to reverse its decision, China delivered a *power insult* to demonstrate its jurisdiction over the islands and undermine Japan's ability to control the situation: Chinese patrol vessels in the islands waters, aircraft flights over the islands, and the use of a weapons-guiding radar lock. The frequent displays of Chinese power created a *generalization* of the insult, increasing its impact on the other side and provoking more antagonistic reactions by Japan. Through the use of a *projection insult*, China countered Japanese actions, presenting them as based on fabrications, and portrayed Japan as solely responsible for tensions over the islands.

Like the conflict between Japan and China, the dispute over the islands between Japan and Korea included several evolving *power* and *legitimacy* insults. The conflict started with the dominance of *legitimacy insults*, but later in the dispute *power insults* prevailed. The *legitimacy insults* were strengthened by the employment of the dimensions of international law and victory over imperial Japan. The *power insults* were produced on different levels—diplomacy, international law, and the economy. Both countries developed *projection insults*, legitimizing their claims by attributing all responsibility for growing tensions on the other side.

To challenge Korean ownership of the islands, the Japanese government brought in the issue of international geographic names and sent Coast Guard ships to survey waters surrounding the islands. This action created a *legitimacy insult* that underscored Japanese claims to the territory and invalidated the current ownership of Korea on the level of international law. Responding to this insult, Korea also created a *legitimacy insult* that stressed the legality of Korean ownership and the unlawful nature of Japanese actions in the framework of the history of aggression by imperial Japan. Presenting the rights of Korea to the islands as a symbolic opportunity for Japan to compensate for its offenses, the Korean government created the *reactivation* of insult. Thus, both countries used internationally accepted dimensions to create *legitimacy insults*: international law and the victory over imperial Japan.

To further support its rights to the islands, the Korean government created a *power insult*—the first-ever visit of a Korean president to the islands. The insult helped present Japan as powerless to change or challenge the existing ownership. When an individual soccer player repeated this *power insult* demonstrating the Korean rights to the islands, Korea rewarded the player and created a new *legitimacy insult*. Japan immediately responded with a *legitimacy insult*, stressing that Japan has full rights to the islands based on historic evidence and international law. To strengthen this insult, Japan added a *projection insult*, depicting itself as a peacekeeper in the region and positioning Korean action as extremely provocative—and a *power insult*. Japan further stressed differences in foreign policy and revoked its ambassador to Korea.

To reinforce its *legitimacy insult*, the Korean government continued to invoke the frame of an aggressive imperialist Japan and Korean victimhood to demand an apology from the Japanese emperor. This *legitimacy insult* provoked a strong reaction in Japan that underlined its own *legitimacy insult*, calling the Korean presence on the island an "illegal occupation." These two *legitimacy insults* provoked generalized *power insults* when both returned each other's official letters, demonstrating their control over the situation. Unable to change the ownership of the islands, Japan also created a *power insult* on international level, bringing the issue to the international court, and a *power insult* on the economic level, postponing its financial aid to Korea. All these repeating power insults on different levels—diplomatic, economic, and international—created the *conglomeration* of insult, increasing their potency and producing multifaceted effects. The Japanese government also sensitized public to the *legitimacy insult* through a massive informational campaign in newspapers, stressing the lawful and genuine foundations for its ownership of the islands and presenting the Korean interpretation as ambiguous and vague. Korea responded with the fusion of *power* and *legitimacy insults*, refusing to participate at the ICJ, thus neutering the Japanese application as well as presenting the lawful foundations for its ownership—historic, geographic, and legal—at the level of domestic and international mass media.

Comparative analysis of both conflicts shows that *legitimacy* insults were central in official statements and actions of all sides. The *legitimacy insults* helped participating countries validate their own rights to the islands while delegitimizing claims of the other parties. These insults gradually evolved, including more dimensions and increasing their scope. If in the beginning they were based on interpretations of history and domestic law, in the process of conflict development they involved criteria of international law, national sovereignty, and peace in the region. In their conflicts with Japan, both China and Korea reactivated the insults of victimization by imperial Japan during World War II, drawing parallels between aggressive imperialistic policies and current Japanese policies.

The framework of invasions by Japan helped both Korea and China strengthen their *legitimacy insults* as well as create *projection* insults, blaming Japan for aggressively expanding its territory and creating the conflicts in the region, while presenting their countries as peace–loving and concerned about stability in the region. Japan also responded with *projection insults* that reinforced its *legitimacy insults* and raised them to the level of regional security.

All three countries used *power* insults to support their *legitimacy insults*. However, more *power insults* were used by the sides that did not have ownership over the islands, China in the Sino-Japanese conflict and Japan in Japanese-Korean conflict. Unable to change the existing ownership of the islands, these countries created a series of *power insults* to showcase their control over the situation and downgrade the strength of their opponent. China demonstrated its military power, sending ships and aircraft to the islands, while Japan created *power insults* on different levels, including diplomacy, international law, and the economy.

The cases also show how a *divergence insult* was used to strengthen the *legitimacy insult*: it created a social boundary between loyal patriotic supporters of the official position over the islands and "renegades" who questioned this position. This *divergence insult* together with mass media campaigns aimed to sensitize the public, increasing the homogeneity of public opinion and thus the perceived legality of the government's assertions.

The analysis of insults in both cases reveals that the legitimacy of the ownership of the islands in the region is still under question. While one side uses historic evidence and international and domestic law to validate its rights, the other side employs its interpretation of history and law to delegitimize existing ownership and increase the legality of its claims. The history of Japanese imperial aggression is still a sensitive issue in the region and is utilized as a framework to assess current disputes. The uncompleted process of forgiveness and reconciliation creates the possibility for reactivation of insults in belligerent invasions of the disputed islands. The use of force and demonstrations of power are considered acceptable by all involved sides that create the *generalization* and *conglomeration* of *power insults,* thereby increasing the intensity of the conflicts.

CHAPTER 6

Declaration of War

In 2012, North Korea launched a long-range rocket that instead of reaching its target disintegrated, falling into the sea. Embarrassed by the technological failure and needing to save face in the international community, North Korea then conducted nuclear bomb tests despite world wide protests, including statements by the United Nations and the United States. Several months later North Korea announced that it was scrapping of the ceasefire agreement that ended the Korean War in 1953 and nullifying the declaration on the denuclearization of the Korean Peninsula. It also cut direct phone lines with South Korea, released a propaganda video showing a possible missile attack on the United States, and named possible targets on US territory. Finally, North Korea declared that it was "entering a state of war" and was ready to "make a strike of justice at any target any time as it pleases without limit."[1]

Were these actions and statements demonstrations of real intentions, or were they were constructed insults? What was a motivation behind these threats and insults? How did reactions of the United States reduce tensions in this growing conflict? The following analysis of insults helps answer these questions and better understand the conflict between North Korea and the United States over Korean nuclear ambitions.

The Korean War of 1950–1953 was supported by different countries on each side of the conflict: China supported northern forces, while the United States and the UN backed southern forces. On July 27, 1953, a ceasefire agreement was signed, stopping open warfare. As a part of the agreement, a demilitarized zone (DMZ) was established along the 38th parallel to separate the two sides of the conflict. The Democratic People's Republic of Korea

(DPRK), based on communist ideology and totalitarian political structures, formed the government in the north, while the Republic of Korea (ROK), which promoted democratic principles, was established on the south.

The DPRK's Communist Party charter clearly states that the aim of the DPRK is to "ensure the complete victory of socialism in the northern half of the Democratic People's Republic of Korea and the accomplishment of the revolutionary goals of national liberation and the people's democracy on the entire area of the country."[2] Over the six decades since the end of the Korean War, North Korea has attached labels such as "human scum" and "political idiot" to describe South Korea and the United States. Additionally, the North Koreans have often threatened to turn South Korea into "a sea of fire." The DPRK also has blamed "US hostile policy" for the status quo on the peninsula.

The conflict incidents between the United States and North Korea started in 1968, when the Korean military captured the USS *Pueblo*, an American intelligence-gathering ship. The ship's crew was released, but the North Korean government seized the ship. The following year, North Korea shot down a US reconnaissance plane, killing 31 Americans. In 1998, North Korea sent a missile over Japan, an incident perceived by the international community as a missile test. In 2006, North Korea conducted more missile tests. The US response to this test and similar provocations was angry. In 2002, in his State of the Union Address, President George W. Bush labeled North Korea, Iran, and Iraq the "Axis of Evil" and in 2005, during her confirmation testimony to the Senate for the position of the secretary of state, Condoleezza Rice described North Korea as an "Outpost of Tyranny."

The United States stopped oil shipments to North Korea in 2002, reacting to the secretiveness of the North Korean nuclear program. In response, North Korea expelled international nuclear inspectors and withdrew from the Nuclear Nonproliferation Treaty six-party talks with the United States, China, Russia, Japan, and South Korea. In 2007, following the nuclear test in North Korea, several diplomatic breakthroughs occurred in international efforts to shut down North Korea's nuclear enrichment program. In December 2007, President G. W. Bush sent a handwritten letter to Kim Jong-il discussing a bilateral agreement. Bush officially removed the DPRK from the terror-watch list in October 2008, following a Department of State announcement that the DPRK would catalog and dismantle its entire nuclear program by the year's end.

In 2010, South Korea conducted a military exercise within its own waters—a fact that was confirmed by the international community. Despite this confirmation, North Korea saw the exercise as artillery fire in its territorial waters and responded by bombing the Yeonpyeong Islands with 170 shells and rockets. The attack killed four people and injured 19 and caused widespread damage.³ South Korea responded by shelling North Korean gun positions. This incident escalated tensions on the Korean Peninsula. In turn, the United States reiterated its commitment to the defense of South Korea, stating that the United States is "firmly committed" to South Korea's defense, and to the "maintenance of regional peace and stability."⁴

THE "DECLARATION OF WAR"

In March 2012, North Korean president Kim Jong-un announced his intention to launch a rocket to commemorate the one hundredth anniversary of the birth of Kim Il-sung, the Great Leader of Korea, and Kim Jong-un's grandfather. In spite of warnings from President Obama, the rocket was launched in April. The rocket disintegrated before reaching its target, to the great humiliation of the North Korean leaders. The following August, while the United States and South Korea were planning annual war games, Kim accused the United States and South Korea of conducting a "war rehearsal" as a preparation to invade the North Korea. He visited the military unit that had attacked South Korea's Yeonpyeong Island in 2010 and called for all troops to be ready to wage a sacred war against South Korea. In October 2012, the North Korean government announced that it had developed missiles with the capability of reaching the US mainland. A few months later, North Korea declared that it would conduct another missile-launch test in a renewed effort to launch a satellite into space. The mission was declared a success.

On January 1, 2013, Kim reached out to his incoming counterpart in South Korea, calling for bettering of relationships between the two nations in his new year's address: "An important issue in putting an end to the division of the country and achieving its reunification is to remove confrontation between the north and the south.... The past records of inter-Korean relations show that confrontation between fellow countrymen leads to nothing but war." However, Kim also added that "the military might of a country represents its national strength. Only when it builds up its military might in every way can it develop into a thriving country." He echoed his predecessors' military-centric thinking and stressed the importance of economic development: "Let us bring about a radical turn in the building of an economic giant with the same spirit and mettle as were displayed in conquering space."⁵

The two rocket launches—one failed and one successful—were created as a fusion of *projection* and *power insults*. North Korean leaders presented the actions of South Korea and the United States as an attempt to exercise power in the region and show dominance over North Korea. The international nuclear security summit was presented as a threat to the North Korean nuclear program and the war games were positioned as a security threat and demonstration of military power. North Korean leadership even attributed to the United States the intention to invade their country, thus projecting onto the United States the willingness to reduce North Korea's power and increase control over the country. In his statement, President Kim stressed that his actions were designed to further his country's economic development and that military development was a part of this economic growth. Thus, he denied any aggressive intentions on the part of North Korea, at the same time stressing that the actions of South Korea, and the United States as its ally, threatened the fragile peace on the peninsula.

The two rocket launches demonstrated North Korea's power and its readiness to defend its sovereignty and territory by any means. They also indicated that North Korea could not be held to any warnings or restrictions established by the United States, which it does not consider significant. North Korea's actions were designed to emphasize the equal status of both countries and their equivalent powers. Thus, through this fusion of *projection* and *power insults* North Korea projected aggressive action against the United States and demonstrated its power in the region.

Reacting to the rocket launch in December, the UN Security Council passed a resolution on January 22, 2013, to strengthen the sanctions against the North Korean regime. Two days later, in response to the sanctions, North Korea announced plans for further nuclear tests as well as tests for a long-range rocket. Korean Central News Agency said that North Korea would carry out another nuclear test as part of an "all-out action" against the United States: "We are not disguising the fact that the various satellites and long-range rockets we will launch, as well as the high-level nuclear test we will carry out, are targeted at the United States, the arch-enemy of the Korean people.... Settling accounts with the US needs to be done with force, not with words."[6]

On February 12, the DPRK carried out an underground nuclear test. The Foreign Ministry presented the test as designed "to defend the country's security and sovereignty in the face of the ferocious hostile act of the US, which wantonly violated the DPRK's legitimate right to launch satellite for peaceful purposes,"[7] thereby positioning the US sanctions as aggressive acts. The statement also pointed out that "this nuclear test is our first measure, which displayed our maximum restraint.... If the US continues with their hostility and complicates the situation, it would be inevitable to continuously conduct a stronger second or third measure."[8] The statement also emphasized that "the nuclear test will greatly encourage the army and people of the DPRK in their efforts to build a thriving nation with the same spirit and mettle as displayed in conquering space, and offer an important occasion in ensuring peace and stability in the Korean Peninsula and the region."[9] The North Korean spokesperson stressed that "the DPRK's patience reached its limit as the United States intensified such hostile act as implementing before anyone else the UNSC's 'resolution on sanctions,' far from apologizing for its renewed wanton violation of the DPRK's right to satellite launch.... The DPRK's nuclear test is a just step for self-defense not contradictory to any international law. The U.S. has long put the DPRK on the list of preemptive nuclear strike. It is quite natural just measure for self-defense to react to the U.S. ever-increasing nuclear threat with nuclear deterrence."[10] He urged the United States to choose between giving up sanctions in the name of being fair, or continuing its hostilities and thus forcing the DPRK's hand towards harsher steps. "The U.S., though belatedly, should choose between the two options: respect the DPRK's right to satellite launch and open a phase of detente and stability, or continue its current path, leading to the explosive situation by persistently pursuing its hostile policy toward the DPRK. In case the U.S. chooses the road of conflict finally, the world will clearly see the army and people of the DPRK defend its dignity and sovereignty to the end through a do-or-die battle between justice and injustice, greet a great revolutionary event for national reunification and win a final victory."[11]

The nuclear test and statements of the North Korean leadership further developed *power* and *projection insults*. The statements portrayed the United States as an aggressive and brutal nation that intended to take control over North Korea. They blamed the United States for escalating the conflict, describing the United States as "the arch-enemy of the Korean people" that "continues with their hostility and complicates the situation." At the same time, the nuclear test was presented as one of the "efforts to build a thriving nation" in North Korea and "ensuring peace and stability in the Korean Peninsula and the region." Justifying its nuclear tests as actions of development and peace-building, North Korea also described them as provoked acts of self-defense. Thus, North Korea constructed a *projection insult*, blaming the United States for aggressive actions that provoked the peaceful nation of North Korea to enhance its self-protection. This *projection insult* was again interconnected with a *power insult*: North Korean leadership threatened the United States with its intention to "continuously conduct stronger" measures up to "the end through a do-or-die battle between justice and injustice." The statements emphasized the willingness and ability of North Korea to utilize all its power and strength in the fight with the United States. Finally, this fusion of *projection* and *power insult* was strengthened by a *legitimacy insult*. North Korean leadership actively denied any rights of the United States to put sanctions or restrictions on North Korea and its actions, thus delegitimizing US policies. At the same time, North Korea justified its own actions, including rocket launches and nuclear tests, as legitimate and in compliance with international law. Thus, North Korea continued to construct *projection* and *power insults*, reinforcing them by the development of a *legitimacy insult*.

In response, President Obama warned that North Korean provocations violated security in the region. He stated: "This is a highly provocative act that, following its December 12 ballistic missile launch, undermines regional stability, violates North Korea's obligations under numerous United Nations Security Council resolutions, contravenes its commitments under the September 19, 2005 Joint Statement of the Six-Party Talks, and increases the risk of proliferation. North Korea's nuclear weapons and ballistic missile programs constitute a threat to U.S. national security and to international peace and security."[12] He also confirmed the commitments to allies in the region and the readiness to "take steps necessary to defend ourselves and our allies." Thus, President Obama recognized this *legitimacy insult*, making it *congruous*. He responded with the statement that denied the lawfulness of North Korea's actions based on several agreements and laws. He also stressed that actions of North Korea were illegitimate as they endangered the fragile peace in the region and created a threat to the United States. Finally, he confirmed the preparedness of the United States to use all legitimate measures to prevent conflict in the region.

On February 25, 2013, Dennis Rodman and the Harlem Globetrotters began their "Basketball Democracy Tour" visit of North Korea. After the meeting with President Kim, Rodman named him a "friend for life."[13] In an interview, Rodman claimed that Kim was a peace-loving man who was forced to act tough against the West by his generals, adding that "Kim told me to pass on a message that he said is very important. He said, 'Tell President Obama to call me. Because if we can talk, we can work this out.'" Rodman added, "He loves basketball and so does President Obama, so they have that in common—and there is even more they could talk about if Obama would just pick up the phone and call him."[14]

Despite this display of positive intentions in March 2013, angered by the UN sanctions, North Korea for the first time in the conflict threatened a preemptive nuclear strike on both the United States and South Korea. It declared that it would be scrapping the 1953 ceasefire agreement and nullifying the declaration on the denuclearization of the Korean Peninsula.

It also cut direct phone lines with South Korea at Panmunjom—an abandoned village, which sits on the DPRK-ROK border.

Responding to the possibility of a North Korean attack, the Obama administration announced a plan to deploy additional ground-based missile-interceptors on the West Coast. The United States also declared that B-52 bombers would make flights over South Korea in their annual joint military exercises with the South Koreans. Angered by this news, North Korea released a YouTube propaganda video showing a possible missile attack on the United States.[15] It threatened to attack US and South Korean bases and put its troops on full alert. It also declared through state media that the military was ready for combat in response to B-52 bomber flights in the South Korean military drills. North Korea claimed that it planned to lock rockets on US targets, releasing photos of Kim and military officials with strike plans. It also cut the last military hotline with South Korea. The North Korean military command threatened to end the armistice and claimed that it would "make a strike of justice at any target any time as it pleases without limit."[16]

Two days later, the United Nations Security Council released its resolution to strengthen sanctions on North Korea. A North Korean Foreign Ministry spokesman stressed that the United States "is set to light a fuse for a nuclear war," adding that North Korea "will exercise the right to a preemptive nuclear attack to destroy the strongholds of the aggressors and to defend the supreme interests of the country."[17] On March 11 North Korea unilaterally ended the armistice reached at the end of the Korean War.[18] An army general told a Pyongyang rally that the military was ready to fire a long-range nuclear-armed missile to turn Washington into a "sea of fire."[19] The next day, President Kim asked troops to go on "maximum alert" for a potential war, claiming that "war can break out right now."[20]

This exchange of actions and statements created a new spiral in *congruous power insult*: both countries displayed their readiness to use stronger measures in response to the actions of the other. These actions, including the cutting of telephone lines by North Korea and unilaterally ending the armistice, demonstrated unwillingness to negotiate any of its decisions and proved the power to make its own choices. It showed the readiness of North Korean leadership to go to extreme measures without internal or external restrictions. In an interview to CNN, one US senior administration official stated: "The new leader is acting in ways a bit more extreme than his father, who was colder and more calculated.... Kim Jong Il was more aware of the off-ramps to end these escalations. I don't recall he ever went this far in terms of the pace and scope of the rhetoric. Threatening to launch nukes directly against the United States and South Korea confirms what a lot of people have been saying, which is we are dealing with someone new.... Nobody knows what he has planned, what he is thinking or contemplating doing or why the North Koreans are tripling down on this rhetoric.... Unfortunately, he is following the example of his father and grandfather pretty closely. It's hard to be optimistic."[21] Referring to South Korea having elected a new president bent on easing tensions, the official added, "Given that for five years they were so angry at the previous president, Lee Myung-bak, why would they mortgage the next five years by being so difficult when a new South Korean leader is just taking office? It's so very concerning." Another US senior administration official added, "It's dangerous to dismiss these threats as just rhetoric and propaganda.... It's hard to predict."[22] Thus, the *power insults* acted out by North Korean leadership were perceived by the United States as an escalation of the conflict, creating a high level of uncertainty and unpredictability in its relations with North Korea.

The White House intelligence chief said that a North Korean attack on South Korea or the United States was unlikely and would threaten the Kim dynasty, while underlining that Pyongyang remained unpredictable and threatening. He said, "The intelligence community has long assessed that, in Pyongyang's view, its nuclear capabilities are intended for deterrence, international prestige and coercive diplomacy. We do not know Pyongyang's nuclear doctrine or employment concepts.... we do not know what would constitute, from the North's perspective, crossing that threshold." He also labeled North Korean rhetoric as "very belligerent" and added that it was very concerning.[23]

The United States took several steps to bolster missile defenses and "stay ahead of the threat." On March 15, US defense secretary Chuck Hagel declared that with its "very provocative actions and belligerent tone, [North Korea] has ratcheted up the danger and we have to understand that reality," and warned anew that the US military was ready to respond to any eventuality on the peninsula. He added: "The reason that we are doing what we are doing and the reason we are advancing our program here for homeland security is to not take any chances, is to stay ahead of the threat to assure any contingency.... We certainly will not go forward with the additional 14 interceptors until we are sure that we have the complete confidence that we will need.... But the American people should be assured that our interceptors are effective."[24] Admiral James Winnefeld stated: "We believe the KN-08 [a North Korean missile] does have the range to reach the United States."[25] Undersecretary of Defense for Policy James Miller echoed: "I hope that they understand that we need to take steps to protect ourselves from potential threats from Iran and North Korea." Hong Lei, spokesperson for the Chinese Ministry of Foreign Affairs, warned the United States on the consequences of this policy: "Bolstering missile defenses will only intensify antagonism, and it doesn't help solve the issue.... [the antimissile issue] matters to global strategic balance and regional stability. It also matters to strategic trust between relevant countries."[26]

These statements of US officials show that while they were taking the threat seriously and were ready to defend the United States in the event of a nuclear strike, the declarations of North Korean leadership were perceived as a *power insult* rather than a real danger. They recognized that North Korean leaders, facing increasing US and UN sanctions, tried to redefine the balance of power, increase North Korea's might, and preserve international prestige.

North Korea labeled the American antimissile policy as a "hostile policy" and underlined that it would not be negotiating terms of its nuclear program with the United States. A North Korean Foreign Ministry spokesman went on to state that nuclear weapons "serve as an all-powerful treasured sword for protecting the sovereignty and security of the country.... Therefore, they cannot be disputed... as long as the U.S. Nuclear threat and hostile policy persist."[27] North Korean military issued threats, warning that US bases in Guam and Japan were "within [its] striking range." They added, "The U.S. should not forget that the Andersen Air Force Base on Guam where the B-52s take off and naval bases in Japan proper and Okinawa where nuclear-powered submarines are launched are within the striking range of the DPRK's precision strike means."[28] Additionally, in response to a perceived US "nuclear blackmail and threat," North Korea vowed to "take corresponding military actions" and stated that it would take "strong military counteraction" if B-52 flights over the Korean Peninsula continued.

On March 28, President Kim in a meeting with top generals signed orders to put North Korean rocket units on standby to attack US bases, underlining that they "judged the time has come to settle accounts with the U.S. imperialists in view of the prevailing situation."[29] " According to the Korean Central News Agency, President Kim "finally signed the plan on technical preparations of strategic rockets of the KPA (Korean People's Army), ordering them to be on standby for fire so that they may strike any time the US mainland, its military bases in the operational theatres in the Pacific, including Hawaii and Guam, and those in South Korea."[30] In response, US defense secretary Chuck Hagel said: "The North Koreans have to understand that what they're doing is very dangerous.... We must make clear that these provocations by the North are taken by us very seriously and we'll respond to that."[31] US secretary of state, John Kerry, asserted that his country would not accept the DPRK as a "nuclear state."

On March 31, North Korean central committee and military command gave signals that they would pursue the development of WMDs, underlining that "[nuclear weapons] are neither a political bargaining chip nor a thing for economic dealings to be presented to the place of dialogue or be put on the table of negotiations aimed at forcing DPRK to disarm itself.... [DPRK's nuclear armed forces] represent the nation's life, which can never be abandoned as long as the imperialists and nuclear threats exist on earth."[32] The next day, North Korea pledged to restart its Yongbyon Nuclear Complex, including a uranium enrichment facility and a reactor that were closed in October 2007 in accordance with the six-party talks.

In response to a US official declaring that two medium-range missiles were loaded on mobile launchers along North Korea's east coast, Pyongyang warned that it could not guarantee the safety of embassies and international organizations should an armed conflict break out. North Korea warned foreigners to secure shelter or evacuate in case of hostilities in response to Japan activating its missile defense systems at three points in Tokyo. On March 30, North Korea's government, ruling party, and other organizations jointly issued the statement that emphasized: "From this time on, the North-South relations will be entering the state of war and all issues raised between the North and the South will be handled accordingly."[33] North Korea also stated that South Korea and the US mainland were "boiled pumpkin[s]" vulnerable to attack. The following Saturday, however, Russian media reported that a faulty translation might have been to blame for this apparent uptick in bellicose rhetoric. The North Korean original statement apparently stressed that the country would act "in accordance with wartime laws" if attacked, and that "from that time, North-South relations will enter a state of war."[34]

On March 31, at the plenary meeting of the Workers Party of Korea Central Committee, President Kim stated:

> The United States and its following forces fabricated a brigandish resolution on sanctions at the UN Security Council by taking issue with our satellite launch for peaceful purposes successfully carried out in December last year and committed the ruthless and evil hostile act of even outlawing the legitimate right of a sovereign state to launch a satellite. To cope with the prevailing situation, we unavoidably conducted the third underground nuclear test for self-defense as part of practical countermeasures for defending the country's sovereignty and security. The United States and other hostile forces then ran about more madly and cooked up another resolution on sanctions of higher intensity, while also mobilizing vast armed forces of aggression to carry out the Key Resolve and Foal Eagle joint military exercises aimed at instigating a nuclear war.... The United

States' hostile policy toward the DPRK has become more vicious recently, and this is related to the fact that it has switched the strategic center for world domination over to the Asia-Pacific region and set its sights on us as the first target of attack...We should never forget the lesson taught by the Balkan Peninsula and the Middle East region, which did not acquire powerful national defense capabilities for self-defense while looking to big powers and even abandoned their existing war deterrent under pressure and appeasement of imperialists, and ended up as a victim of aggression in the end.[35]

In these statements and actions North Korea continued to exacerbate the *power insult*, creating *conglomeration* of insults. It increased the readiness of its military force to launch the rockets at any time and even emphasized that some US territories and military bases were targets for North Korea. To aggravate this power insult, North Korea also employed a *projection insult*, describing the US actions as "nuclear blackmail and threat" and "evil hostile acts" that provoked the self-defense of North Korea. North Korean leadership portrayed the United States as "hostile," "mad," and "aggressive," presenting it as an invader in the Balkan Peninsula and the Middle East. The reference to these regions aimed to bring the *projection insult* to a new level—international—and present the United States as a global aggressive intruder. North Korean leaders emphasized that the "bellicose intentions of imperialistic" United States could be only deterred by the development of nuclear capabilities. Thus, nuclear tests and rocket launches were presented as an essential measure to prevent invasive plans of the United States and preserve the independence of North Korea.

On April 1 the United States and South Korea started their military exercises amid North Korean threats. North Korean media accused the United States and South Korea of "waging madcap nuclear war maneuvers." A government-run newspaper stressed: "This is aimed at igniting a nuclear war against [the United States] through a pre-emptive strike....The prevailing situation proves that a new war, a nuclear war, is imminent on the peninsula."[36] A North Korean official said: "We do not wish harm on foreigners in South Korea should there be a war," thus indicating that foreigners should evacuate the peninsula now that the two Koreas were on the brink of war.

South Korea claimed that any provocative action from the North would beget a strong response "without any political considerations," especially North Korean rhetoric that it had entered "a state of war." The Obama administration downplayed the North Korean threat through spokesperson Jay Carney, saying the rhetoric was not new and that "we are not seeing large-scale military mobilization and repositioning of the DPRK's forces.... What that disconnect between rhetoric and action means, I'll leave to the analysts to judge."[37] US State Department spokesperson Victoria Nuland said: "As national security adviser Tom Donilon said less than a month ago, the U.S. will not accept the DPRK as a nuclear state. This position has not changed since national security adviser Donilon stated it a month ago," adding that North Korea's reactivation of Yongbyon's facilities would constitute "a clear violation of the DPRK's international obligations and the commitments it made at that time."[38] While stressing the activation would take time, Nuland added, "But were they to be able to put themselves back into position to use the facility, that would obviously be extremely alarming but, as I have said, it's a long way from here."[39] White House spokesperson Jay Carney said that the United States was working with allies in Seoul and Tokyo, adding, "We are regularly reaching out to Beijing and Moscow to encourage them to do more to restrain the North Koreans." He added that Kim Jong-un was not playing a new game, stating that "there is a pattern of behavior here. A pattern that is familiar."[40] Secretary of State Kerry, after a meeting with the South Korean foreign minister, Yun Byung-see, said, "The bottom line is very simply that what Kim Jong Un has been choosing to do is provocative, it is dangerous, reckless, and the U.S. will not accept the DPRK as a nuclear state.... And I reiterate again the U.S. will do what is necessary to defend ourselves and defend our allies, Korea and Japan. We are fully prepared and capable of doing that and the DPRK understands that."[41]

On April 4, in defense of US deployments to the Pacific Region, Victoria Nuland stated that robust measures to account for all possibilities were necessary: "When you have a country that is making the kind of bellicose statements and taking the kind of steps that they have, you have to take it seriously and you have to take steps to defend the U.S. and its allies.... The ratcheting up of tensions on the DPRK side was the cause of us shoring up our defensive posture."[42] Nuland added that diplomatic measures were being considered with Kerry due to visit South Korea, Japan, and China, and that the Department of State was optimistic, as the program would help all parties "recognize the threat we share is common and that we are stronger if we work together."[43] She also added that DPRK should return to the international community, thus ending sanctions, saying that "this does not have to get hotter.... They just have to comply with their international obligations."[44]

Two days later, the US national intelligence director, James Clapper, stressed that the United States believes that Kim was attempting to "consolidate and affirm his power" and to show he is "in control of North Korea."[45] Admiral Samuel Locklear said that while using the same playbook as his father and grandfather, Kim appeared incapable of taking de-escalatory channels when available, while agreeing with Republican John McCain's assessment that US–North Korean relations were at their worst. President Obama noted: "We agree now is the time for North Korea to end the kind of belligerent approach they have been taking and try to lower temperatures. No one wants to see a conflict on the Korean Peninsula. But it's important for North Korea, like every other country in the world, to observe the basic rules and norms that are set forth, including a wide variety of UN resolutions."[46]

These statements of US officials show that they recognized the *power*, *projection*, and *legitimacy* insults developed by North Korean leadership. They saw all North Korean declarations as a "belligerent rhetoric" rather than real threats and acknowledged the attempts of North Korea to redefine the existing balance of power. Moreover, US officials understood that North Korea used its nuclear program as a tool in its quest for international prestige and power. This understanding of the motivations and mechanisms of insults helped US officials react objectively to the North Korean threats.

To reduce tensions, on April 7, the United States postponed a missile launch for a month. A senior defense official noted: "This is the logical, prudent and responsible course of action to take."[47] John Kerry visited South Korea and noted that North Korea had not demonstrated any nuclear capability, adding that "the rhetoric that we are hearing is simply unacceptable." Kerry also warned that a North Korean missile launch would be "a huge mistake"; he also underlined that Washington and Seoul were committed to the now-defunct 2005 six-party denuclearization agreements should the North take "meaningful" steps in a call for dialogue—albeit the DPRK declaring that its nuclear program was a nonnegotiable security matter. Kerry also said: "If Kim Jong Un decides to launch a missile.... he will be choosing to willfully ignore the entire international community.... And it will be a provocation and unwanted act that will raise people's temperatures."[48] Kerry also pointed out that "relations between the North and South can improve very quickly if leaders of the North, and one in particular, can make the right decisions."[49] Kerry then suggested dialogue, and said, "We have a lot of issues, including the Kaesong industrial zone. So should we not meet them and ask: 'Just what are you trying to do?'" However, Kerry also added that "they have to be really serious. No one is going to talk for the sake of talking."[50] North Korea refused Kerry's and South Korea's calls for a dialogue, dubbing the offer "a crafty trick" to disguise Seoul's hostility.

CONCLUSION

In its quest for international prestige and right to pursue its policies, North Korea employed several insults. The core type was a *power insult* used during all stages of the conflict. To strengthen this insult, North Korea developed *legitimacy* and *projection insults*, aiming to demonstrate its military might but attribute all responsibility for the growing conflict to the United States and South Korea. In the dynamic of this fight, the *projection insult* became more salient, finally resulting in the declaration of war, and the *legitimacy insult* developed into a more complex one, incorporating new levels of interpretation. The United States recognized these insults and reacted to them as confrontational rhetoric rather than real threats. At the same time, the US leadership responded to the *legitimacy insult* by correcting the North Korean statements and emphasizing the actual legal situation concerning nuclear tests and rocket launches.

During the entire conflict, North Korea used a *power insult* aimed at demonstrating the strength of North Korea and its readiness to defend it sovereign right to make its own decisions. It also implied that North Korea would ignore all warnings and restrictions imposed by the United States and follow its own method of economic and military development. The actions of North Korea, including rocket launches, nuclear tests, cutting of telephone lines, and putting rocket units on standby, were designed to suggest equal status and powers equivalent to those of the United States. North Korean leaders threatened the United States to raise the ante in this fight, unilaterally ended the armistice, increased the readiness of its military force, named some targets on US territories, and finally declared a "state of war." These *power insults, conglomerated* over time, emphasized the readiness of North Korea to utilize all of its might in the fight with the United States.

The *power insults* were interconnected with *projection insults*: descriptions of the United States as a "hostile evil" aggressor intending to exercise its power in the region and invade North Korea helped justify North Korean actions. Different events, including the international nuclear security summit and the war games, were portrayed as a threat to North Korean political and territorial sovereignty. North Korea strengthened this *projection insult* over time, blaming the United States for escalating the conflict, portraying it as "the arch-enemy of the Korean people," and attributing to the United States the intention to invade North Korea. The *projection insult* was aggravated by bringing the attribution of aggressive intentions on the global level and describing the United States as "vicious" invader on the Balkans and Middle East. The use of this dimension attempted to present North Korea as a next victim of the "hostile imperialistic" United States. Thus, North Korea presented the development of nuclear capabilities as a necessary means of self-defense, provoked by the United States. It also described its actions as designed to further its own economic development—"efforts to build a thriving nation" and ensure "peace and stability in the Korean Peninsula and the region." This *projection insult* denied any aggressive intentions on the part of North Korea, at the same time stressing that the actions of the United States threatened the fragile peace on the peninsula.

This fusion *of projection* and *power insults* was reinforced by the construction of a *legitimacy* insult. North Korea repudiated the rights of the United States to impose sanctions or restrictions on North Korea and delegitimized policies of the United States as unacceptable in the international community. The actions of North Korea, including rocket launches and nuclear tests, were justified as completely legitimate and lawful in the framework of international law. Thus, North Korea continuously constructed *power insults*, reinforcing them by the development of *projection* and *legitimacy insults*.

US leaders perceived the declarations and actions of North Korea as insults rather than real danger. However, they were ready to prevent the development of the North Korean nuclear program and defend the United States in case of a nuclear strike. The most significant response was provoked by the *legitimacy insult*: President Obama denied the lawfulness of North Korean actions based on several agreements and laws, and stressed that North Korea's actions were illegitimate as they created a dangerous situation in the region. The US leadership understood that North Korean leaders, facing increasing US and UN sanctions, were trying to redefine the balance of power using its nuclear program. This understanding of the motivations and mechanisms of insults helped US officials objectively react to the North Korean threats and not to contribute to the spiraling conflict by creating new insults.

This analysis of insults helps us understand the dynamics of conflict between North Korea and the United States. The actions of the international community and the United States aimed to prevent the development of nuclear capabilities of North Korea were perceived by its leadership as an insult intended to reduce North Korea's international status and strip it of power. To redefine this balance of power and increase its perceived might, North Korea constructed a series of *power insults*, threatening the United States with rocket launches, nuclear bomb tests, and aggressive statements, including a declaration of war. These actions helped North Korea promote its independence, rights to make own decisions, and ability to ignore imposed restrictions. To support and justify these power insults, North Korea also used *legitimacy* and *projection insults*, blaming the United States for unlawful and aggressive policies.

However, while taking situation seriously, US officials were able to distinguish aggressive rhetoric from a real threat. The *power, legitimacy,* and *projection insults* constructed by North Korea did not provoke aggressive statements or actions by the United States, as North Korean leadership expected. The actions of the United States following North Korea's aggressive stance, such as postponing missile launches and calling for a dialogue, helped reduce tensions in a conflict that had a potential to escalate militarily.

CHAPTER 7

Dealing with Insult

The analysis of five cases in this book shows that insults were incorporated in the very body of these conflicts. In some instances insults were central to conflict dynamics, while in others they helped support in-group claims and position the out-group in a particular way. But in all cases they shaped conflict and contributed to the increase of tensions between groups. In each conflict, some insults appear to be core offenses, strengthened through the processes of *conglomeration* and *generalization*.

In the case of the murder of the Armenian soldier and the subsequent release of his murderer, different insults were central to the actions of two national groups. The Armenian side mostly used *identity insults* to create a negative image of the Azerbaijani society. These insults depicted Azeris as cruel, barbaric, xenophobic, and full of anti-Armenian hysteria. The Azerbaijani side predominantly employed *projection insults* to deny its responsibility for the development of the conflict and presented its actions as provoked by the brutal aggressiveness of Armenians.

In the example of Pussy Riot, Russian leadership constantly used *legitimacy insults* to demolish the voices of the opponents and posited actions of opposition as *identity insults* to the faith and patriotic feelings of the masses. The opposition continuously employed *legitimacy insults* to invalidate the close connections between the Russian Orthodox Church (ROC) and the government.

In the case of Ukraine, the major form of insult constructed by both sides of the conflict was a *divergence insult*, which emphasized the core differences between parties, fortified social boundaries, and precluded imposition of alien values and beliefs. These *divergence insults* were gradually *transferred* to other in-group members and even some members of the out-group.

In the conflict between North Korea and the United States, North Korea employed a *power insult* as a core offense at all stages of the conflict. This insult was instrumental in North Korea's quest for international prestige and rights to pursue its own policies, which were considered controversial by international community.

In the dispute over islands between China and Japan, the core form of insult used by both sides during all stages of the conflict was a *legitimacy insult* that helped increase validity of in-group claims over out-group ones. The dispute over the islands between Japan and South Korea included several evolving *power* and *legitimacy insults*, moving from the dominance of *legitimacy insults* to the prevalence of *power insults*. While *legitimacy insults* involved the dimensions of international law and victory over Imperial Japan, *power insults* were produced on different levels—diplomacy, international law, and economy.

These core insults were strengthened through the employment of other insults. In the Armenian-Azerbaijani conflict, both sides used a *legitimacy insult* to position themselves as the rightful side and present the other side as illegitimate and nondeserving of the trust of the international community. Russian leadership used a *divergence insult* to create the boundary between the opposition on one side and national patriots and true believers on the other side. In Ukraine, *divergence insults* were strengthened by the development of *legitimacy* and *relative insults* that aimed at diminishing the validity and rights of the out-group. In the dispute between China and Japan, Japanese leadership utilized a *divergence insult*, aiming to increase internal support for its action, and both countries developed *power* and *projection insults*, aiming to demonstrate their force but attribute all responsibility for growing tensions to the other side. Similarly, in the dispute between Japan and China, both countries developed *projection insults*, legitimizing their claims by attributing all responsibility for growing tensions on the other side. In the conflict between North Korea and the United States, North Korea developed *legitimacy* and *projection insults*, aiming to demonstrate its military might but attribute all responsibility for growing conflict to the United States and South Korea.

Many of these insults were gradually *transferred* to other in-group members and even some members of the out-group. For example, Russian leadership transferred an *identity insult* from Orthodox believers to the general public, and veterans from the Eastern Ukraine transferred *legitimacy insult* to fellow veterans in L'viv. Governments and leaderships *sensitized* their public as well as the international community to insults produced by or attributed to out-groups. For instance, Armenia and Azerbaijan actively used their diasporas, international institutions, and mass media to emphasize insults by out-groups. Some in-groups employed *reactivation of insult* to present current actions and policies of the out-group in the framework of historic abuses, revalidating past experiences of trauma. For example, both China and South Korea used memories about the aggressiveness of imperial Japan to present Japanese claims of ownership over the contested islands as belligerent. The more often these insults were repeated, the more offensive and abusive they became, thus increasing the *conglomeration of insults*. Based on their similarity to a previous insults, new actions and words of out-groups were perceived as an insult, producing *generalization of insult*. This can also be seen in North Korea, which repeated power insults over and over again, presenting each new insult as a continuation of previous ones.

The main task of this analysis was to demonstrate that specific forms of insults are indicative of particular conflict; therefore, the employment of one or another form of insult can help reveal the main issues that underlie conflict dynamics. To deal with the encounters that involve specific insults, it is important to use appropriate tools of resolution and management of conflict. Table 7.1 shows the connections between the form of the insult, connotation of conflict, and approaches to intervention. The following discussion explains these interconnections and provides recommendations to deal with each case of insult.

IDENTITY INSULT

Identity insult was employed in the cases of Pussy Riot, the murder of the Armenian soldier, and celebration of Victory Day in Ukraine. In the first case, both parties in the conflict used *identity insults*, while in the two latter cases only one side employed this tactic. The analysis shows that both insulting and insulted sides can construct an *identity insult*. The insulting side attributes a negative identity, dishonest motivations, and foul values to the out-group and portrays its actions as destructive or flawed. An *identity insult* helps develop a negative depiction of the out-group, especially in the comparison with the in-group. The insulting part recognizes or creates an identity insult if group members feel that their main values and positive features are under the attack and their self-esteem is targeted by the out-group.

In the case of Pussy Riot, some committed Orthodox Christians created the *attributed identity insult*, recognizing the corruption of the Russian Orthodox Church (ROC) leadership as a deep offense to their faith and religious identity. Similarly, progressive people in Russia employed the

Table 7.1 CONCEPTUAL FRAMEWORK FOR MITIGATION OF INSULTS

Form of insult	Short description	Indicator for	Recommendations
Identity	Attribution of negative features, wrong motivations or foul values to out-group or accusation in performing destructive or erroneous actions	Conflicts that involve a fight between two identities, in which each party aims at increasing self-esteem by creating a negative image of the out-group and presenting its values and beliefs as corrupt and flawed	Transformation of collective axiology
Projection	Justification of particular actions or eradication of the negative features of the in-group by imposing them on an out-group	Conflicts with previous history of aggression and offense that was not reconciled or forgiven. The in-group can use history of out-group's aggression toward other groups or countries.	Reconciliation, forgiveness, transitional justice, history education
Divergence	Enhancing of differences and the social boundary if one or both groups feel a threat to their values and beliefs, deny any similarities, or aim at alienation of the out-group	Conflicts that involve divergence and a strong need for separation between two groups or resistance to imposition of the values and beliefs of one group on another one	Agonistic dialogue
Relative	Denial of certain rights of the out-group and emphasis on the in-group's privileged position and right to make decisions, and define the connotations of historic and current events and holidays.	Conflicts in which the in-group denies specific rights of the out-group and places itself as superior to the in-group	Shared society, identity dialogue
Power	Decrease of absolute power of the out-group or relative coercive power in comparison with the in-group	Conflicts that involve competition for control over specific territory, social groups, or political and ideological positions	Negotiation, mediation
Legitimacy	Initiation and promotion of a recategorization process that legitimizes one side and delegitimizes the other	Conflicts in which one group or both groups aim at diminishing the legitimacy and rightfulness of the out-group's position and increasing of in-group validity	Aknowledgment, negotiation of identities

attributed identity insult to depict the fusion of the ROC with the Russian government as a promotion of extremely conservative values and views on society, sexual relations, and the role of women. They believed that this value system is wrong and in contradiction with the meaning of their national identity. The actions of Pussy Riot were an example of a reaction to this *identity insult.*

The ROC and the Russian government also created the *attributed identity insult*, presenting the actions of Pussy Riot as an offense to the Orthodox faith, *sensitizing* Orthodox believers to this deep harm to their faith and identity. They also *transferred* the *identity insult* to nonreligious people by comparing it with an offense to the memory of the Great Patriotic War veterans. Thus, they presented "Punk Prayer" as an *identity insult* to Orthodox believers as well as to the patriotic feelings of all Russian citizens, uniting religious feelings with national ones and blending religious identity with national identity. By appealing to the patriotic feelings of Russian citizens, Russian leaders shifted the insult to the fusion of the ROC and the state into an insult to the sacral history and patriotic foundations of Russia. This *attributed identity insult* helped the ROC and the government to mask the political motivation of their actions and deny any political inspiration behind Pussy Riots performance, repudiating the *legitimacy insult* created by the group.

The use of the identity insult by both parties reveals the nature of the conflict in Russia: there is a major contradiction between two concepts of national identity presented, on the one side, by the government and ROC and, on the other side, by progressive democratic movements. *Identity insults* are used to impose negative identity on the out-groups and portray their values, beliefs, and views as amoral and erroneous. The government depicts all actions of the opposition as targeting national identity and national pride, portraying the opposition as unpatriotic. It impacts the perception of the opposition among the general public who believe that the opposition aims to destroy a strong state and the unique Russian Orthodox society. The government is positioned as a defender of national values and the superiority of Russia.

In the case of the murder of the Armenian solder, the Armenian side used an *identity insult* to present this killing and the subsequent release and glorification of the murderer as an illustration of the policy of aggression and hatred among Azerbaijani people. Armenian officials depicted the Azerbaijani government as promoting a culture of hate and justifying aggressive actions against Armenians, including violent crimes and ethnic cleansing before and during the war. They also positioned Azerbaijani society as driven by ethnic and religious animosity, as violating human rights, and as vigorously supporting brutal retaliations and killings. In contrast, the Armenian side was presented as peace-loving and actively seeking the resolution of existing conflicts.

The use of *identity insult* by the Armenian side reveals the problems in resolution of the Nagorno-Karabakh conflict. Armenia completely denied accountability for the conflict and presented Azerbaijani society as bigoted, aggressive, and an impediment to the peace process. Attributing all responsibility for the conflict to the Azerbaijani side, Armenians demonstrated to the international community their willingness to come to an agreement to terminate the conflict. At the same time Armenian leadership insisted on an agreement that would confirm the independence of the Nagorno-Karabakh.

In Ukraine, a group of young people created the *identity insult* by frying eggs on the eternal flame of the Tomb of the Unknown Solder. Their actions were intended to diminish the value and victories of the Red Army during World War II and present them as erroneous and alien to contemporary Ukraine. These actions were perceived as offensive by the majority of the population, who saw them as an *identity insult* to the memory of people who gave their life in the fight against fascism.

The use of *identity insult* by the young Ukrainians reveals the conflict between two political identities, a dissonance of values, beliefs, and perceptions. Young people have a pro-Western and pro-democratic identity and protest values of the older generation that, in their view, are pro-Soviet and totalitarian. They employed an *identity insult* to weaken the foundation of the pride of the older generation—the victory in the Great Patriotic War—and increase their own self-esteem by putting down the out-group.

Thus, an *identity insult* is indicative of conflicts that involve a fight between two identities, in which each party aims to increase self-esteem and improve in-group image by creating a negative image of the out-group and define its values and beliefs as corrupt and flawed. Often, these two identities are presented as opposite and contradictory to each other, with each side denying the core of the other identity and diminishing its main values. If parties use an *identity insult*, such conflicts should be treated as identity-based conflicts.

While an *identity insult* targets the out-group's values, beliefs, and perceptions, portraying them as erroneous or vicious and differing from the in-group's, it is possible to reduce the effects of this insult through redefinition of collective axiology and altering the negative images of the out-group. Collective axiology is

> a system of value-commitments that define which actions are prohibited, and which actions are necessary for specific tasks. It provides a sense of life and

world, serves to shape perceptions of actions and events, and provides a basis for evaluating group members. A collective axiology defines boundaries and relations among groups and establishes criteria for ingroup/outgroup membership. Through its collective axiology, a group traces its development from a sacred past, extracted from mythic episodes beyond the life of mortals, and seeks permanence. Transcending the finitude of individual life, a collective axiology extends retrospectively from the salient episodes of the past to a prospective vision, presumably into the otherwise uncertain future. An individual's identity and values that are acquired at birth and left behind at death exist before that birth and behind that death.[1]

Two variables characterize the dynamics of collective axiology: the degree of collective generality and the degree of axiological balance.

1. *Collective generality*. The degree of collective generality refers to the ways in which in-group members categorize the Other, how they simplify, or not, their defining (essential) character. The collective generality includes four main characteristics:
   (i) Homogeneity of perceptions and behaviors of out-group members
   (ii) Long-term stability of their beliefs, attitudes, and actions
   (iii) Resistance to change
   (iv) The scope or range of the out-group category

A high level of collective generality is connected with the viewing an out-group as consistent, homogeneous, demonstrating fixed patterns of behaviors, committed to durable rigid beliefs and values, and widespread in the region or the whole world. A low degree of collective generality reflects the perception of the out-group as differentiated, ready for transformation, exhibiting various kinds of behaviors, and relatively limited in scope.

The degree of collective generality can change over time, especially in the situation of strengthening intergroup tensions or violence. For example, the escalation of conflict can lead to the perception of an enemy not as a small local group but as an entire race, ethnic group, nationality, or culture. The image of an out-group can became more rigid, firm, and homogeneous. During violent conflicts, people tend to deny the diversity and competing priorities of an out-group and its multicultural and political structure and to perceive it as a single "entity" with similar beliefs and attitudes and supporting common policies toward other groups.

2. *Axiological balance*. Axiological balance refers to a kind of parallelism of virtues and vices attributes to groups. When applied to stories about

the Other, a balanced axiology embeds positive and negative characteristics in group identities. Balanced axiology leads to the recognition of decency and morality as well as immorality and cruelty of both the Other and the in-group. A high degree of axiological balance reflects recognition of one's own moral faults and failings, while a low degree of axiological balance is connected with the perception of an in-group as morally pure and superior and an out-group as evil and vicious. This tends to promote a "tunnel consciousness" and a diminished capacity for independent thought. "In its extreme form, a low axiological balance is correlated to exaggeration, inflation, and fabrication of out-group vices and in-group glories. The 'Them/Us' duality seems fixed in the timeless social order. With a fabricated sense of its collective virtues, the in-group promotes a sense of moral supremacy over the outgroup. Such an unbalanced depiction of group differences provides a ground for a struggle against criminal elements of the world."[2]

The transformation of negative perceptions of others into positive ones includes two interrelated processes: (1) the increase in the axiological balance and (2) decrease in axiological generality. The first goal can be achieved through the alteration of the positive images of one's own group and negative images of others into complex images that contain both positive and negative features. The second goal can be achieved through the reassessment of the homogeneity of the other groups and perception of others as having multiple views and opinions.

The values, needs, and traditions of each social group have to be perceived not as contradictory to those of other group, but in the framework of the respect for such values as peace, justice, and humanity. This approach can help resolve contradictions between groups; change people's conceptions of the groups, from distinct groups in conflict to a larger, more inclusive group; and make attitudes toward other groups more positive, even if they share a long history of offenses.

One of the ways for the transformation of negative perceptions into positive ones involves redefinition of in-group identity and acceptance of in-group deeds as negative. The recognition of in-group violent actions and human rights of out-groups poses a threat to in-group identity, which rests on the idea of "positive We, negative They." The acknowledgment of negative in-group actions requires review and reconceptualization of in-group identity, a process that always invokes strong resistance. In-group members have a strong aspiration to defend the positive self-image and reject negative information that can destroy it. Stressing other important components of the meaning of identity, such as cultural heritage, deep traditions, history of peaceful coexistence with other groups, and so on, can help preserve a high level of self-esteem and in-group pride.

Narrative intervention has to emphasize positive features in the self-description of an in-group, such as "peaceful people" who "value tolerance," are "open-minded and understanding," and take "pleasure in forgiveness." These images exist in the self-portrayal of all groups and serve as powerful sources for self-esteem and pride. The emphasis on peaceful images of the in-group and out-group can provoke supporting narratives that describe the in-group's peaceful history and glory and evidences of positive intergroup relations. Such storytelling by different people will reinforce these images through complimentary ideas and constructive character. The positive emotions produced during this process will strengthen the formation of peaceful self-concepts and positive perceptions of others, with an emphasis on tolerance, reconciliation, and goodwill.

Thus, reconstruction of collective axiology can encumber the production of a negative portrayal of the out-group, a presentation of its values and beliefs as corrupt and flawed, and an invidious comparison with the in-group, thus decreasing the effects of *identity insults*. In identity-based conflicts, in which an *identity insult* is employed as a tool in a fight between two identities, reconstruction of collective axiology prevents denial of the core of out-group identity and creation of negative out-group images.

PROJECTION INSULT

A *projection insult* was employed in the cases of the murder of the Armenian solder, the conflict between the United States and North Korea, and disputes over the contested islands between Japan, China, and South Korea. In the first two cases, only one side used a *projection insult*, while in the latter case, both sides actively employed this form of insult. In all cases, all parties used *projection insults* to justify particular actions or eradicate the negative features of the in-group by imposing them on an out-group. The in-group depicted the out-group as aggressive, brutal, and provoking. The offensive actions of the in-group were validated as a response to this aggressiveness and as a defensive behavior.

In the case of the killing of the Armenian soldier, the Azerbaijani murderer used a *projection insult* to justify his act. He attributed all responsibility to the Armenian side, emphasizing that the killing of innocent Azerbaijani people in Nagorno-Karabakh by Armenian soldiers was unprovoked brutality and justified retaliation. In the context of the Nagorno-Karabakh conflict, he saw all actions of Armenian soldiers at the NATO school as insulting and provoking. Through the *projection insult*, he posited the murder as an honorable and obligatory action the helped avenge the murders of Azerbaijani people and ease the pain of their relatives. Azerbaijani officials and mass media supported this presentation of the murder as a need for defense provoked by the cruelty of Armenians in Nagorno-Karabakh and the offensive behavior of Armenian officers. Using a *projection insult*, Azerbaijani officials presented the imprisoning of Safarov in parallel with Azerbaijani sufferings in the Nagorno-Karabakh conflict and legitimized the decision to release Safarov as a symbolic act of victory in this war. Therefore, the *projection insult* was employed to annul the accountability of Safarov and justify the Azerbaijani government's decision to release him by ascribing provocative and threatening actions to the Armenian side.

This use of this *projection insult* by the Azerbaijani side reveals the nature of impediments to peace in the Nagorno-Karabakh conflict. The Azerbaijani side denied all responsibility for the ongoing conflict and imposed it on Armenia. The *projection insult* also helped Azerbaijan prolong peace negotiations, justifying its action by presenting Armenia as a terrorist state that could not participate in serious negotiations. Using the constant threat from aggressive Armenia, the Azerbaijani government imposed a robust control within the country, avoided the development of a peace agreement that could finally determine the status of Nagorno-Karabakh, prevented informal contacts across conflict lines, and disrupted ongoing dialogue projects.

In the case of conflict between the United States and North Korea, *projection insults* were actively used by the North Korean leadership to describe the United States as a "hostile evil" aggressor intending to exercise its power in the region and invade North Korea. These insults helped justify North Korean nuclear bomb tests and rocket launches. To strengthen the insults, North Korea employed different events, including the international nuclear security summit and the US war game exercise with South Korea, to portray the United States as a threat to North Korean political and territorial sovereignty. This attribution of aggressive intentions was brought on the global level by positioning the United States as a "vicious" invader of the Balkans and Middle East, and claiming that North Korea would be the next victim of the "hostile imperialistic" United States. Thus, North Korea presented the development of nuclear capabilities as a necessary means of self-defense, provoked by the United States, which threatened the fragile peace on the peninsula.

The use of a *projection insult* sheds light on the nature of the ongoing conflict between North Korea and the United States. North Korea wants to develop its positive image among the international community and gain the support of those that feel victimized by US foreign policy. It posits itself as a victim of aggression that has to defend itself by any means. Thus, all aggressive actions of the North Korean leadership, including the declaration of war, were justified by the attribution of responsibility to the United States. All preventive policies of the United States and the UN only worsened the situation because were portrayed by North Korea as examples of imperialistic plans.

In the case of disputed islands between Japan, China, and South Korea, Japanese leaders employed a *projection insult* to justify Japan's position as a country that encouraged peace and cooperation in the region and blamed China and North Korea for increasing tensions, exacerbating conflict, and intruding into sovereign Japanese territory. Both China and South Korea employed *projection insults* to deny their hostile actions and present them as Japanese speculations and fabrications. They used imperial Japan's historical invasions to blame Japan for aggressively expanding its territory and creating conflicts in the region, while presenting their own countries as peace-loving and concerned about stability in the region.

The use of *projection insult* by all sides in the dispute over islands shows the specificity of these two conflicts. The history of Japanese imperial aggression still has a significant effect on relations in the region. Both China and South Korea effectively utilized this memory as a framework for assessing current disputes, presenting Japan as a belligerent invader into their territory. The uncompleted process of forgiveness and reconciliation creates the possibility of blaming the out-group for aggressive action and justification of one's own offensive policies.

Thus, a *projection insult* points to conflicts that have a previous history of aggression and offense that was not reconciled or forgiven. The in-group can invoke previous aggressions that not only targeted the in-group but also involved other groups as victims. For instance, the Azerbaijani invoked the history of Armenian brutality in both the Nagorno-Karabakh region, and an Armenian operation in the 1920s to assassinate Turkish leaders who were planning the mass killing of Armenian people. These were intended to present Armenia as a terrorist state, unwilling to be peaceful towards Azerbaijanis.

North Korea employed the war game exercises by the United States and South Korea as well as US military operations in Bosnia and Iraq to portray the United States as aggressive and imperialist. China and South Korea used the history of invasions by imperial Japan in different countries in the region. These memories create a framework for the assessment of the current actions of the out-group and justification of actions of the in-group as defensive.

To deal with *projection insults*, it is important to avoid responding with offensive or aggressive statements and actions. The insulting side specifically provokes the insulted side to react this way in order to confirm its accusations. The actions of the United States, such as postponing a missile launch and calling for dialogue, helped reduce tensions in the conflict between the United States and North Korea that had the potential to escalate into military action.

If sides in a conflict use *projection insults*, reconciliation, forgiveness, and restorative justice must be used together with other conflict resolution techniques. Reconciliation is a restoration of relationships in the aftermath of conflict to build a stable and peaceful future where respect and security prevail. Reconciliation is a process of building long-term peace between former enemies through bilateral initiatives and institutions across governments and societies. It involves reestablishing cooperation between conflicting parties who have harmed each other and implicates management of social identities and the process of reckoning with the past. Reconciliation processes depend on interrelations between conflict, power, social identity, and collective memory/historic narratives. These processes aim to explore and overcome the traumatic experiences and injustices that occurred during the conflict and define ways to build trust, cooperation, and mutual coexistence. These techniques include truth and reconciliation commissions, which can help reconcile human rights abuses and victimization and provide mercy in sentencing—with the possibility of amnesty—to those who show genuine repentance for their actions.

Similar actions of forgiveness and reconciliation help restore positive relations between nations. For example, in 1958, Charles de Gaulle and Konrad Adenauer redefined the relationship between France and Germany. This required a reconsideration of perceptions and memories, reconstruction of their common past, and the development of the basis for a common interpretation of future events and collaboration. This process included the acceptance of complexity and all contradictions of the past and the understanding of the other party's interpretation of events and actions. In 1958–1962, de Gaulle and Adenauer had several meetings designed to overcome negative perceptions rooted in past events and to achieve reconciliation. They stressed that former enemies were determined to become friends. One of the most important steps was mutual understanding and the official recognition of the sufferings of the other nation. Changes in the German national identity included confrontation with the past and acceptance of responsibility for the most difficult episodes in national history. De Gaulle also recognized the negative actions of France and described Germany as a "great nation." Both nations decided not to emphasize the conflictual past, but rather highlight the solidarity that also characterized relations between them. Past wars and conflicts between the French and Germans were redefined as a common past of collective sufferings, and both nations became allies that mutually endured a common tragedy.

History education also plays a crucial role in the formation of the concepts of society during processes of reconciliation and peace-building, especially in societies with a long history of conflict, violence, and mistrust among ethnic and religious groups. The politics of reconciliation presented in historic narratives affect psychological healing and recovery on a personal level. Thus, history education in postconflict societies is one of the major mechanisms that can unite political and social reconciliation with the processes of individual healing and recovery. History education as a social practice of construction of sociopolitical memories influences public discourse and supports a specific ethno-political order at the same time developing personal values, perceptions, and beliefs. Seixas defines the main function of history education as providing identity, cohesion, and social purpose.[3] Therefore, history education can address the collective traumas and contribute to reconciliation through development of a common inclusive identity, facilitation of social cohesion, and development of a compelling moral framework. Accountability for the past and the rewriting of history to include different perspectives, voices, and understandings of previous violent actions create a platform for the society to move forward. The acknowledgment of past events and of the responsibilities of perpetrators is critical for the processes of reconciliation.

History education in postconflict societies faces the complex task of reconciling the wrongdoings of all parties: "In most societies recovering from violence, questions of how to deal with the past are acute, especially when the past involves memories of death, suffering, and destruction so widespread that a high percentage of the population is affected."[4] Reconciliation, apology, and forgiveness become vital factors in the restoration of a society and promotion of tolerance and, thus, are a critical task of history education. Yet the effective approach to teaching about conflicts of the past is often debated: "They are sensitive because they relate to particularly painful, tragic, humiliating or divisive times in a country's past, and there is a fear or concern that reference to them in history lessons might renew old wounds and divisions and bring back too many painful memories."[5]

The presentation of the past poses serious challenges for countries, but ignoring history can lead to even more severe problems. History curricula should highlight the ways in which all groups within a society have suffered, include discussions of why and how these groups were dehumanized and demonized, and show how acts of discrimination and violence were justified. History textbooks should not deny or disregard the antagonism of, or cruel actions committed by, various groups; only acknowledgment and understanding of the roots and effects of conflict can undermine harmful nationalistic and ethnocentric ideologies. History curricula should present "memories of the past...for everyone in a community to own up to—if it is not to be a community forever divided by clashing assessments of the crimes of ancestors."[6] Such curricula can develop the basis for the prevention of possible future acts of aggression, hostility, and dominance by any state or actor.

To transform postconflict societies, history curricula should compliment the reconciliation process, including acknowledgment, truth-telling, apology, repair, and democratization.[7] One of the tasks of history education is to recognize the victims of violence and repression, as well as their suffering and the need for justice. Younger generations have to understand the complex—and sometimes controversial—relationship between justice and reconciliation, which can lead to further clashes in societies recovering from conflict. The quest for justice and prosecution of perpetrators can jeopardize fragile processes of reconciliation and endanger efforts to foster a dialogue among former enemy groups. At the same time, reconciliation is not complete without some form of punishment and retribution for past crimes committed. These controversies should not be ignored or undermined and must be presented in history textbooks. The processes of democratization provide the basis for open discussions about the positions of victims and perpetrators and policies toward reconciliation.

During last decade, common history projects have been introduced as a new approach for trauma healing and reconciliation.[8] Common history projects can provide an optimistic forecast for a shared future based on an understanding and acknowledgment of past issues and relations between them. Common history projects have become one of the best vehicles through which to address issues of victimization and violence and create mutual understanding between societies formerly in conflict. Thus, through common history textbook projects, history education can contribute to the healing and reconciliation processes in postconflict societies.

Furthermore, in postconflict societies in which political and diplomatic approaches are not always successful, history education can encourage dialogues within and between communities. Common history textbooks encourage future generations of leaders to foster partnerships and good relations with neighbors. History curricula that promote respect for other nations' voices and perspectives can profoundly transform and strengthen relationships between states; they can destroy old stereotypes of enemies and endorse tolerance, mutual understandings, and future cooperation.

While it is very difficult to revise historical narratives in weak states or regions that are still enmeshed in conflict, many political leaders in post-conflict states have recognized that efforts to revise biased historical narratives can heal traumas and improve the relationship between former enemies. Once violence subsides and states become more secure and confident, citizens are better prepared to examine their history with more scrutiny.[9] As stressed by Adwan and Bar-On, children are better able to embrace more than one narrative from their early stages of development, but this capacity generally declines with the onset of adulthood.[10] Thus, teaching multiple narratives through history curricula might be one of the most effective ways of trauma healing and reconciliation, thus reducing the effects of projection insults and preventing future offenses.

Processes of reconciliation and forgiveness, as well as the use of history education, hamper *projection insults* that present antagonistic in-group action as defensive behavior and as a response to out-group provocations and aggressiveness. Because these types of intervention facilitate reconciliation and forgiveness for a previous history of aggression and offense, they block projection insults and prevent the use of historic traumas for justification of particular in-group actions or denial of the negative features of the in-group through imposition them on an out-group.

DIVERGENCE INSULT

Divergence insults were employed in the cases of the celebration of Victory Day in Ukraine, disputes over the islands around Japan, China, and South Korea, and Pussy Riot in Russia. In the first case, two major groups in Ukraine employed this type of insult, while in the two latter cases, governments used a *divergence insult* to create a border between the majority and a small opposition group. In all cases, the *divergence insult* enhanced differences and social boundaries between the majority and a group that wanted to highlight differences and distance themselves. from the out-group. This aim is accomplished by emphasizing the negative characteristics of an out-group and differences between the in-group and the out-group.

In the case of Ukraine, *divergence insults* helped both sides reinforce social boundaries between them and prevent imposition of alien values, beliefs, and traditions. Representatives of Western Ukraine opposed totalitarian values and Russian imperial aggressiveness, symbolized by the red flag. They used *divergence insults* to defend Ukrainian independence from the imposition of pro-Soviet and pro-Russian values and ideology. Similarly, representatives of Eastern Ukraine saw the promotion of Ukrainian nationalism as an imposition of both Nazi and pro-Western ideology and wanted to separate themselves from these ideas. These *divergence insults* stressed the alien nature of ideals of the opposite side and emphasized the importance to preserve social boundaries between these groups.

The use of a *divergence insult* in this emergent conflict emphasized an essential necessity to preserve the ideological divide between two regions of the country, and showed that opposite interpretations of history are central to interethnic relations in Ukraine. This situation could be described as an unstable coexistence in which any attempts to infiltrate the social boundary and impose ideas on the other side are vigorously rejected. Actions like passing the red flag law and the representatives' visit to the southeast of L'viv work as triggers that initiate the exchange of offenses.

In the case of disputes around the contested islands, Japan employed a *divergence insult* in the beginning of the conflict when the purchases of the islands were only considered. This insult helped increase Japanese public support and position all criticism and opposition disloyal to the country. Creating a social boundary between faithful compatriots and opponents, the Japanese government dismissed all disagreements within its borders as well as presented the island issue as a domestic matter that should not be a concern for any other country. This *divergence insult*, together with mass media campaigns that *sensitized* the public to the insults, increased the homogeneity of public opinion, and silenced the "renegades" who questioned this position. The employment of a *divergence insult* also highlights the internal problems regarding the government's claims over the islands. Japanese leadership recognized the disputed nature of its policies toward the islands and used the *divergence insult* as a means to promote the legality of the government's assertions.

In the case of Pussy Riot, the ROC created a *divergence insult* portraying the rock group as essentially different from Russian Christian society, and "Punk Prayer" as a delinquent intentional offense to the sacral faith. The ROC positioned the church as defender of freedom and morality against Pussy Riot. Similarly, during the trial, the prosecution and the judge also used a *divergence insult* to strengthen the boundary between the girls and Russian society. Thus, a *divergence insult* was used to establish a social boundary between Pussy Riot and the rest of society and present the opposition as offenders of national values and the religious faith of all Russian people. The use of the *divergence insult* shows the nature of the conflict in Russia, where the government emphasizes the alien nature of opposition groups and presents them as divergent from the rest of Russia. This policy helps place the opposition on the outskirts of the society as inorganic and fundamentally distinct from main Russian values.

Divergence insults are indicative of the conflicts that involve the divergence and of a strong need for separation between two groups. Additionally, they can represent resistance to imposition of values and beliefs of one group over another and usually demonstrate a certain level of insecurity connected with the threat of out-group infiltration into in-group boundary. This divergence can occur between two groups in a society, each of which defies any attempts of the out-group to inflict its perceptions and ideology on the in-group, defending its geographic, social, and political space from intrusion by the out-group. It also can occur when governments try to silence the opposition or discredit it among the public. The former is indicative of societies with a deep divide between social groups, the latter of totalitarian societies or societies with controversial social issues.

To deal with a *divergence insult*, it is important to introduce agonistic dialogue in the society. Only through systemic dialogue can common ground be established and a cohesive national identity develop, one based on unifying ideas, including ideas of civic society and a civic concept of national identity, human rights, and the equality of every citizen independent of his or her religion, ethnicity, and language. Such dialogue rests on ideas of agonistic pluralism[11] that convert antagonism into agonism, promotes engagement of adversaries across profound differences, and involves "a vibrant clash of democratic political positions."[12] In divided societies, agonistic dialogue becomes an essential political practice that contributes to building relationships and expands understanding between groups. Dialogue in divided society should not illuminate conflict, but rather transform the nature of that conflict. Any democratic society includes conflicts as an essential part of political life; thus the dialogue's aim is to transform "violent conflict into non-violent forms of ongoing political struggle."[13] Thus, agonistic dialogue practice is less about finding the "truth" or some form of consensus about the history of the conflict, than about "seeking accommodation between conflicting accounts in such a way as to make a conflict more liveable."[14]

Starting with disagreements as a starting point, agonistic dialogue does not aim to overcome these disagreements through the finding or creation of a consensus. "Acknowledging issues of power and conflict as a central feature of dialogue," it "highlights the shifting nature of relationships concerned with power, identity, and vulnerability, and continues to privilege conflict as a crucial and potentially productive element of social change."[15] Agonistic dialogue helps expand existing political spaces and create new ones; it promotes openness to distinction and conflicting views, and the development of new understandings of social identity. The practice of agonistic dialogue is based on "the need to acknowledge the dimension of power and antagonism and their ineradicable character" as well as their impact on the development and functioning of social identities.[16] Such dialogue should be sustainable over time; embroil deep level of engagement of all parties involved; create positive relationship and trusts between participants; build a "safe space" for expressions of deep hopes, fears and interests; and increase understanding of the complex, multidimensional character of the problems. These procedures help create a democratic society where people can "live together productively, even harmoniously, with conflict."[17]

Thus, agonistic dialogue can serve as an antidote to *divergence insult* or can reduce its effects by diminishing intergroup differences and the social boundary. Agonistic dialogue diminishes threats associated with the acknowledgment of similarity or resemblance between groups as well as removes motivation for alienation of the out-group. It could be an effective tool in conflicts that involve a strong need for separation between two groups or resistance to imposition of values and beliefs of one group over another.

RELATIVE INSULT

Relative insult was used in the cases of the celebration of Victory Day in Ukraine and of the murder of the Armenian soldier. In the former case both sides used this insult, while in the latter only the Azerbaijani side employed it. *Relative insults* deny certain rights of the out-group and emphasize the in-group's privileged position, inclusive rights to make decisions and define the connotations of historic and current events and holidays. *Relative insult* also rejects the rights of the out-group to make particular decisions or take certain actions, bringing a normative dimension to the conflict and defining what the out-group can and cannot do as a result of its subordinate position.

Through the use of *relative insults* representatives of Southeastern Ukraine positioned their group as the only one that has rights and capacities to define the meaning of Victory Day. They denied the rights of the population of Western Ukraine to delineate the connotation of the Great Patriotic War and discuss who were its winners and losers. Representatives of Southeast Ukraine came to L'viv to celebrate the victory of the Red Army together with veterans from Western Ukraine and demonstrate their right to glorify their ideals. Ukrainian nationalists saw this visit of as *relative insult*, perceiving it as a denial of their right to treat this date according to their own values and beliefs. In response, the young Ukrainian nationalists created another *relative insult*, using violent actions to demonstrate their exclusive right to control the celebration of Victory Day in L'viv, thus denying the rights of pro-Soviet groups to celebrate it in their town.

The use of *relative insult* helps reveal the core of the conflict in Ukraine. Two regional groups have different perceptions of Ukraine's history and conflicting beliefs about the role of the Red Army and Ukrainian nationalists in the Great Patriotic War. Both sides deny the rights of the out-group to define the meaning of the victory in this war and perceive the out-group as subordinate to the in-group because of its faulty ideological position.

In the case of the murder of the Armenian soldier, the Azerbaijani side created a *relative insult* through denial of the rights of Armenia to condemn actions of the murderer and the government. The Azerbaijani side used a *relative insult* to deny the ability of the Armenian president to influence perceptions in other countries, and to emphasize that Armenia had no leverage in the international community. Moreover, Azerbaijani officials furthered this *relative insult,* denying such characteristics of the Armenian president as reason, intelligence, and authority. The *relative insult* posited Armenia as vulnerable and weak in comparison with a strong and effective Azerbaijan.

The employment of *relative insult* helps us understand the problems that impede the resolution of the Nagorno-Karabakh conflict. Azerbaijani officials positioned the Armenian president and Armenian society as weak and without influence, while emphasizing the triumph of Azerbaijani foreign policy. The denial of Armenia's right to define the meaning of the conflict and appeal for international support presents Armenia as inferior to Azerbaijan, and impedes any attempts to find an equal approach to resolution of the conflict.

Thus, *relative insult* is indicative of conflicts in which the in-group denies specific rights to the out-group and regards itself as superior to this out-group. Areas of conflict include the right to define the connotations of national history, the meaning of specific events and ways of celebrating certain holidays—as in Ukrainian case—or the right to influence the international community and request actions of international third parties—as the Nagorno-Karabakh conflict. In both cases, the out-group is positioned as mediocre in comparison with the in-group. Such perceptions often lead to resentment, ignorance, and fear in relations between groups and produce inequalities and exclusions on the societal level.

To deal with a *relative insult*, it is important to approach this resentment on different levels, including societal, communal, and institutional, creating a sustainable and equal society. If the sides of the conflict employ *relative insults*, the most effective way of dealing with them is through the development of a shared society, including equality, impartiality, and dialogue.[18] "Shared societies are stable, safe and just, and are based on the promotion and protection of all human rights, as well as on non-discrimination, tolerance, respect for diversity, equality of opportunity, solidarity, security and participation of all people including disadvantaged and vulnerable groups and persons."[19] A shared society supports equality of all cultural, ethnic, and religious identities, recognizing their values and interdependence. This approach addresses divisions between groups and creates positive connections between communities. Accountable governments and inclusive decision-making, including administration, representative bodies, an accessible judicial system, free and fair elections, and equal access for basic needs and services, help develop trust and positive social relations.[20] Education also can contribute to the development of respect between communities with contradictory histories and values. The development of a shared society must be collaborative, adaptive to social environments, and inclusive of all stakeholders in consensus-oriented efforts.

Another approach to relative insult is identity dialogue. Identity dialogue aims to transform dominant identities into multiple identities with polymodal meanings. The structure of narratives that are based on "They as inferior" perceptions and that reflect supercilious attitudes, feeling, and stereotypes, can be replaced by a new structure rooted in a more equal approach to out-group. This type of dialogue has to involve participants in a discussion of the values, needs, and traditions of each group and the possibilities for the creation of a relationship that would satisfy and respect the values and needs of all involved groups. This new relationship expands people's conceptions of membership from exclusive groups in conflict to a more inclusive group, and makes attitudes toward other groups more positive, in spite of a long history of mutual offenses. On the basis of a positive balance between differences and similarities, members of all groups develop positive attitudes and stereotypes of each other.

The first step for identity reconstruction involves increasing awareness of the role of identity in conflicts, of We-They perceptions, and of collective axiology that leads to violence. Stories of different conflicts and violent actions, analyzed through the prism of identity, provide insights into salience and dominance of identity, alterations of perception, misbalanced and projective axiologies, and accepted or expected aggressive behaviors. It is important that the cases of conflict discussed at this stage of the dialogue be different from the conflict in which the participants are themselves involved. Similar events and situations will provoke comparisons and strengthen negative attitudes and emotions. The more distant the cases are from the participants' experience, the lower their resistance to understanding the possibility of misperceptions. Thus, in Crimea, where conflict developed between Muslim Crimean Tartars and Orthodox Russians, the discussion of conflict in Bosnia exacerbates strong negative feelings and aggravates aggressive attitudes toward other ethnic groups. On the other hand, the discussion of conflicts perceived as very different from the Crimean situation, such as discriminative practices in the Dominican Republic or violence in Sudan and Rwanda, allows more objective analysis, which increases the understanding of the roots of vicious actions and which facilitates changes in perceptions, leading to the recognition of aggressive behaviors of one's own group.

The recognition of the equal rights of out-groups may pose a threat to in-group identity, which rests on the idea of "superior We, inferior They." The values, needs, and traditions of each group must be perceived not as mutually contradictory, but in the framework of a shared society that would satisfy and respect the values and needs of all identity groups. This approach can also help resolve contradictions between different identities, change people's conceptions of belonging to one of two groups that are locked in struggle, to belonging to a much more inclusive group, and make attitudes toward other groups more positive, even of they had a long history of offenses.

To turn such models into positive attitudes and actions, the intervener has to take the next step: form a shared overarching identity that can lead to the de-escalation of conflict. These shared identities can reduce intergroup hostility by minimizing attention to ethnic/racial/religious differences and instead create the sense that all involved are "one unit." Sources for an overarching identity can be found in a common geographic location, common national ideas, shared community problems, and so forth. By asking questions about positive present and future developments and the possibilities of collaboration with others, the intervener can reinforce the formation of a shared identity. The intervener's task is to facilitate the creation of narratives of productive partnership, which are based on peaceful concepts of the in-group and which emphasize possible positive images of out-groups.

The formation of a new common identity is possible only if in-group members do not perceive that the new overarching identity being created poses a threat to their primary identity (ethnic/racial/religious). If values, core ideas, or new identity needs contradict the possible (perceived) values and ideas of the existing identity, a new circle of violence can begin as a response to this sense of threat. The intervener has to construct the concept and perception of the new shared identity very carefully, using narratives of existing collaboration and situations of successful teamwork. By asking such questions as "What can we do together to make our future better?" and "What can we do for our children?" practitioners can shift the emphasis of narratives from past opposition to mutual understanding, mutual responsibilities, and the mutual defense of human rights among former enemies. In this case, concepts of a peaceful in-group and of a new "We-ness" will develop simultaneously and will reinforce each other. These concepts will reduce the effects of *relative insults* that deny the rights of the other group.

Thus, development of a shared society and identity dialogue helps deal with *relative insults* through the mutual acknowledgment of certain rights of the out-group and the equal position of both groups. Through these types of intervention both groups accept the rights of the out-group to make particular decisions and take certain actions and do not attribute to the out-group a subordinate position. The development of a shared society and identity dialogue can be an effective tool in conflicts, in which *relative insults* are employed to increase fear in relations between groups and produce inequalities and exclusions on a societal level.

POWER INSULT

A *power insult* was employed in the case of conflict between North Korea and the United States and in disputes around the contested islands. In the former case only one side, North Korea, used a *power insult*, while in the latter case all sides used them. These *power insults* occurred in situations of competition for coercive power, both real and perceived. They were aimed at decreasing the absolute power of the out-group or its power in comparison with in-group.

During the entire conflict between North Korea and the United States, North Korean leadership used a *power insult* to exhibit its strength and readiness to defend its sovereign rights. It also defiantly ignored all warnings and restrictions imposed by the United States and displayed the will to follow its own economic and military development processes. To emphasize the equal status and equivalent powers of the United States and North Korea, North Korean leadership employed various *power insults*, including rocket launches, nuclear tests, the cutting of telephone lines to South Korea, putting rocket units on standby, unilaterally ending the armistice, and declaring a "state of war."

These *power insults* revealed the nature of the conflict between North Korea and the United States. North Korean leaders, facing increasing US and UN sanctions, were trying to redefine the balance of power using its nuclear program. *Power insults* targeted the threat of North Korean independence, the right to make its own decisions, and the ability to ignore imposed restrictions. They also emphasized the readiness of North Korea to utilize all its might and strength in a fight with the United States.

In the case of disputes of the islands between Japan, China, and South Korea, all sides created *power insults* to support the validity of their claims by demonstrating their power. To demonstrate their supremacy, each side employed various actions like landing on the islands by activists from both countries, visits by officials to the islands, sailing official ships in island waters, flights of aircrafts over the islands, the use of weapons-guiding radar locks, and violent protests on the streets. All these actions were aimed at demonstrating the in-group's jurisdiction over the islands and the inability of the out-group to control the situation. *Power insults* were also included in international legal processes through appeals to the international court, and economically through postponing financial aid to the out-group. All these *power insults* helped the in-group posit the out-group as powerless to challenge existing ownership of the islands.

The use of *power insults* helped reveal the core of the conflict over island territory. The sides that did not have ownership of the islands used more *power insults*: China in the Sino-Japanese conflict and Japan in the Japanese-Korean conflict. These countries employed *power insults* to demonstrate their control over the situation and denigrate the power of the out-group. The Chinese demonstrated its military power, sending ships and aircraft to the islands, while Japan created power insults on different levels, including diplomacy, international law, and economy.

Thus, *power insults* are indicative of conflicts that involve competition for control over a specific territory, social group, or political and ideological positions. Usually *power insults* are used by the side that feels less powerful and has less abilities to change the situation or alter out-group behavior. In these conflicts the inferior group desperately tries to restore the balance of power and uses coercive actions to demonstrate its force. If the out-group responds with more demonstration of power, it creates a security dilemma and provokes a spiral of aggressive and violent actions.

Dealing with power insults requires involvement in negotiations that encourage a search for agreement rather than open aggression.[21] Negotiations are usually undertaken when the parties recognize the conflict of interest between them and believe that a third party's influence will help them to get a better deal.[22] The fight for power usually involves interdependence, but the meaning of the balance of power can differ across the parties. This interdependence can be either "win-lose" or "win-win" in nature, defining the type of negotiation that is more appropriate for resolution of the conflict.[23] Positively interdependent goals normally result in cooperative approaches to negotiation, because any participant can "attain his goal if, and only if, the others with whom he is linked can attain their goals."[24] "Negative interdependence means the chance of one side attaining its goal is decreased by the other's success."[25]

During the negotiation, parties "will either attempt to force the other side to comply with their demands, to modify the opposing position and move toward compromise, or to invent a solution that meets the objectives of all sides."[26] Depending on the content of parties' interdependence, negotiations can be in form of *distributive* bargaining processes or *integrative* bargaining. The former is based on a principle of competition between participants and can result in "win-lose" outcomes or incomplete satisfaction of groups' needs. The latter rests on collaborative practices to find a "win-win" solution to the dispute, focusing on the development of mutually beneficial agreements that satisfy the interests of both sides. Integrative bargaining "refers to the potential for the parties' interests to be [combined] in ways that create joint value or enlarge the pie"[27] and usually produces more satisfactory outcomes for the parties involved.

Many scholars believe the two approaches should be used together. Usually negotiations involve both "creating" and "claiming" value: "parties' negotiators work cooperatively to create value (that is, 'enlarge the pie') but then they must use competitive processes to claim value (that is, 'divide up the pie')."[28] Because both parties are aware that they have mutual influence on the other's outcome, mutual adjustment is one of the main strategies during a negotiation. The readiness of one party to readjust its positions depends on its expectations regarding the other party's approaches. Through changes in parties' positions, compromises, and concessions, a settlement can be reached. The rejection of proposals by one party can lead to a break in negotiations. Thus, the effective solution takes into account the requirements of each party and optimizes the outcomes for both. In positional bargaining, the mutual focus on interests, issues, and positions brings both parties toward satisfactory agreement.[29]

Another approach to *power insults* is mediation. In mediation, parties seek the assistance of a third party to change their positions and behavior without resorting to aggressive actions. As a voluntary form of conflict management, mediation provides a choice for parties to begin or continue mediation, and ensures that they retain control over the outcome and are free to accept or reject any agreement. These features make mediation less threatening to the parties than other possible conflict management options. "It is non-evaluative and non-judgmental and it is particularly suited to the reality of international relations, where states and other actors guard their autonomy and independence quite jealously. It offers both parties the prospects of a better outcome without necessarily having any direct meetings with a sworn enemy."[30]

In the process of mediation, the parties can make their own decision on any outcome. The mediator facilitates communication between the parties, helping them focus on the main problems of the conflict and produce decisions that meet the interests and needs of all involved parties. The aim of the mediator is to create a more productive discussion, helping the parties determine facts, demonstrate empathy, and generate new ideas. "A successful mediation effort has an outcome that is accepted and owned by the parties themselves."[31]

There are two types of mediation: problem-solving mediation and transformative mediation. "Problem-solving mediation is aimed at resolving specific disputes between parties and coming up with a mutually acceptable solution to the immediate, short-term problem. In problem-solving mediation, the mediator normally plays a very active role in guiding the process."[32] Transformative mediation is a better fit in dealing with *power insults*. This mediation targets deeper changes within parties and their intergroup relations: "mediation's greatest value lies in its potential not only to find solutions to people's problems but to change people themselves for the better, in the very midst of conflict."[33] The main aim of transformative mediation is the empowerment and mutual recognition of the parties involved, enabling them to define their own issues and to understand the other party's point of view. This type of mediation helps the parties make better choices regarding the process and outcomes and better understand the position of the other party, developing a mutually satisfactory solution.

Thus, negotiation and mediation can be useful tools for dealing with and preventing *power insults* in situations of competition for coercive power, both real and perceived. They help in discussing a balance of absolute or relative power of the out-group and in-group and finding a satisfactory decision for both groups regarding control over specific territory, social groups, or political and ideological positions. Negotiation and mediation can help empower a group that feels less dominant and prevent the use of *power insults* as a tool for changing the situation or altering out-group behavior.

LEGITIMACY INSULT

Legitimacy insults were employed in all cases, including in the murder of the Armenian soldier, the Pussy Riot case in Russia, celebration of Victory Day in Ukraine, disputes over islands, and the conflict between North Korea and the United States. These *legitimacy insults* initiated and promoted a recategorization process that legitimizes the in-group and delegitimizes the out-group. As a foundation for legitimacy, groups can use interpretations of history and domestic law, morality, international law, national sovereignty, peace in the region, and meta-frames of internationally accepted concepts like fascism, totalitarianism, and imperialism. Sometimes, the same dimension can be used by both sides to portray the out-group as illicit and illegitimate.

In the case of the murder of the Armenian soldier, both sides vigorously employed *legitimacy insults*. The Azerbaijani side denied the legitimacy of the Armenian government, claiming that it had orchestrated ethnic cleansing in Nagorno-Karabakh, presenting Armenia as a terrorist state. Azerbaijani actions were legitimized as a response to victimization and suffering as a result of the aggressive, terrorist policies of Armenia. The release of Safarov despite Armenia's protests was also presented as a symbol of Armenian weakness in comparison with a rightful Azerbaijan, which enjoyed the support of the international community. The Armenian side also used a *legitimacy insult* to delegitimize the Azerbaijani government for ruining the negotiation process and legitimized the Armenian government, which had the strong support of the international community. This legitimacy insult helped Armenia depict Safarov's release as an unlawful action by an aggressive and bigoted Azerbaijani government that was destroying the fragile possibility for peaceful resolution of the Nagorno-Karabakh conflict.

The employment of *legitimacy insults* shows the nature of the Nagorno-Karabakh conflict. Both countries actively delegitimized the other and legitimized their position in the eyes of the international community. While Azerbaijani officials used terrorism as a legitimacy frame and presented Armenia as a terrorist state that could not be involved in negotiations, the Armenian side employed the success of a negotiation process as a frame for legitimacy, thus presenting Azerbaijan as an impediment to negotiations through its aggressive actions. Thus, both sides appealed to the international community to destroy the validity of the other based on internationally accepted values and categories.

In the case of Pussy Riot, the ROC legitimized its close connection with the government, referring to the need to prevent the infiltration of sinful ideas into society. It also delegitimized its opponents as enemies of Orthodoxy, offenders of the Orthodox faith, and supporters of evil. The opposition, in its turn, delegitimized the fusion of the Russian government and the ROC as appropriate to a third-world dictatorship, characterized by corruption and absence of the rule of law and human rights. As representatives of this opposition, Pussy Riot created *legitimacy insults* to portray the ROC-government tandem as a sexist order that promoted the prevalence of men over women and denied LGBT rights. Members of Pussy Riot promoted their legitimacy as defenders of human rights, especially rights of women and LGBT.

The use of *legitimacy insults* helps reveal the specificity of the conflict in Russia. The government, preserving the stability of the existing regime, delegitimized opposition and denied the political reasons behind these protests. The Russian leadership shifted the discourse of the opposition from a political to a moral sphere and presented defenders of women and LGBT rights as sinful and illegitimate. Thus, there was a little support for the ideas of the opposition among the general public and little readiness to approve collective actions.

In Ukraine, both sides employed *legitimacy insults*, decreasing each other's validity by linking to other side to fascist and totalitarian ideologies. They also legitimized values of the in-group, associating it with fighters for freedom. These *legitimacy insults* invoke meta-frames, positioning both sides within widely accepted dichotomies of good and evil. Both groups used internationally accepted criticisms of fascism and totalitarianism as a reference frame for the legitimacy of the in-group's values. Thus, interpretation of the history of the middle of twentieth century is a core issue in the conflict between the Ukrainian regions.

In the case of disputes over islands, Japan used *legitimacy insults* during the entire conflict with China, legitimizing its exclusive rights of ownership of the islands and delegitimizing Chinese claims to them. To increase this legitimacy insult, Japanese leaders utilized the concept of historic truth and international law, raising the conflict to the level of international relations. China responded with a *legitimacy insult*, reaffirming its rights over the islands and invalidating Japanese claims to them, questioning the adequacy of Japanese foreign policy as a whole. To strengthen this *legitimacy insult*, China employed criteria accepted by the international community, including national sovereignty and victimization by imperialist aggressors. The Chinese government introduced the dispute as an integral part of the contentious history of Sino-Japanese conflicts and *reactivated* previous insults and humiliations of the Chinese people by Japanese invaders.

To challenge Korean ownership of disputed islands, the Japanese government also created a *legitimacy insult*, questioning international geographic names and current ownership of islands by South Korea at the international court. Responding to this insult, South Korea also created a *legitimacy insult*, emphasizing the legality of its ownership and the unlawful nature of Japanese actions in the framework of Japan's historical aggressions. Japan immediately responded with a new *legitimacy insult*, stressing that it had full rights to the islands based on historic evidence and international law, and that the Korean presence on the island was an "illegal occupation."

The use of *legitimacy insults* reveals the nature of the disputes over islands. *Legitimacy insults* were used as a core insult in official statements and actions on all sides, helping them validate their own rights to the islands while delegitimize claims of the other side. These legitimacy insults progressively evolved, including new dimensions and increasing in their scope. Starting from interpretations of history and domestic law, they progressed to involve international law, national sovereignty, and peace in the region. In addition, both China and South Korea reactivated the insults of victimization by imperial Japan during World War II, emphasizing parallels between aggressive imperialistic policies and current Japanese claims.

In the case of conflict between North Korea and the United States, *legitimacy insults* were employed by the North Korean leadership, which repudiated the rights of the United States to impose sanctions or restrictions on North Korea, and delegitimized US policies as unacceptable in the international community. North Korea justified its own actions, including rocket launches and nuclear bomb tests, as legitimate in the framework of international law. The *legitimacy insult* revealed the specificity of the conflict between North Korea and the United States. The declarations and actions of North Korea were insults rather than real danger. The United States emphasized the unlawful nature of North Korean actions based on several agreements and laws and stressed that these actions were illegitimate, as they created a dangerous situation in the region.

Thus, *legitimacy insults* are indicative of conflicts in which one group or both groups aim at diminishing the legitimacy and rightfulness of the out-group's position and increasing the in-group's validity. This dual process of legitimization and delegitimization helps validate in-group actions for the general public within the country and for the international community, securing support for specific actions. To emphasize its validity, the in-group can use historic interpretations as well as legal, moral, and security dimensions accepted nationally or internationally.

Thus, to deal with *legitimacy insults* it is essential to employ such conflict resolution practices as acknowledgment and identity negotiation. Both sides should acknowledge the legitimacy of the other side and its claims, treating historic narrative as a deep belief in a particular state of intergroup relations rather than truth. This acknowledgment can be based on public rituals and symbolic actions that address former "group suffering, offer apology, and signify future good" as well as promote "acceptance of moral responsibility for past events that victimized the other group, along with assurances that similar events will not happen in the future."[34] Acknowledgment also involves acceptance the validity of the out-group, its legitimate position and concerns, the lawfulness of its sovereignty, national policies, or a particular governing institution.[35]

This could be done during specially organized workshops on identity negotiation. While *legitimacy insults* target the positions, policies, and actions of out-group, portraying them as erroneous or vicious, it is possible to reduce the effects of this insult through negotiation over group identities. As Kelman[36] stresses, the possibility of negotiating identity rests on two features of social identity: (1) identities are not zero-sum concepts like territory and resources; and (2) as social constructs, they can be reconstructed and redefined. "In fact, the reconstruction of identity is a regular, ongoing process in the life of any national group. Identities are commonly reconstructed, sometimes gradually and sometimes radically, as historical circumstances change, crises emerge, opportunities present themselves, or new elites come to the fore."[37]

Undoubtedly, national identities contain some core elements that cannot be negotiated: a sense of peoplehood, attachment to the land, confidence in history, and commitment to culture and religion.[38] In order to protect the essential components of identity, only a few central elements can be reconsidered and redefined. To reduce intergroup tensions and develop a common understanding and acceptance of out-group legitimacy, these elements can be discussed and negotiated during specially organized workshops.

One of the basic assumptions of the theory of protracted identity-based conflict is that basic needs are not negotiable and that people need universal justice. In reality, basic needs and conceptions of justice are also identity-based concepts, and their meaning depends on the meaning and structure of particular in-group identities. Security, freedom, and community have different meanings and are perceived in various ways among people with different social identities. Even for the same person, a basic human need can have a different meaning depending on which social identity is most salient for that individual at that moment.

Understanding of the different meanings associated with concepts like justice, lawfulness, and basic human needs can help reconcile different identities and approaches to legitimacy. An identity negotiation workshop includes dialogue, which considers differences in the meaning of these basic concepts, and which develops ways to accommodate them. Because of variations in the perception of basic human needs, legality, and justice among different groups, it is possible to negotiate these concepts among groups in order to develop new common perceptions, reconciling the legitimacy of existing identities.

The process of identity negotiation in a workshop setting has been described by Kelman[39] as an informal, unofficial progression of give-and-take among groups whose ideas of the validity of respective national identities conflict with one another. Such a practice can be organized in different forms, ranging from mediation between social groups in the process of nation building to the redefinition of identity through reconsidering history, and from negotiations among political leaders to discussion workshops in communities.

In addition to addressing legitimacy, the negotiation of identities is also essential in developing peaceful coexistence between former adversaries. Conflictual identities have to be reconfigured to accommodate a new type of intergroup relation and to accept multiple meanings of events and policies. Such a step-by-step process of recreating identity demands the cooperation of both parties. This cooperation depends on the mutual understanding that employment of legitimacy insults demolishes positive international acceptance of both parties in the conflict.

The processes of acknowledgment and identity negotiation can deter *legitimacy insults* that rest on recategorization, legitimizing the in-group, and delegitimizing the out-group. Acknowledgment and identity negotiation emphasize the validity of different interpretations of history and domestic law, morality, international law, national sovereignty, peace in the region, and meta-frames of internationally accepted concepts. Thus, these types of interventions also help validate policies and actions of both groups for the general public within the country and for the international community, thus decreasing the prospects for the employment of legitimacy insults.

COMPLEX INTERVENTIONS

In many conflicts both parties employ simultaneously several insults; thus the resolution of these conflicts should involve a complex of different intervention methods and tools. The proper intervention approach depends on the forms of the core and secondary insults, their application to both or only one party (types of insult), and the specificity of the dynamics of these insults.

For example, in the conflict over the killing of the Armenian solder, the Armenian side mostly used *identity insults* and the Azerbaijani side predominantly employed *projection insults*. In addition, both sides used *relative* and *legitimacy insults*. Thus, the resolution of this conflict should involve reconstruction of collective axiology and revision of history education in both countries, reconciliation and forgiveness, identity dialogues, and acknowledgment.

In the case of Pussy Riot, Russian leadership used *legitimacy* insults and *attributed identity insults*, while the opposition continuously employed *legitimacy insults*. In addition, Russian leadership also employed a *divergence* insult. Thus, the approach to this conflict must be based on negotiation of national and religious identity and agonistic dialogue in the society.

In the case of Ukraine, the major form of insult constructed by both sides of the conflict was *divergence* insult. In addition, both sides used *identity, relative*, and *legitimacy insults*. The approach to the resolution of this conflict should rest on agonistic dialogue and the formation of shared society in Ukraine and include such tools as identity dialogue and identity negotiation.

In the case of the conflict between North Korea and the United States, North Korea was employing a *power* insult as a core offense and also used *legitimacy* and *projection insults*. The resolution of this conflict requires negotiation and mediation, as well as elements of reconciliation and negotiation of identities.

In the dispute over islands between China and Japan, both sides employed *legitimacy insult* as the core form of insult; the dispute over the islands between Japan and South Korea included several evolving *power* and *legitimacy* insults. The sides also used *projection* and *divergence* insults. The approach to these conflicts should involve negotiation, mediation, acknowledgment, and agonistic dialogue. It is important to revise history education in all three countries and to promote forgiveness and reconciliation.

All these methods should be sensitive to the issues around which each insult is built. As insults indicate the central problems in conflicts, careful analysis of insults employed in conflict dynamics is essential to the planning of intervention approaches. Addressing core insults helps improve relations between the parties involved, decrease tensions, and mitigate feelings of anger and motivation for revenge.

While not a panacea to all world conflicts, it is my hope that this methodology brings us one step closer to a lasting peace and mutual prosperity.

NOTES

INTRODUCTION
1. Yannis Gabriel, "An Introduction to the Social Psychology of Insults in Organizations," *Human Relations* 51, no. 11 (1998): 1329–54, 1331.
2. Richard B. Felson, "Impression Management and the Escalation of Aggression and Violence," *Social Psychology Quarterly* 45, no. 4 (1982): 245–54, doi:10.2307/3033920.
3. Leonard S. Newman and Ralph Erber, *Understanding Genocide* (New York: Oxford University Press, 2002).
4. Ishani Maitra and Mary Kate McGowan, eds., *Speech and Harm: Controversies over Free Speech* (Oxford: Oxford University Press, 2012); Gabriel, "Social Psychology of Insults"; Didier Eribon, *Insult and the Making of the Gay Self*, trans. Michael Lucey (Durham, NC: Duke University Press, 2004).
5. Gabriel, "Social Psychology of Insults."
6. Jerome Neu, *Sticks and Stones: The Philosophy of Insults* (New York: Oxford University Press, 2008).
7. Yoshihisa Kashima, Klaus Fiedler, and Peter Freytag, *Stereotype Dynamics: Language-Based Approaches to the Formation, Maintenance, and Transformation of Stereotypes* (New York: Lawrence Erlbaum Associates, 2008).
8. Gabriel, "Social Psychology of Insults."
9. Marc D. Hauser, *Moral Minds* (New York: Ecco, 2006).
10. Eribon, *Insult and Gay Self*.
11. Khari Enaharo, *Race Code War* (Chicago: African American Images, 2003).
12. Mari Matsuda, *Words That Wound* (Boulder, CO: Westview Press, 1993).
13. William K. Jones, *Insult to Injury: Libel, Slander, and Invasions of Privacy* (Boulder: University Press of Colorado, 2003); and Maitra and McGowan, *Speech and Harm*.
14. Linda G. Mills, *Insult to Injury: Rethinking Our Responses to Intimate Abuse* (Princeton: Princeton University Press, 2003).
15. Jonathan Culpeper, *Impoliteness: Using Language to Cause Offence* (New York: Cambridge University Press, 2011).
16. William I. Miller, *Humiliation: And Other Essays on Honor, Social Discomfort, and Violence* (Ithaca, NY: Cornell University Press, 1995).
17. Gabriel, "Social Psychology of Insults."
18. Evelyn G. Lindner, "Humiliation as the Source of Terrorism: A New Paradigm," *Peace Research* 33, no. 2 (2001): 59–68, 59.

19. Gabriel, "Social Psychology of Insults."
20. Michael Linden, Max Rotter, Kai Baumann, and Barbara Lieberei, *The Post-traumatic Embitterment Disorder (PTED)* (Cambridge, MA: Hogrefe & Huber, 2007).
21. Linden et al., *Post-traumatic Embitterment Disorder*, 159.
22. Ed Cairns and Miles Hewstone, "Embitterment and Forgiveness in the Context of the Conflict in Northern Ireland," in *Embitterment: Societal, Psychological, and Clinical Perspectives*, ed. Michael Linden and Andreas Maercker (Leipzig: Springer-Verlag Wien, 2011), 220–29.
23. Ulich Orth, Leo Montada, and Andreas Maercker, "Feelings of Revenge, Retaliation Motive, and Posttraumatic Stress Reactions in Crime Victims," *Journal of Interpersonal Violence* 21, no. 2 (2006): 229–43.
24. Ian R. McKee and N. T. Feather, "Revenge, Retribution, and Values: Social Attitudes and Punitive Sentencing," *Social Justice Research* 21, no. 2 (2008): 138–63.
25. Nico H. Frijda, "On the Functions of Emotional Expression," in *The (Non)expression of Emotions in Health and Disease*, ed. Ad Vingerhoets, Frans van Bussel, and Jan Boelhoewer (Tilburg: Tilburg University Press, 1997), 1–14.
26. Ira Gabler and Andreas Maercker, "Revenge after Trauma: Theoretical Outline," in Linden and Maercker, *Embitterment*, 42–69.
27. Tammy Greer, Mitchell Berman, Valerie Varan, Lori Bobrycki, and Sheree Watson, "We Are a Religious People; We Are a Vengeful People," *Journal of Scientific Study of Religion* 44, no. 1 (2005): 45–57; Orth, Montada, and Maercker, "Feelings of Revenge."
28. Lynne M. Andersson and Christine M. Pearson, "Tit for Tat? The Spiraling Effect of Incivility in the Workplace," *Academy of Management Review* 24 (1999): 452–71, 455.
29. Brianna B. Caza, and Lilia M. Cortina, "From Insult to Injury: Explaining the Impact of Incivility," *Basic and Applied Social Psychology* 29, no. 4 (2007): 335–50, 335.
30. Eribon, *Insult and Gay Self*.
31. Crystal L. Z. Matsibekker, *The Snob Effect: The Psychology of Negotiation Tactics in the Salesroom* (Ann Arbor, MI: ProQuest, 2008).
32. Eugene Weinstein, and Paul Deutschberger, "Some Dimensions of Altercasting," *Sociometry* 26 (1963): 454–66.
33. It is worth noting that the perception of insult depends on a person or group's ego-syntonic self-identity: an identity of being weak can be accepted by some people (some women, for example).
34. Robert J. Rydell, Diane M. Mackie, Angela T. Maitner, Heather M. Claypool, Melissa J. Ryan, and Eliot R. Smith, "Arousal, Processing, and Risk Taking: Consequences of Intergroup anger," *Personality and Social Psychology Bulletin* 34 (2008): 1141–52; Eliot R. Smith, Charles Seger, and Diane M. Mackie, "Can Emotions Be Truly Group-Level? Evidence regarding Four Conceptual Criteria," *Journal of Personality and Social Psychology* 93 (2007): 431–46.
35. Richard B. Felson, "Aggression as Impression Management," *Social Psychology* 41, no. 3 (1978): 205–13; Felson, "Impression Management and the Escalation of Aggression and Violence."
36. Diane M. Mackie, Lisa Silver, and Eliot R. Smith, "Emotion as an Intergroup Phenomenon," in *The Social Life of Emotions*, ed. Colin W. Leach and Larissa A. Tiedens (New York: Cambridge University Press, 2004), 227–45; Angela T. Maitner, Diane M. Mackie, and Eliot R. Smith, "Evidence for the Regulatory Function of Intergroup Emotion: Emotional Consequences of Implemented or Impeded Intergroup Action," *Journal of Experimental Social Psychology* 42 (2006): 720–28.;

Smith, Seger, and Mackie, "Can Emotions Be Truly Group-Level?"; Vincent Yzerbyt, Muriel Dumont, Daniel Wigboldus, and Ernestine Gordijn, "I Feel for Us: The Impact of Categorization and Identification on Emotions and Action Tendencies," *British Journal of Social Psychology* 42 (2003): 533–49.
37. Rydell et al., "Arousal, Processing, and Risk Taking."
38. Matthew J. Hornsey, Mark Trembath, and Sasha Gunthorpe, "'You Can Criticize Because You Care': Identity Attachment, Constructiveness, and the Intergroup Sensitivity Effect," *European Journal of Social Psychology* 34 (2004): 499–518.
39. William B. Irvine, *A Slap in the Face: Why Insults Hurt—and Why They Shouldn't* (New York: Oxford University Press, 2013).
40. *Issues in Social Psychology and Conflict Resolution: 2011 Edition* (Atlanta: Scholarly Editions, 2012).
41. The analysis of insults and their dynamics was based on five case studies. In the study of such complex phenomena as insults "the boundaries between phenomenon and context are not clearly evident" (R. K. Yin, *Case Study Research: Design and Methods*. SAGE, 2009) and "no basic laws exist to determine which factors and relationships are important" (R. Fidel, The case study method: A case study. *Library and Information Science Research*, 6(3) (1984), 273–288). Case study as a methodological approach helps overcome these issues through in-depth investigation and detailed examination of a particular phenomenon based on a variety of sources of data. Multiple case studies that use a replication strategy help capture the complexity of a phenomenon while revealing rich understandings about the context in which it is based. Such replication requires a careful selection of cases based on purposive sampling. Purposive sampling provides an opportunity to select a case based on presence of particular social phenomena or process.
42. The process tracing method involves examination of causation through causal relations between the observed events in case studies and involves the inductive observation of causal mechanisms and processes of their functioning.
43. David Collier, "Understanding Process Tracing," *Political Science and Politics* 44, no. 4 (2011): 823–30; Alexander L. George and Andrew Bennett, *Case Studies and Theory Development in the Social Sciences* (Cambridge: MIT Press, 2005).
44. Addressing a set of different criteria ensured the validity and reliability of this research. Construct validity was achieved through the development of specific operational measures for each form, type of insult, and features of its dynamics. Internal validity was established through the analysis of the indicative nature of insults: that is, connections between specific form of insult and the core issues of conflicts. The descriptions of the type of conflicts for which the study's findings can be generalized ensured external validity. Reliability and validity were also achieved through triangulation—the use of multiple sources of evidence.

CHAPTER 1

1. Charles Tilly, *Identities, Boundaries, and Social Ties* (Boulder, CO: Paradigm Publishers, 2005).
2. Y. Gabriel, "An Introduction to the Social Psychology of Insults in Organizations," *Human Relations 51*, no. 11 (1998): 1329–54, 1339.
3. E. Goffman, *Behavior in Public Places: Notes on the Social Organization of Gatherings* (New York: The Free Press, 1963) and Goffman, *Relations in Public: Microstudies of the Public Order* (New York: Basic Books, 1971).
4. Henri Tajfel and John C. Turner, "The Social Identity Theory of Intergroup Behaviour," in *Psychology of Intergroup Relations*, ed. Stephen Worchel and

William G. Austin, 2nd ed. (Chicago: Nelson-Hall, 1985), 7–24; Henri Tajfel, ed., *Differentiation between Social Groups: Studies in the Social Psychology of Intergroup Relations* (New York: Academic Press, 1979).

5. Marilynn B. Brewer, "The Many Faces of Social Identity: Implications for Political Psychology," *Political Psychology* 22, no. 1 (March 2001): 115–25; Marilynn Brewer, *Intergroup Relations*, 2nd ed. (Buckingham, England: Open University Press, 2003).

6. Nyla R. Branscombe and Daniel L. Wann, "Collective Self-Esteem Consequences of Outgroup Derogation When a Valued Social Identity Is on Trial," *European Journal of Social Psychology* 24, no. 6 (1994): 641–57, doi:10.1002/ejsp.2420240603; M. Canidu and Cinzia Reggiori, "Discrimination of Low-Status Outgroup: The Role of Ingroup Threat," *European Journal of Social Psychology* 32 (2002): 501–15; Jay W. Jackson, "The Relationship between Group Identity and Intergroup Prejudice Is Moderated by Sociostructural Variation 1," *Journal of Applied Social Psychology* 32, no. 5 (2002): 908–33, doi:10.1111/j.1559-1816.2002.tb00248.x.

7. Branscombe and Wann, "Collective Self-Esteem Consequences"; Peter R. Grant and Rupert Brown, "From Ethnocentrism to Collective Protest: Responses to Relative Deprivation and Threats to Social Identity," *Social Psychology Quarterly* 58, no. 3 (September 1995): 195, doi:10.2307/2787042.

8. Vamik Volkan, *Bloodlines: From Ethnic Pride to Ethnic Terrorism* (New York: Basic Books, 1998), 90.

9. Volkan, *Bloodlines*, 27.

10. Volkan, *Bloodlines*, 27.

11. John H. Herz, "Idealist Internationalism and the Security Dilemma," *World Politics* 2, no. 2 (1950): 157–80, doi:10.2307/2009187.

12. Volkan, *Bloodlines*; Vamik D. Volkan, *Blind Trust: Large Groups and Their Leaders in Times of Crisis and Terror* (Charlottesville, VA: Pitchstone Publishing, 2004).

13. J. A. Davis, "A Formal Interpretation of the Theory of Relative Deprivation," *Sociometry* 22 (1959): 280–96; W. G. Runciman, *Relative Deprivation and Social Justice: A Study of Attitudes to Social Inequality in Twentieth Century England* (New York: Penguin, 1972); Raymond Tanter and Ted R. Gurr, "Why Men Rebel," *Midwest Journal of Political Science* 14, no. 4 (November 1970): 725, doi:10.2307/2110363.

14. Runciman, *Relative Deprivation*.

15. Faye Crosby, "The Denial of Personal Discrimination," *American Behavioral Scientist* 27, no. 3 (January 1, 1984): 371–86, doi:10.1177/000276484027003008.

16. Kerry Kawakami and Kenneth L. Dion, "The Impact of Salient Self-identities on Relative Deprivation and Action Intentions," *European Journal of Social Psychology* 23, no. 5 (1993): 525–40, doi:10.1002/ejsp.2420230509; Iain Walker and Thomas F. Pettigrew, "Relative Deprivation Theory: An Overview and Conceptual Critique," *British Journal of Social Psychology* 23, no. 4 (1984): 301–10, doi:10.1111/j.2044-8309.1984.tb00645.x.

17. Dorwin Cartwright, ed., *Studies in Social Power* (Ann Arbor: Research Center for Group Dynamics, Institute for Social Research, University of Michigan, 1959); Morton Deutsch and Harold B. Gerard, "A Study of Normative and Informational Social Influences upon Individual Judgment," *Journal of Abnormal and Social Psychology* 51, no. 3 (1955): 629–36, doi:10.1037/h0046408; Leon Festinger, "A Theory of Social Comparison Processes," *Human Relations* 7, no. 2 (May 1, 1954): 117–40, doi:10.1177/001872675400700202; J. R. P. French and B. Raven, "The Bases of Social Power," in Cartwright, *Studies in Social Power*, 150–67; Herbert

C. Kelman, "Compliance, Identification, and Internalization: Three Processes of Attitude Change," *Journal of Conflict Resolution* 2, no. 1 (March 1, 1958): 51–60, doi:10.1177/002200275800200106.
18. Serge Moscovici, *Social Influence and Social Change* (New York: Published in cooperation with European Association of Experimental Social Psychology by Academic Press, 1976).
19. Gene Sharp, *The Politics of Nonviolent Action* (Boston: P. Sargent, 1973).
20. John C. Turner, "Explaining the Nature of Power: A Three-process Theory," *European Journal of Social Psychology* 35, no. 1 (2005): 1–22, doi:10.1002/ejsp.244.
21. French and Raven, "Bases of Social Power."
22. Serge Galam and Serge Moscovici, "Towards a Theory of Collective Phenomena: III. Conflicts and Forms of Power," *European Journal of Social Psychology* 25 (1995): 217–29.
23. Herbert Kelman, "Reflections on the Social and Psychological Processes of Legitimization and Delegitimization," in *The Psychology of Legitimacy: Emerging Perspectives on Ideology, Justice, and Intergroup Relations*, ed. J. T. Jost and B. Major (New York: Cambridge University Press, 2001), 54–73.
24. Kelman, "Reflections," 67.
25. D. Cohen et al., "Insult, Aggression, and the Southern Culture of Honor: An 'Experimental Ethnography,'" *Journal of Personality and Social Psychology* 70, no. 5 (1996): 945–60.
26. Burke A. Hendrix, "Moral Error, Power, and Insult," *Political Theory* 35, no. 5 (October 1, 2007): 550–73, doi:10.1177/0090591707304586.
27. John C. Turner et al., "Failure and Defeat as Determinants of Group Cohesiveness," *British Journal of Social Psychology* 23, no. 2 (1984): 97–111, doi:10.1111/j.2044-8309.1984.tb00619.x.
28. Volkan, *Bloodlines*; Volkan, *Blind Trust*.
29. Daniel Rothbart and Karina Korostelina, eds., *Identity, Morality, and Threat: Studies in Violent Conflict* (Lexington, MA: Lexington Books, 2006); Anthony Douglas Smith, *Ethno-Symbolism and Nationalism: A Cultural Approach* (New York: Routledge, 2009).

CHAPTER 2

1. L. Shevtsova, "Russia under Putin: Titanic Looking for Its Iceberg?" *Communist and Post-Communist Studies* 45, nos. 3–4 (2012): 209.
2. Levada Center, Indeksy.
3. L. Gudkov, "Presidentskie vybory v Rossii 2012 goda," Levada Center, 2012, 5, available at
4. Gudkov, "Presidentskie vybory v Rossii 2012 goda," 6.
5. L. Stan, "Eastern Orthodox Views on Sexuality and the Body," *Women's Studies International Forum* 33, no. 1 (January–February 2010): 38.
6. Levada Center, "Byli 'Sovetskimi,' stali 'provoslavnymi,'" November 12, 2012, available at http://www.levada.ru/21-11-2012/byli-sovetskie-stali-pravoslavnye.
7. Bureau of Democracy, Human Rights and Labor, "International Religious Freedom Report 2010: Russia," November 17, 2010, available at http://www.state.gov/j/drl/rls/irf/2010/148977.htm.
8. Levada Center, "Rossiyane o religii i tserkvi," November 10, 2012, available at http://www.levada.ru/11-10-2012/rossiyane-o-religii-i-tserkvi.
9. Levada Center, "Byli 'Sovetskimi,' stali 'provoslavnymi.'"
10. J. Anderson, *Religion, State and Politics in the Soviet Union and the Successor State* (New York: Cambridge University Press, 1994); K. Behrens, *Die Russische*

Orthodoxe Kirche. Sergen für die "neuen Zaren" (Paderborn: Ferdinand Schöningh Verlag, 2002); T. Biechelt, "Two Variants of the Russian Radical Right: Imperial and Social Nationalism," *Communist and Post-Communist Studies* 42, no. 4 (December 2009): 505–26.

11. "About the Freedom of Conscience and Religious Organizations," *Federal Law*, October 26, 1997.
12. Bureau of Democracy, Human Rights and Labor, "International Religious Freedom Report 2010: Russia."
13. Bureau of Democracy, Human Rights and Labor, 2011. "International Religious Freedom Report 2011: Russia," available at http://www.state.gov/j/drl/rls/irf/2011religiousfreedom/index.htm#wrapper.
14. Bureau of Democracy, Human Rights and Labor, "International Religious Freedom Report 2010: Russia."
15. RIA Novosti, "Mevedev nazval chudom vazrozhdenie pravoslaviya v Rosii za 20 let," November 5, 2011, available at http://ria.ru/religion/20111105/481348877.html.
16. RIA Novosti, "Mevedev nazval chudom vazrozhdenie pravoslaviya v Rosii za 20 let."
17. Russkaya Pravoslavnaya Sterkov', "Molit'sya, dymat'i deistvivat'," February 27, 2012, available at http://www.patriarchia.ru/db/text/2039212.html.
18. Russkaya Pravoslavnaya Sterkov', "Molit'sya, dymat'i deistvivat'."
19. Bureau of Democracy, Human Rights and Labor, "International Religious Freedom Report 2011: Russia."
20. I. Papkova and D. P. Gorenburg, "The Russian Orthodox Church and Russian Politics," *Russian Politics and Law* 49, no. 1 (January–February 2011): 3–7.
21. Maranatha, "Patriarh Kirill chitaet politicheskiy pluralism "igrushkoi" I dan'yu mode," March 18, 2010, available at http://www.maranatha.org.ua/cnews/r/68203.
22. Levada Center, "Rossiyane o religii i tserkvi."
23. Russkaya Pravoslavnaya Sterkov', "Vstrecha Svyateishego Patriarha Kirilla s uchastnikami V Mezhdunarodnogo festivalya pravoslavnyh SMI," November 1, 2012, available at http://www.patriarchia.ru/db/text/2560710.html.
24. Russkaya Pravoslavnaya Sterkov', "Interv'yu Predstoyatelya Russkoi Pravoslavnoi Sterkvi telekanaly 'Rossiya,'" September 9, 2012, available at http://www.patriarchia.ru/db/text/2457657.html.
25. Russkaya Pravoslavnaya Sterkov', "Interv'yu Predstoyatelya Russkoi."
26. Russkaya Pravoslavnaya Sterkov', "Vstrecha Svyateishego Patriarha Kirilla."
27. Russian Service of Deutsch Welle, "Patriarh Kirill bez retushi ili chasy nevidimki,"April 7, 2012, available at http://korrespondent.net/russia/1337668-dw-patriarh-kirill-bez-retushi-ili-chasy-nevidimki.
28. A. Sedov, "Patriarch Kirill rasskazal of chasah Breguet 1 kvartire d Dome na naberezhnoi," *Komsomol'skaya Pravda*, March 29, 2012, available at http://www.kp.ru/daily/25859.4/2827010.
29. Korrespondent Ru, "Na sajte rpc s fotografii Patriarha Kirilla sterli chasy ostavir ih otrazhenie," April 4, 2012, available at http://korrespondent.net/world/russia/1336758-na-sajte-rpc-s-fotografii-patriarha-kirilla-sterli-chasy-ostaviv-ih-otrazhenie.
30. Korrespondent Ru, "Original fotografii Patriarha Kirilla s dorogimi chasami vernuli na sajt rpc," April 5, 2012, available at http://korrespondent.net/video/world/1336855-original-fotografii-patriarha-kirilla-s-dorogimi-chasami-vernuli-na-sajt-rpc.

31. Korrespondent Ru, "Original fotografii Patriarha Kirilla s dorogimi chasami vernuli na sajt rpc."
32. H. Langston, "Meeting Pussy Riot," *Vice*, March 12, 2012, available at http://www.vice.com/read/A-Russian-Pussy-Riot.
33. Langston, "Meeting Pussy Riot."
34. Langston, "Meeting Pussy Riot."
35. J. Rothman, "Still a Hot Topic," *New Yorker*, September 14, 2012, available at http://www.newyorker.com/online/blogs/backissues/2012/09/feminism-riot-grrrl-and-pussy-riot.html.
36. RussMuss.net, "Putin Wet Himself," 2012, available at http://russmus.net/song/12000#1; translation modified.
37. C. Rumens, "Pussy Riot's Punk Prayer is Pure Protest Poetry," *Guardian*, August 20, 2012, available at http://www.theguardian.com/books/2012/aug/20/pussy-riot-punk-prayer-lyrics.
38. Free Pussy Riot, "Nadia Tolokonnikova's Closing Statement," available at http://freepussyriot.org/content/nadia-tolokonnikovas-closing-statement.
39. Russkaya Pravoslavnaya Sterkov', "Interv'yu mitropolita Volokolamskogo Ilariona telekanaly 'Dozhd,'" March 15, 2012, available at http://www.patriarchia.ru/db/text/2075242.html.
40. V. R. Legoyda, "Somnevat'sya mozhno v voih silah, a ne v vere," Russkaya Pravoslavnaya Sterkov', March 13, 2012, available at http://www.patriarchia.ru/db/text/2071283.html.
41. D. Sinyakov, "Russia's Rights Ombudsman Calls for Pussy Riot Release," Reuters, April 11, 2012, available at http://en.ria.ru/society/20120411/172743927.html.
42. Levada Center, "Aktsii grupp Femen i Pussy Riot," March 22, 2012, available at http://www.levada.ru/22-03-2012/aktsii-grupp-femen-i-pussy-riot.
43. B. Dubin, "Aktsiya gruppy Pussy Riot v khrame Khrista Spasitelya," April 3, 2012, available at http://www.levada.ru/03-04-2012/aktsiya-gruppy-pussy-riot-v-khrame-khrista-spasitelya-kommentarii-b-dubina.
44. Sinyakov, "Russia's Rights Ombudsman."
45. Levada Center, "Rossiyane o dele Pussy Riot," July 31, 2012, available at http://www.levada.ru/31-07-2012/rossiyane-o-dele-pussy-riot.
46. M. Lipman, "The Absurd and Outrageous Trial of Pussy Riot," *New Yorker*, August 7, 2012, available at http://www.newyorker.com/online/blogs/newsdesk/2012/08/the-absurd-and-outrageous-trial-of-pussy-riot.html.
47. M. Elder, "Pussy Riot Trial: Vladimir Putin Calls for Leniency," *Guardian*, August 3, 2012, available at http://www.theguardian.com/world/2012/aug/03/pussy-riot-trial-vladimir-putin.
48. Lipman, "Absurd and Outrageous Trial."
49. Levada Center, "Rossiyane o dele Pussy Riot."
50. Free Pussy Riot, "Nadia Tolokonnikova's Closing Statement."
51. Free Pussy Riot, "Katja Samutsevich's Closing Statement in the Criminal Case against the Feminist Punk Group Pussy Riot," available at http://freepussyriot.org/content/katja-samutsevich%E2%80%99s-closing-statement-criminal-case-against-feminist-punk-group-pussy-riot.
52. Lipman, "Absurd and Outrageous Trial."
53. Free Pussy Riot, "Masha Alyokhina's Closing Statement," available at http://freepussyriot.org/content/masha-alyokhinas-closing-statement.
54. Lipman, "Absurd and Outrageous Trial."
55. Free Pussy Riot, "Nadia Tolokonnikova's Closing Statement."

56. O. Shishkin, "Uchastnisty gruppy Pussi Riot poluchuli real'nye sroki v kolonii obshego regima," August 17, 2012, available at http://www.1tv.ru/news/social/213588?refresh.
57. Grani.Ru, "Putin: Pussy Riot pravil'no posadili," October 7, 2012, available at http://grani.ru/Politics/Russia/President/m.207091.html.
58. Russkaya Pravoslavnaya Sterkov', "Zayavlenie Vyshego Sterkovnogo Soveta Russkoi Pravoskavnoi Sterkvi d svyazi s sudebnym prigovorom po delu list, oskvernivshih svyashennoe prostranstvo Khramf Khrista Spasitelya," August 17, 2012, available at http://www.patriarchia.ru/db/text/2411921.html.
59. Russkaya Pravoslavnaya Sterkov', "Zayavlenie Vyshego Sterkovnogo Soveta Russkoi."
60. Russkaya Pravoslavnaya Sterkov', "Protoirei Vladimir Vigilyanskiy. Kak zashchitit' nashi khramy?" September 11, 2012, available at http://www.patriarchia.ru/db/text/2461772.html.
61. Levada Center, "Rossiyane o religii i tserkvi."
62. Levada Center, "Tret' rossiyan verit v chestnyi sud nad Pussy Riot," August 17, 2012, available at http://www.levada.ru/17-08-2012/tret-rossiyan-verit-v-chestnyi-sud-nad-pussy-riot.
63. Levada Center, "Nakazanie uchastnistam gruppy Pussy Riot tret' rossyan sochla adekvatnym," October 2, 2012, available at http://www.levada.ru/02-10-2012/nakazanie-uchastnitsam-gruppy-pussy-riot-tret-rossiyan-sochla-adekvatnym.
64. M. Bennets, "Anger as Pussy Riot Jailed for Two Years," RIA Novosti, August 17, 2012, available at http://en.ria.ru/russia/20120817/175287463.html.
65. V. R. Legoyda, "Spilivanie kresta v Kieve-pretenziya na demontazh khristianskoy stivilizastii," *Ruskaya Pravoslavnaya Sterkov'*, August 22, 2012, available at http://www.patriarchia.ru/db/text/2422141.html.
66. Mitropolit Chelyabinskiy Feofan, "Religiosnyi factor vsegda pytayutsya ispol'zovat' te, kto stremitsya sprovozhirovat' razdelenie v obshestve," August 29, 2012, available at http://www.patriarchia.ru/db/text/2435502.html.
67. Shevtsova, "Russia under Putin."
68. Levada Center, "O blagopoluchii naseleniya i demokratii v strane," August 11, 2011, available at http://www.levada.ru/10-08-2011/o-blagopoluchii-naseleniya-i-demokratii-v-strane.

CHAPTER 3
1. P. D'Anieri, "Structural Constraints in Ukrainian Politics," *East European Politics & Societies* 25, no. 1 (January 7, 2011): 28–46, doi:10.1177/0888325410388559; T. J. Colton, "An Aligning Election and the Ukrainian Political Community," *East European Politics & Societies* 25, no. 1 (January 7, 2011): 4–27, doi:10.1177/0888325410388561. Kuzio, "Political Culture and Democracy"; Dr Wsevolod Isajiw and Taras Kuzio, eds., "Ukraine's Post-Soviet Transition: A Theoretical and Comparative Perspective," in *Society in Transition: Social Change in Ukraine in Western Perspectives* (Canadian Scholars Press, 2003).
2. Lucio Malan, *Post-Orange Ukraine: Internal Dynamics and Foreign Policy Priorities*. Draft. Committee Report (NATO: Parliamentary Assembly, 2011), http://www.nato-pa.int/default.asp?SHORTCUT=2439.
3. Karina V. Korostelina, "Identity and Power in Ukraine," *Journal of Eurasian Studies*, 4, no. (1) (2013): 34–46; "National Identity Formation and Conflict Intensions of Ethnic Minorities," in *The Psychology of Resolving Global Conflicts: From War to Peace*, ed. Mari Fitzduff and Chris E. Stout, vol. 2 (Praeger Press, 2006), 147–171,

http://scar.gmu.edu/book-chapter/9625; "Concepts of National Identity and the Readiness for Conflict Behaviour," *National Identities* 10, no. 2 (June 2008): 207–223, doi:10.1080/14608940801999131.
4. Censor.Net, "Krasnoznamennyi Krum: parlament poluostrova rehil ezhegodno v den' Pobedy bybeshivat' krasnue flagi s izobrazheniem serpa I molota," available at http://censor.net.ua/ru/news/view/119408/krasnoznamennyyi_krym_parlament_poluostrova_reshil_ejegodno_v_den_pobedy_vyveshivat_krasnye_flagi_s_izobrajeniem_serpa_i_molota.
5. A. Fin'ko, "Ukrainskaya oppositsiya ssoredotochilas' na national-populizme," Analytic, May 15, 2011, available at http://www.analitik.org.ua/publications/finko/4dce2863b8845/.
6. I. Vlasyk, "9 travnay u L'vovi yak dzerkalo ukrayinskoyi polityky," Ukrainskaya Pravda, May 12, 2011, available at http://www.pravda.com.ua/articles/2011/05/12/ 6188285/.
7. Vlasyk, "9 travnay u L'vovi yak dzerkalo ukrayinskoyi polityky."
8. For more details on Magdeburg Law see http://www.encyclopediaofukraine.com/pages%5CM%5CA%5CMagdeburglaw.htm.
9. K. V. Korostelina, "Mapping National Identity Narratives in Ukraine," *Nationalities Papers* 41, no. 2 (2013): 293–315; K. V. Korostelina, "Ukraine Twenty Years after Independence: Concept Models of the Society," *Communist and Post-Communist Studies* 46, no. 1 (2013): 53–64; K. V. Korostelina, "Identity and Power in Ukraine," *Journal of Eurasian Studies* 4, no. 1 (2013): 34–46.
10. T. Vozniak, "Taras Vozniak's Vision of May 9 Events in Ukraine," ZIK, May 7, 2011, available at http://zik.ua/en/news/2011/05/07/286403.
11. M. Riabchuk, "The V-Day Spectacle and Beyond," Ukraine Analysis, May 16, 2011, available at http://ukraineanalysis.wordpress.com/2011/05/.
12. Censor.Net, "V Lutske zapretili sovetskuyu simvoliku: 'communism—huzhe fashizma,'" available at http://censor.net.ua/ru/news/view/165946/v_lutske_zapretili_sovetskuyu_simvoliku_kommunizm__huje_fashizma.
13. Segodnya, "Kommunisty ponyali pochemy dlya nachionalistov 9 maya—den' skorbi" (Communists understood why nationalists see May 9 is a day of grief), April 15, 2011, available at http://www.segodnya.ua/news/14242098.html.
14. The name of the city L'viv has a different pronunciation in Russian—"L'vov." The spelling "L'vov" will be used in translations of citations from Russian.
15. InoTV, "L'vovskie nasionalisty zapretili prazdnivat' poedy nad Gitlerom" (L'viv nationalists banned celebrations of victory over Hitler), May, 8, 2011, available at http://inotv.rt.com/2011-05-08/Lvovskie-nacionalisti-zapretili-prazdnovat- pobedu.
16. Riabchuk, "V-Day Spectacle."
17. O. Tyagnybok, "Na popytki vernut' krasnoe proshloe reakstiya budet vsegda," FoRum, May 10, 2011, available at http://for-ua.com/interview/2011/05/10/140201.html.
18. Riabchuk, "V-Day Spectacle."
19. Lenta.Ru, "9 maya vo L'vove otmetili strel'boi I potasovkami," May 10, 2011, available at http://lenta.ru/articles/2011/05/09/lviv/.
20. O. Tyagnybok, "Na popytki vernut' krasnoe proshloe reakstiya budet vsegda," FoRum, May 10, 2011, available at http://for-ua.com/interview/2011/05/10/140201.html.
21. My South, "Lviv Regional Council Found in the Events of May 9 'scenario FSB,'" May 13, 2011, available at http://mysouth.su/2011/05/lviv-regional-council-found-in-the-events-of-may-9-quot-scenario-fsb/.

22. N. Vitrenko, "Ukraine grozit ustanovlenie fashistskoi diktatury," FoRum," May 10, 2011, available at http://for-ua.com/authornews/2011/05/11/070905.html.
23. V. Kornilov, "Neobanderovskiy bespredel v Den' pobedy: mneniya ekspertov," Informashionno-Analiticheskiy Portal Materik, May 11, 2011, available at http://www.ia-centr.ru/expert/10454/.
24. Kievpost, "Ukrainian Nationalists Detained over May 9 Events in Lviv," May 16, 2011, available at http://www.kyivpost.com/news/nation/detail/104457/#ixzz1i7SxZQyY.
25. Y. Kotova, "Yanukovich zastavil Rossiyu zdat' 'dezhurnuh fraz' o besporayadkah na 9 maya," Gazeta Ru, May 10, 2011, available at http://www.gzt.ru/topnews/world/-yanukovich-zastavil-rossiyu-zhdatj-dezhurnyh-fraz-/360292.html.
26. I. Diskin, "Neobanderovskiy bespredel v Den' pobedy: mneniya ekspertov," Informashionno-Analiticheskiy Portal Materik, May 11, 2011, available at http://www.ia-centr.ru/expert/10454/.
27. Kuzio. T. Twenty years as an independent state: Ukraine's ten logical inconsistencies. Communist and Post-Communist Studies, 45, Issues 3–4, 2012, Pages 429–438
28. V. Sinel'nikov, "Prigovor Kievlyanke, zharivshei yaichnistu na Vechnom ogne, budet obzhalovan," Vesti, October, 5, 2012, available at http://www.vesti.ru/doc.html?id=925182.
29. RiaNovosti, "Progovor studentke, zharivshei yaichnistu na Vechnom ogne, mogut uzhestochit'," October 4, 2011, available at http://ria.ru/world/20121004/766294519.html.
30. T. Kuzio. "Twenty Years as an Independent State: Ukraine's Ten Logical Inconsistencies," *Communist and Post-Communist Studies* 45, nos. 3–4 (2012): 429–38.

CHAPTER 4

1. A. Saparov, "Why Autonomy? The Making of Nagorno-Karabakh Autonomous Region 1918–1925," *Europe-Asia Studies* 6, no. 4 (2012): 281.
2. T. Ambrosio, "Unfreezing the Nagorno-Karabakh Conflict? Evaluating Peacemaking Efforts under the Obama Administration," *Ethnopolitics* 10, no. 1 (2011): 93.
3. S. Cornell, "Autonomy as a Source of Conflict: Caucasian Conflicts in Theoretical Perspective," *World Politics* 54 (2002): 2; Shale Horowitz, "Explaining Post-Soviet Ethnic Conflicts: Using Regime Type to Discern the Impact and Relative Importance of Objective Antecedents," *Nationalities Papers* 29, no. 4 (2001): 636–60; Ronald G. Suny, *The Revenge of the Past: Nationalism, Revolution, and the Collapse of the Soviet Union* (Stanford: Stanford University Press, 1993).
4. Stanley Kaufmann, "Ethnic Fears and Ethnic War in Karabagh," *CSIS*, October 1998, available at http://csis.org/files/media/csis/pubs/ruseur_wp_008.pdf.
5. V. Tishkov, *Ethnicity, Nationalism and Conflict in and after the Soviet Union: The Mind Aflame* (London: Sage, 1997).
6. Thomas de Waal, "The Karabakh Trap: Dangers and Dilemmas of Nagorno-Karabakh Conflict," Conciliation Resources, December 2008; M. Croissant, *The Armenian-Azerbaijani Conflict: Causes and Implications* (London: Praeger, 1998).
7. V. Cheterian, "The Origins and Trajectory of the Caucasian Conflicts," *Europe-Asia Studies* 64, no. 9 (2012): 1625.
8. Cheterian, "Origins and Trajectory."
9. Thomas de Waal, "Remaking the Nagorno-Karabakh Peace Process," *Survival*, August 2010, available at http://www.carnegieendowment.org/2010/08/01/remaking-nagorno-karabakh-peace-process/bll6.

10. Cheterian, "Origins and Trajectory."
11. Thomas de Wall, "Time to Shine a Light on a Hidden Conflict: Nagorno-Karabakh in 2011," *Journal of Conflict Transformation*, February 2011, available at http://www.carnegieendowment.org/2011/02/01/time-to-shine-light-on-hidden-conflict-nagorno-karabakh-in-2011/bks4.
12. Cheterian, "Origins and Trajectory."
13. Thomas de Waal, "Challenging the Language of Estrangement in the Caucasus," Eurasianet, December 15, 2011, available at http://www.carnegieendowment.org/2011/12/15/challenging-language-of-estrangement-in-caucasus/8qss.
14. de Waal, "Time to Shine a Light."
15. de Waal, "Remaking the Nagorno-Karabakh Peace Process."
16. H. Barseghyan and S. Sultanova, "History Lessons in Armenia and Azerbaijan," *IWPR*, February 27, 2012, available at http://iwpr.net/report-news/history-lessons-armenia-andazerbaijan.
17. Barseghyan and Sultanova, "History Lessons."
18. R. Garagozov, "Do Woes Unite Foes? Interplay of Narratives, Memory, Emotions and Attitudes in the Karabakh Conflict," *Dynamics of Asymmetric Conflict: Pathways toward Terrorism and Genocide* 5, no. 2 (2012): 116.
19. M. Grono, *Nations in Transit: Azerbaijan* (Washington, DC: FreedomHouse, 2011); F. Guliyev, "Political Elites in Azerbaijan," in *Challenges of the Caspian Resource Boom: Domestic Elites and Policy-Making*, ed. Andreas Heinrich and Heiko Pleines (New York: Palgrave Macmillan, 2012), 117–30.
20. K. E. Pearce and S. Kendzior, "Networked Authoritarianism and Social Media in Azerbaijan," *Journal of Communication* 62 (2012): 283.
21. S. Abbasov, "Civil Society in Azerbaijan: Under Fire but Still Resisting," *Caucasus Analytical Digest* 12 (2010), available at http://www.css.ethz.ch/publications/pdfs/CAD-12-13-14.pdf.
22. A. Gahramanova, "Internal and External Factors in the Democratization of Azerbaijan," *Democratization* 16 (2009): 777.
23. C. Tokluoglu, "The Political Discourse of the Azerbaijani Elite on the Nagorno-Karabakh Conflict (1991–2009)," *Europe-Asia Studies* 63, no. 7 (2011): 1225.
24. Tokluoglu, "Political Discourse," 1247.
25. Ramil Safarov, "Ramil Safarov's First Interrogation," n.d., available at http://budapest.sumgait.info/safarov-interrogation.htm.
26. Safarov, "Ramil Safarov's First Interrogation."
27. K. Pearce, "Deep Dive: Filling in the Gaps—Reading the Ramil Safarov Case in Azerbaijan," Radio Free Europe, September 10, 2012, available at http://www.rferl.org/content/filling-in-the-gaps-azerbaijani-media-construction-of-narrative-over-ramil-safarov-case-armenia/24703619.html.
28. Safarov, "Ramil Safarov's First Interrogation."
29. Safarov, "Ramil Safarov's First Interrogation."
30. Safarov, "Ramil Safarov's First Interrogation."
31. Safarov, "Ramil Safarov's First Interrogation."
32. Safarov, "Ramil Safarov's First Interrogation."
33. Kuti Balazs, "Kuti Balazs: An Eyewitness," 2004, available at http://budapest.sumgait.info/kuti-balazs-account.htm.
34. Ministry of Foreign Affairs of Armenia, "Armenian Response: Statement by the Ministry of Foreign Affairs of Armenia on the Murder of an Armenian Lieutenant in Budapest by an Azerbaijani Military Officer," 2004, available at http://budapest.sumgait.info/armenian-response.htm.

35. J. Tabibian, speech at the Permanent Council of OSCE, 2004, available at http://budapest.sumgait.info/tabibyan.htm.
36. Tabibian, speech.
37. Pearce, "Deep Dive."
38. Pearce, "Deep Dive."
39. Pearce, "Deep Dive."
40. Pearce, "Deep Dive."
41. D. Sindelar and A. Kazimova, "Passions, History Run Deep in Safarov Case," Radio Free Europe, September 5, 2012, available at http://www.rferl.org/content/passions-and-history-run-deep-in-safarov-case/24699074.html.
42. Sindelar and Kazimova, "Passions, History Run Deep."
43. Sindelar and Kazimova, "Passions, History Run Deep."
44. Sindelar and Kazimova, "Passions, History Run Deep."
45. Trend, "Union of Liberation Movements Protests Unfair Sentence on Azeri Officer in Hungary," April 14, 2006, available at http://en.trend.az/news/politics/852805.html.
46. P. Marton, "The Ramil Safarov Case and Orban's Bumpy Ride East," *Budapest Times*, September 9, 2012, available at http://www.budapesttimes.hu/2012/09/09/the-ramil-safarov-case-and-orbans-bumpy-ride-east/.
47. Marton, "Ramil Safarov Case."
48. Reuters, "Azerbaijan Denies Plans to Buy Hungary Debt," September 4, 2012, available at http://www.reuters.com/article/2012/09/04/hungary-azeri-debt-idUSL6E8K40OR20120904.
49. Reuters, "Azerbaijan Denies Plans."
50. Radio Free Europe, "EU Suggests Azerbaijan Broke Pledges, Pardon 'Endangers' Region," September 5, 2012, available at http://www.rferl.org/content/eu-ashton-spokeswoman-suggests-azerbaijan-abandoned-pledges-pardon-killer-armenia/24698123.html.
51. News.Az, "Release of Safarov Will Improve Psychological Mood of Society," September 1, 2012, available at http://news.az/articles/politics/67396.
52. Azerbaijan State Telegraph Agency, "Orders," August 31, 2012, available at http://www.azertag.com/en/node/995825.
53. Contrarian Hungarian, "Hungary Extradites Azerbaijani Axe Murderer: The Repercussions," September 2, 2012, available at http://thecontrarianhungarian.wordpress.com/2012/09/02/hungary-extradites-azerbaijani-axe-murderer-the-repercussions/.
54. "Azerbaijan Delivers Note to Hungary," *Turkish Weekly*, September 6, 2012, available at http://www.turkishweekly.net/news/141396/azerbaijan-delivers-note-to-hungary.html.
55. Trend, "Azerbaijani Foreign Ministry Appreciates Cooperation of Hungarian Side for Return of Safarov to Homeland," August 31, 2012, available at http://en.trend.az/regions/scaucasus/azerbaijan/2060625.html.
56. "Azerbaijan Delivers Note."
57. News.Az, "Release of Safarov."
58. Thomas de Waal, "Setback for Peace in the Caucasus," *BBC News*, September 4, 2012, available at http://www.carnegieendowment.org/2012/09/04/setback-for-peace-in-caucasus/drre.
59. Radio Free Europe, "EU Suggests Azerbaijan Broke Pledges."
60. Radio Free Europe, "Baku Slammed by Brussels over Safarov," September 13, 2012, available at http://www.rferl.org/content/safarov-azerbaijan-armenia-europeanparliament/24707701.html.

61. Radio Free Europe, "EU Suggests Azerbaijan Broke Pledges."
62. Trend, "Azerbaijan's Ruling Party: Release of Ramil Safarov Is Triumph of Courage and Justice," August 31, 2012, available at http://en.trend.az/news/politics/2060692.html.
63. Trend, "Top Official: Ramil Safarov's Return Possible Thanks to Azerbaijani President's Political Will and Personal Authority," August 31, 2012, available at http://en.trend.az/news/politics/2060742.html.
64. Trend, "MP: Council of Europe Should Be Concerned about Occupied Azerbaijani Lands' Liberation Rather Than Safarov's Release," September 7, 2012, available at http://en.trend.az/news/karabakh/2062650.html.
65. Trend, "Ruling Party: Pardon of Ramil Safarov Is Example of Azerbaijani President's Concern for Patriots," August 31, 2012, available at http://en.trend.az/news/politics/2060696.html.
66. http://www.president.am/en/press-release/item/2012/08/31/President-Serzh-Sargsyan-ambassadors-meeting/
67. H. E. Mr. Edward NALBANDIAN Minister of Foreign Affairs of the Republic of Armenia at the General Debate of the 67th Session of the UN General Assembly, Ministry of Foreign Affairs of the Republic of Armenia, available at http://www.mfa.am/en/speeches/item/2012/10/01/67sesion/.
68. Radio Free Europe, "Row Erupts after Azerbaijan Pardons Armenian Officer's Repatriated Killer," August 31, 2012, available at http://www.rferl.org/content/azerbaijani-officer-who-killed-armenian-officer-pardoned/24694081.html.
69. "Armenians Hold Anti-Hungary Rally over Azeri Killer Pardon," *BBC News*, September 1, 2012, available at http://www.bbc.co.uk/news/world-europe-19450438.
70. ArmeniaNow.Com, "Safarov Reactions: Sargsyan Asks Nation Not to Burn Hungarian Flag; Hungarians Say 'We Are Sorry, Armenia,'" September 5, 2012, available at http://armenianow.com/news/39733/armenia_hungary_azerbaijan_ramil_safarov_serzh_sargsyan_flag.
71. Trend, "Armenian President Admits His Untenability," September 1, 2012, available at http://en.trend.az/news/karabakh/2060829.html.
72. Trend, "Azerbaijani Foreign Ministry: Safarov's Return Not Contrary to International Law," September 1, 2012, available at http://en.trend.az/news/politics/2060944.html.
73. Trend, "Top Official: Weakness and Feebleness Provoke Armenian President to Voice High-Flown Phrases toward Azerbaijan," September 3, 2012, available at http://en.trend.az/news/society/2061300.html.
74. de Waal, "Setback for Peace."
75. de Waal, "Challenging the Language."

CHAPTER 5

1. T. W. Burkman, *Japan and the League of Nations* (Honolulu: University of Hawaii Press, 2007), 162.
2. I. Chang, *The Rape of Nanking* (New York: Penguin, 1997), 166.
3. C. Johnson, "The Patterns of Japanese Relations with China, 1952–1982," *Pacific Affairs 59*, no. 3 (1986): 402.
4. Y. Chung, *Korea under Siege, 1876–1945: Capital Transformation and Economic Transformation* (New York: Oxford University Press, 2006).
5. J. W. Steinberg, Bruce W. Menning, David Schimmelpenninck van der Oye, David Wolff, and Shinje Yokete, eds., *The Russo-Japanese War in Global Perspective: World War Zero* (Boston: Brill, 2005).

6. Steinberg et al., *Russo-Japanese War*.
7. Steinberg et al., *Russo-Japanese War*.
8. K. Yi, *A New History of Korea*, trans. E. W. Wagner (Cambridge: Harvard University Press, 1984).
9. S. Conrad, "Entangled Memories: Versions of the Past in Germany and Japan, 1945–2001," *Journal of Contemporary History 38*, no. 1 (2003): 85.
10. Glenn D. Hook, Julie Gilson, Christopher W. Hughes, and Hugo Dobson, *Japan's International Relations: Politics, Economics and Security*, 3rd ed. (New York: Routledge, 2012).
11. C. S. Soh, *The Comfort Women: Sexual Violence and Postcolonial Memory in Korea and Japan* (Chicago: University of Chicago Press, 2009).
12. Yi, *New History of Korea*; Liu and Atsumi, "Constructing Trauma and Its Treatment"; Johnson, "Patterns of Japanese Relations"; Hook et al., *Japan's International Relations*; L. Hein and M. Selden, eds., *Censoring History: Citizenship and Memory in Japan, Germany, and the United States* (Watertown, MA: Eastgate Books, 1999).
13. Johnson, "Patterns of Japanese Relations."
14. Ministry of Foreign Affairs of the People's Republic of China, Sino-Japanese Treaty of Peace and Friendship, November 17, 2000, available at
15. K. Togo, "Japan's Territorial Problem: The Northern Territories, Takeshima, and the Senkaku Islands," National Bureau of Asian Research, May 8, 2012, available at http://www.nbr.org/research/activity.aspx?id=247#.UkDJOIY3v7U.
16. W. Wan, "Collision at Sea Sparks Anger, Breakdown in China-Japan Talks," *Washington Post*, September 20, 2010, available at http://www.washingtonpost.com/wp-dyn/content/article/2010/09/20/AR2010092000130.html.
17. Wan, "Collision at Sea."
18. Associated Press, "China Lashes Out at Japan over Reported Insult," *Jakarta Post*, October 21, 2010, available at http://www.thejakartapost.com/news/2010/10/21/china-lashes-out-japan-over-reported-insult.html.
19. Wada Haruki, "Resolving the China-Japan Conflict over the Senkaku/Diaoyu Islands," *Asia-Pacific Journal: Japan Focus*, October 25, 2010, available at http://www.japanfocus.org/-Wada-Haruki/3433.
20. Phuket News, "Tokyo to Buy Disputed Islands: Governor," available at http://www.thephuketnews.com/tokyo-to-buy-disputed-islands-governor-29945.php.
21. J. McCurry, "Tokyo's Right-Wing Governor Plans to Buy Disputed Senaku Islands," *Guardian*, April 19, 2012, available at http://www.theguardian.com/world/2012/apr/19/tokyo-governor-senkaku-islands-china.
22. M. Dickie, "Tokyo Warned over Plans to Buy Islands," *Financial Times*, June 6, 2012, available at http://www.ft.com/cms/s/0/af98fc54-aef7-11e1-a4e0-00144feabdc0.html#axzz2flRN2Vib.
23. Japan Today, "Gemba Rebukes Japan's Envoy to China over Senkaku Remarks," June 9, 2012, available at http://www.japantoday.com/category/politics/view/gemba-rebukes-tokyos-ambassador-to-china-over-senkaku-remarks/comments/popular/id/2444385.
24. M. Dickie, "Japan Cautions Diplomat on China Remarks," *Financial Times*, June 7, 2012, available at http://www.ft.com/intl/cms/s/d2b90060-b0a2-11e1-a79b-00144feabdc0.html#axzz2O68nRlK.
25. Japan Today, "Gemba Rebukes Japan's Envoy."
26. "Ishihara Adds Another Senkaku Isle to Shopping List; Niwa Says Sorry," *Asahi Shumbun*, June 9, 2012, available at http://ajw.asahi.com/article/behind_news/politics/AJ201206090024.

27. "Japan Protests at Chinese Ships Near Disputed Islands," *BBC News*, July 11, 2012, available at http://www.bbc.co.uk/news/world-asia-china-18792556.
28. Reuters, "China Dismisses Japan Plan to Buy Disputed Islands," July 8, 2012, available at http://www.reuters.com/article/2012/07/08/us-china-japan-islands-idUSBRE86701A20120708.
29. "Japan Protests at Chinese Ships."
30. "Japan Activists Land on Disputed Islands amid China Row," *BBC News*, August 19, 2012, available at http://www.bbc.co.uk/news/world-asia-china-19303931.
31. "Japan Activists Land."
32. L. Sieg and K. Takenaka, "Japan Says Disputed Islands Should Not Hurt Key China Ties," Reuters, August 20, 2012, available at http://www.reuters.com/article/2012/08/20/us-japan-china-idUSBRE87I00F20120820.
33. Sieg and Takenaka, "Japan Says."
34. Sieg and Takenaka, "Japan Says."
35. AlJazeera, "Japan Vows No Compromise on Islands Row," September 27, 2012, available at http://www.aljazeera.com/news/asia-pacific/2012/09/201292722139105715.html.
36. AlJazeera, "Japan Vows No Compromise."
37. AlJazeera, "Japan Vows No Compromise."
38. K. Voigt, "Dangerous Waters: Behind the Islands Dispute," *CNN*, September 24, 2012, available at http://www.cnn.com/2012/09/24/world/asia/china-japan-dispute-explainer/.
39. "Japan Government 'Reaches Deal to Buy' Disputed Islands," *BBC News*, September 5, 2012, available at http://www.bbc.co.uk/news/world-asia-19485565.
40. O. Fujimura, "Press Conference by the Chief Cabinet Secretary," Prime Minister of Japan and His Cabinet, September 10, 2012, available at http://www.kantei.go.jp/foreign/tyoukanpress/201209/10_p.html.
41. "China's Statements over Daiyou Islands," *People's Daily Online*, September 11, 2012, available at http://english.people.com.cn/90883/7943813.html.
42. "China's Statements over Daiyou Islands."
43. "China's Statements over Daiyou Islands."
44. "China's Statements over Daiyou Islands."
45. "China's Statements over Daiyou Islands."
46. Z. Shengnan, Q. Zhongwei, and W. Jiao, "Xi Slams Daiyou 'Purchase,'" *China Daily*, September 20, 2012, available at http://usa.chinadaily.com.cn/china/2012-09/20/content_15769455.htm.
47. EnglishNews.cn, "China Slams Noda's UN Speech," September 28, 2012, available at http://news.xinhuanet.com/english/video/2012-09/28/c_131878975.htm.
48. AlJazeera, "China Accuses Japan of Stealing Islands," September 28, 2012, available at http://www.aljazeera.com/news/asia-pacific/2012/09/20129283645792866.html.
49. "Japan and China Trade Barbs over Islands at UN," *BBC News*, September 28, 2012, available at http://www.bbc.co.uk/news/world-asia-19754353.
50. "Japan and China Trade Barbs."
51. Ministry of Foreign Affairs of Japan, "Position Paper: Japan-China Relations Surrounding the Situation of the Senkaku Islands," November 9, 2012, available at http://www.mofa.go.jp/region/asia-paci/senkaku/position_paper_en.html.
52. Ministry of Foreign Affairs of Japan, "Position Paper."

53. "Chinese Ships Approach Islands in Dispute with Japan," *Guardian*, September 14, 2012, available at http://www.theguardian.com/world/2012/sep/14/chinese-ships-disputed-islands-japan.
54. "Chinese Ships Approach Islands."
55. "Chinese Ships Approach Islands."
56. S. Wee and L. Sieg, "China Surveillance Ships Near Islands Disputed with Japan," Reuters, September 14, 2012, available at http://www.reuters.com/article/2012/09/14/us-china-japan-islands-idUSBRE88C1LG20120914.
57. Ministry of Foreign Affairs of Japan, "Position Paper: Japan-China Relations Surrounding the Situation of the Senkaku Islands," February 7, 2013, available at http://www.mofa.go.jp/region/asia-paci/senkaku/position_paper3_en.html.
58. "China Media: Japan Radar Lock," *BBC News*, March 19, 2013, available at http://www.bbc.co.uk/news/world-asia-china-21840243.
59. "Senkaku (Daiyou) Islands Dispute: China Warns Japan Ahead of Legislative Session," HuffingtonPost, March 2, 2013, available at http://www.huffingtonpost.com/2013/03/02/senkaku-islands-dispute-china-japan_n_2796559.html.
60. Dokdo-Research.com, "Liancourt Rocks Bombing Range: 1947–1952," 2002, available at http://dokdo-research.com/temp.html.
61. ForTheNextGeneration.com, "The Territorial Dispute over Dokdo," available at http://www.forthenextgeneration.com/dokdo/dokdo_01.htm.
62. AlJazeera, "S Korea to Block Japan Survey Vessels," April 19, 2006, available at http://www.aljazeera.com/archive/2006/04/20084916130256831.html.
63. AlJazeera, "S Korea to Block Japan."
64. Kim Tai Kyung, "South Korea President Takes Tough Stand on Japan," April 25, 2006, available at http://english.ohmynews.com/articleview/article_view.asp?no=288099&rel_no=1.
65. Kyung, "South Korea President."
66. J. McCurry, "South Korea and Japan Face Off over Disputed Islands," *Guardian*, August 10, 2012, available at http://www.theguardian.com/world/2012/aug/10/south-korea-japan-disputed-islands.
67. C. Sang-Hun, "South Korean's Visit to Disputed Islets Angers Japan," *New York Times*, August 10, 2012, available at http://www.nytimes.com/2012/08/11/world/asia/south-koreans-visit-to-disputed-islets-angers-japan.html?_r=0.
68. "South Korea's Lee Myung-bak Visits Disputed Islands," *BBC News*, August 10, 2012, available at http://www.bbc.co.uk/news/world-asia-19204852.
69. "South Korea's Lee Myung-bak."
70. TheHankyoreh, "Japan Taking Lee's Dokdo Visit 'Extremely Seriously,'" August 11, 2012, available at http://www.hani.co.kr/arti/english_edition/e_international/546710.html.
71. McCurry, "South Korea and Japan Face Off."
72. TheHankyoreh, "Japan Taking Lee's Dokdo Visit."
73. T. Yokota, "Why Japan and South Korea Are Feuding over a Cluster of Rocks," *Newsweek*, September 3, 2012, available at http://www.thedailybeast.com/newsweek/2012/09/02/why-japan-and-south-korea-are-feuding-over-a-cluster-of-rocks.html.
74. M. Fackler, "Japan Places Pressure on South Korea amid Islets Dispute," *New York Times*, August 24, 2012, available at http://www.nytimes.com/2012/08/25/world/asia/japan-vows-to-press-claims-over-disputed-islands.html?_r=0.
75. C. Sang-Hun, "South Korea Returns Letter on Islets from Japanese Leader," *New York Times*, August 23, 2012, available at http://www.nytimes.com/2012/08/24/

world/asia/south-korea-returns-letter-from-japanese-leader-or-tries-to.html?_r=2&.
76. Sang-Hun, "South Korea Returns Letter."
77. Sang-Hun, "South Korea Returns Letter."
78. Sang-Hun, "South Korea Returns Letter."
79. Yokota, "Why Japan and South Korea Are Feuding."
80. Yokota, "Why Japan and South Korea Are Feuding."
81. Fackler, "Japan Places Pressure."
82. Fackler, "Japan Places Pressure."
83. T. Nakagawa, "South Korea Refuses to Take Takeshima to ICJ," *Yomiuri Shimbun*, August 31, 2012, available at http://www.accessmylibrary.com/article-1G1-301268635/south-korea-refuses-take.html.
84. Fackler, "Japan Places Pressure."
85. The Chosunilbo, "Japan Advertises Dokdo Claim in Newspapers," September 24, 2013, available at http://english.chosun.com/site/data/html_dir/2012/09/13/2012091300905.html.
86. The Chosunilbo, "Japan Advertises Dokdo Claim."

CHAPTER 6

1. J. Kim, "North Korea Enters 'State of War' against South," Reuters, March 30, 2013, available at http://www.reuters.com/article/2013/03/30/us-korea-north-war-idUSBRE92T00020130330.
2. Constitution of North Korea 2009, available at http://en.wikisource.org/wiki/Constitution_of_North_Korea_(1972).
3. Korea News Service (KPA), "Supreme Command Issues Communique," November 23, 2010, available at http://www.kcna.co.jp/item/2010/201011/news23/20101123-19ee.html.
4. "N. Korea Fires Artillery onto S. Korean Island; 2 Dead," *USA Today*, November 23, 2010, available at http://usatoday30.usatoday.com/news/world/2010-11-23-korea-artillery_N.htm.
5. Korea News Service (KNS), "New Year Address Made by Kim Jong Un," January 1, 2013, available at http://www.kcna.co.jp/item/2013/201301/news01/20130101-13ee.html.
6. "North Korean Sanctions: Nuclear Reaction," *Economist*, January 24, 2013, available at; J. McCurry and T. Branigan, "North Korea: Pyongyang Plans Nuclear Test Targeted at US," *Guardian*, January 25, 2013, available at
7. Korean Central News Agency, "KCNA Report on Successful 3rd Underground Nuclear Test," February 12, 2013, available at http://www.ncnk.org/resources/publications/KCNA_3rd_Nuke_Test.pdf
8. Korean Central News Agency, "KCNA Report."
9. Korean Central News Agency, "KCNA Report."
10. DPRK Foreign Ministry, "Spokesman for DPRK Foreign Ministry Urges U.S. to Choose between Two Options," National Committee on North Korea, 2013, http://www.kcna.co.jp/item/2013/201302/news12/20130212-19ee.html.
11. DPRK Foreign Ministry, "Spokesman for DPRK."
12. Barack Obama, "The White House, Office of the Press Secretary, Statement by the President on North Korean Announcement of Nuclear Test," February 12, 2013, available at http://www.whitehouse.gov/the-press-office/2013/02/12/statement-president-north-korean-announcement-nuclear-test.

13. "Rodman Tells North Korea's Kim Jong-un: You Have a Friend for Life," *Guardian*, March 1, 2013, available at http://www.guardian.co.uk/world/2013/mar/01/dennis-rodman-kim-jong-un.
14. M. Williams, "Dennis Rodman Calls Kim Jong-un 'a Great Guy' and Defends North Korea Trip," *Guardian*, March 3, 2013, available at http://www.guardian.co.uk/world/2013/mar/03/dennis-rodman-kim-jong-un.
15. "North Korea Blows Up White House in Propaganda Video," video clip, 2013, available at http://www.youtube.com/watch?v=Qd1qR66gcLQ.
16. "N. Korea, Facing New Sanctions, Threatens to Cancel 1953 Armistice," *Los Angeles Times*, March 5, 2013, available at http://articles.latimes.com/2013/mar/05/world/la-fg-wn-north-korea-threatens-armistice-us-sanctions-20130305.
17. "North Korea Threatens Pre-emptive Nuclear Strike against US," *Guardian*, March 07, 2013, available at http://www.guardian.co.uk/world/2013/mar/07/north-korea-threatens-nuclear-strike-us.
18. "North Korea Ends Armistice with South amid War Games on Both Sides of Border," *Guardian*, March 11, 2013, available at http://www.guardian.co.uk/world/2013/mar/11/north-korea-declares-end-armistice.
19. "North Korea Ends Armistice."
20. T. Branigan, "North Korea Puts Troops on 'Maximum Alert' for Possible War with South," March 12, 2013, available at http://www.theguardian.com/world/2013/mar/12/north-korea-maximum-alaert-war.
21. E. Labott, "Is Kim Jong Un More Dangerous Than His Father?" *CNN*, March 7, 2013, available at http://security.blogs.cnn.com/2013/03/07/is-kim-jong-un-more-dangerous-than-his-father/.
22. Labott, "Is Kim Jong Un More Dangerous."
23. "US Officials: Unpredictable North Korea with Its Nukes and Missiles Poses Serious Threat," Fox News, March 12, 2013, available at http://www.foxnews.com/us/2013/03/12/us-officials-unpredictable-north-korea-with-its-nukes-and-missiles-poses/.
24. AFP, "US 'Prepared for Any Eventuality' from N. Korea," March 28, 2013, available at http://www.afp.com/en/news/topstories/us-prepared-any-eventuality-nkorea.
25. M. Hosenball and P. Stewart, "North Korea Lacks Means for Nuclear Strike on U.S., Experts Say," Reuters, April 4, 2013, available at http://www.reuters.com/article/2013/04/04/us-korea-north-usa-capabilities-idUSBRE9331A920130404.
26. F. Greenwood, "China Warns US against 'Antagonizing' North Korea," *Global Post*, March 18, 2013, available at http://www.globalpost.com/dispatch/news/regions/asia-pacific/south-korea/130318/china-warns-us-against-antagonizing-north-kore.
27. S. Park, "Pentagon to Add Missile Interceptors to Deter North Korea," Bloomberg, March 17, 2013, available at http://www.bloomberg.com/news/2013-03-17/pentagon-to-add-missile-interceptors-to-deter-north-korea.html.
28. J. Mullen, "North Korea Warns That U.S. Bases in Guam, Japan Are within Range," *CNN*, March 22, 2013, available at http://edition.cnn.com/2013/03/20/world/asia/north-korea-threats.
29. D. Chance and P. Stewart, "North Korea Readies Rockets after U.S. Show of Force," Reuters, March 29, 2013, available at http://www.reuters.com/article/2013/03/29/us-korea-north-idUSBRE92R13R20130329.
30. Chance and Stewart, "North Korea Readies Rockets."

31. "North Korea Rocket Units on Standby to Attack US Bases," *Guardian*, March 28, 2103, available at http://www.guardian.co.uk/world/2013/mar/28/north-korea-standby-attack-us.
32. Korea News Service, "Report on Plenary Meeting of WPK Central Committee," March 31, 2013, available at http://www.kcna.co.jp/item/2013/201303/news31/20130331-24ee.html.
33. J. Kim, "North Korea Says Enters "State of War" against South," Reuters, March 30, 2013, available at http://www.reuters.com/article/2013/03/30/us-korea-north-war-idUSBRE92T00020130330.
34. Global Research, "From Korean into English, North Korea's 'State of War' Statement May Have Been the Result of Faulty Translation," March 30, 2013, available at http://www.globalresearch.ca/from-korean-into-english-north-koreas-state-of-war-may-have-the-result-of-faulty-translation/5329040.
35. Korean Central Broadcasting Station, "Full Text of a Report by Kim Jong Un at the 31 March 2013 Plenary Meeting of the Workers Party of Korea Central Committee," April 1, 2013, available at http://www.ncnk.org/resources/news-items/kim-jong-uns-speeches-and-public-statements-1/KJU_CentralCommittee_KWP.pdf.
36. J. Chung, "Embassies Staying Put in North Korea Despite Tension," Reuters, April 6, 2013, available at http://www.reuters.com/article/2013/04/06/us-korea-north-idUSBRE93408020130406.
37. M. Landler and C. Sang-Hun, "U.S. Sees North Korea Blustering, Not Acting," *New York Times*, April 1, 2013, available at http://www.nytimes.com/2013/04/02/world/asia/south-korea-gives-military-leeway-to-answer-north.html?pagewanted=all&_r=0.
38. E. MacAskill and J. McCurry, "North Korea: US Acts to Calm Fears over 'Alarming' Atomic plan," *Guardian*, April 3, 2013, available at http://www.guardian.co.uk/world/2013/apr/02/us-north-korea-nuclear-plan.
39. MacAskill and McCurry, "North Korea."
40. T. McCarthy, "John Kerry: North Korean Rhetoric 'Provocative, Dangerous, Reckless'—as It Happened," *Guardian*, April 2, 2013, available at http://www.guardian.co.uk/world/2013/apr/02/north-korea-us-live-blog.
41. McCarthy, "John Kerry."
42. D. Roberts and J. McCurry, "US Defends Military Deployments in Response to North Korea Threats," *Guardian*, April 4, 2013, available at http://www.guardian.co.uk/world/2013/apr/04/us-north-korea-military-response.
43. Roberts and McCurry, "US Defends Military Deployments."
44. Roberts and McCurry, "US Defends Military Deployments."
45. J. Mullen, B. Starr, and J. Sterling, "N. Korea May Be Able to Deliver Nuke, Pentagon Intel Says," *CNN*, April 12, 2013, available at http://edition.cnn.com/2013/04/11/world/asia/koreas-tensions.
46. Mullen, Starr, and Sterling, "N. Korea May Be Able to Deliver."
47. "US Delays Missile Test to Avoid Exacerbating North Korea Tensions," *Guardian*, April 7, 2013, available at http://www.guardian.co.uk/world/2013/apr/07/us-missile-test-north-korea.
48. T. Branigan, "China and US Push for Dialogue with North Korea," *Observer*, April 13, 2013, available at http://www.guardian.co.uk/world/2013/apr/13/north-korea-south-kim-missiles.

49. T. Branigan, "John Kerry: North and South Korea Tensions Can Ease with Serious Talks," *Guardian*, April 12, 2013, available at http://www.guardian.co.uk/world/2013/apr/12/john-kerry-north-korea-south-tensions.
50. Branigan, "John Kerry."

CHAPTER 7

1. D. Rothbart and K. V. Korostelina, *Identity, Morality and Threat* (Lexington, MA: Lexington Books, 2006), 6.
2. Rothbart and Korostelina, *Identity, Morality and Threat*, 46.
3. P. Seixas, "*Schweigen! die Kinder!* or Does Postmodern History Have a Place in the Schools?" in *Knowing, Teaching and Learning History: National and International Perspectives*, ed. P. Stearns, P. Seixas, and S. S. Wineburg (New York: New York University Press, 2000), 19–37.
4. E. A. Cole, *Teaching the Violent Past: History Education and Reconciliation* (Lanham, MD: Rowman and Littlefield, 2007), 1.
5. R. Stradling, *Teaching 20th-Century European History* (Strasbourg: Council of Europe Publishing, 2001), 100.
6. D. Shriver, *An Ethic for Enemies: Forgiveness in Politics* (New York: Oxford University Press, 1995), 4.
7. Cole, *Teaching the Violent Past*.
8. For detailed analysis of this project see K. V. Korostelina and S. Lassig, eds., *History Education and Post-conflict Reconciliation: Reconsidering Joint Textbook Projects* (New York: Routledge, 2013).
9. D. Newsom, "Reconciling Histories," *Christian Science Monitor*, December 8, 1999, 8.
10. S. Adwan and D. Bar-On, "Leading Forward: The Experience of Palestinians and Israelis in the Learning Each Other's Historical Narratives Project," in *History Teaching, Identities, Citizenship*, ed. L. Cajani and A. Ross (Sterling, VA: Trentham Books, 2007), 155.
11. B. Bashir, "Accommodating Historically Oppressed Social Groups: Deliberative Democracy and the Politics of Reconciliation," in *The Politics of Reconciliation in Multicultural Societies*, ed. W. Kymlicka and B. Bashir (New York: Oxford University Press, 2008), 48–69; A. Hirsch and S. Chakravarti, "Agonism and the Power of Victim Testimony," in *Theorizing Post-conflict Reconciliation: Agonism, Restitution and Repair* ed. A. Hirsch (New York: Routledge, 2011), 11–26; C. Mouffe, *The Democratic Paradox* (New York: Verso, 2000); C. Mouffe, "Democracy as Agonistic Pluralism," in *Rewriting Democracy: Cultural Politics in Postmodernity*, ed. E. D. Ermarth (Burlington, VT: Ashgate, 2007), 36–45; A. Schaap, "Agonism in Divided Societies," *Philosophy & Social Criticism* 32, no. 2 (2006): 255–77.
12. Mouffe, *The Democratic Paradox*, 13.
13. O. Ramsbotham, *Transforming Violent Conflict: Radical Disagreement, Dialogue and Survival* (London: Routledge, 2010), 211.
14. A. Little, "Rhetorics of Reconciliation: Shifting Conflict Paradigms in Northern Ireland," in Hirsch, *Theorizing Post-conflict Reconciliation*, 75.
15. G. Shiv and H. M. Zoller, "Dialogue, Activism, and Democratic Social Change," *Communication Theory* 22 (2012): 77.
16. Mouffe, "Democracy as Agonistic Pluralism," 40.
17. D. L. Schoem, S. Hurtado, T. Sevig, M. Chesler, and S. H. Sumida, "Intergroup Dialogue: Democracy at Work in Theory and Practice," in *Intergroup Dialogue:*

Deliberative Democracy in School, College, Community, and Workplace, ed. D. L. Schoem and S. Hurtado (Ann Arbor: University of Michigan Press, 2001), 15.

18. K. Eyben, D. Morrow, and D. Wilson, *A Worthwhile Venture? Practically Investing in Equality, Diversity, and Interdependence in Northern Ireland* (Coleraine: University of Ulster, 1995), available at http://cain.ulst.ac.uk/issues/reconcile/venture.htm; B. Graham and S. McDowell, "Meaning in the Maze: The Heritage of Long Kesh," *Cultural Geographies* 14, no. 3 (2007): 343–68; C. McCall, "Culture and the Irish Border: Spaces for Conflict Transformation," *Cooperation and Conflict* 46, no. 2 (2011): 201–21; C. McCartney and S. Caroll, "Building a World Safe for Difference," *Global Social Policy* 9, no. 1 (2009): 35–39; J. Nagle and M. A. Clancy, *Shared Society or Benign Apartheid? Understanding Peace Building in Divided Societies* (New York: Palgrave Macmillan, 2010); S. Zeldin, D. Wilson, and J. Collura, "Creating Restorative and Intergenerational Cultures for Youth: Insights from Northern Ireland and the United States," *Youth and Society* 43 (2011): 401–13.
19. Club de Madrid, "The Shared Societies Project," available at http://www.clubmadrid.org/en/ssp/vision_of_a_shared_society.
20. M. C. Fitzduff, *Public Policies for Shared Societies: The Foreigner Next Door* (New York: Palgrave Macmillan, 2013).
21. E. Wertheim, "Negotiations and Resolving Conflicts: An Overview," InterNeg, November 21, 1996, available at http://webarchive.iiasa.ac.at/Research/DAS/interneg/training/conflict_overview.html.
22. R. J. Lewicki, D. M. Saunders, and J. W. Minton, *Negotiation*, 3rd ed. (San Francisco: Irwin McGraw-Hill, 1999).
23. Lewicki, Saunders, and Minton, *Negotiation*.
24. M. Deutsch, *The Resolution of Conflict: Constructive and Destructive Processes* (New Haven: Yale University Press, 1973), 20.
25. M. Deutsch, "Cooperation and Competition," in *The Handbook of Conflict Resolution: Theory and Practice*, ed. M. Deutsch and P. Coleman (San Francisco: Jossey-Bass, 2000), 22.
26. M. Maiese, "Negotiation," Beyond Intractability, October 2003, available at http://www.beyondintractability.org/bi-essay/negotiation.
27. M. Watkins and S. Rosegrant, *Breakthrough International Negotiation: How Great Negotiators Transformed the World's Toughest Post–Cold War Conflicts* (San Francisco: Jossey-Bass, 2001), 31.
28. D. A. Lax and K. Sebenius, "Interests: The Measure of Negotiation," in *Negotiation Theory and Practice*, ed. J. W. Breslin and J. Z. Rubin (Cambridge: Program on Negotiation Books, 1991), 161.
29. R. Fisher and W. Ury, *Getting to Yes: Negotiating Agreement without Giving In*, ed. B. Patton, 2nd ed. (New York: Penguin Books, 1991).
30. J. Bercovitch, "International Mediation and Intractable Conflict," Beyond Intractability, January 2004, available at http://www.beyondintractability.org/bi-essay/med-intractable-conflict.
31. C. Honeyman and N. Yawanarajah, "Mediation," Beyond Intractability, September 2003, available at http://www.beyondintractability.org/bi-essay/mediation.
32. B. Spangler, "Transformative Mediation," Beyond Intractability, October 2003, available at http://www.beyondintractability.org/bi-essay/transformative-mediation.
33. R. A. B. Bush and J. P. Folger, *The Promise of Mediation: The Transformative Approach to Conflict*, 2nd ed. (San Francisco: Jossey-Bass, 2004).
34. I. Shapiro, "Theories of Change," Beyond Intractability, January 2005, available at http://www.beyondintractability.org/bi-essay/theories-of-change.

35. C. Malek and H. Burgess, "Recognition," Beyond Intractability, October 2005, available at http://www.beyondintractability.org/bi-essay/recognition.
36. H. C. Kelman, "Negotiating National Identity and Self-Determination in Ethnic Conflicts: The Choice between Pluralism and Ethnic Cleansing," *Negotiation Journal* 13 (1997): 327–40; H. C. Kelman, "The Role of National Identity in Conflict Resolution," in *Social Identity, Intergroup Conflict, and Conflict Reduction*, ed. R. D. Ashmore, L. Jussim, and D. Wilder (New York: Oxford University Press, 2001), 187–212.
37. Kelman, "Negotiating National Identity," 338.
38. Kelman, "Role of National Identity."
39. H. C. Kelman, "Creating the Conditions for Israeli-Palestinian Negotiations," *Journal of Conflict Resolution* 1 (1982): 39–76; Kelman, "Negotiating National Identity"; Kelman, "Role of National Identity"; H. C. Kelman, "Reconciliation as Identity Change: A Social-Psychological Perspective," in *From Conflict Resolution to Reconciliation*, ed. Y. Bar-Siman-Tov (New York: Oxford University Press, 2004), 111–24.

GLOSSARY

Intergroup insult. A social act constructed mutually by social groups on the boundary between them aiming to strip the out-group of positive identity, justify in-group actions, strengthen intergroup the boundary, and redefine the balance of power.

FORMS OF INSULT
Identity insult. Attribution of negative features, wrong motivations, or foul values to the out-group, or an accusation of performing destructive or erroneous actions.
Projection insult. Justification of particular actions or eradication of the negative features of the in-group by imposing them on an out-group.
Divergence insult. Enhancing differences and the social boundary between groups when an in-group does not want to acknowledge similarity or resemblance, or aims at alienation of the out-group.
Relative insult. Denial of certain rights of the out-group and emphasis on the in-group's privileged position, inclusive right to control a specific territory or group, make decisions, and define the connotations of historic events and identities.
Power insult. Decrease of absolute power or relative coercive power of the out-group in comparison with the in-group.
Legitimacy insult. Initiation and promotion of a recategorization process that legitimizes one side and delegitimizes the other.

TYPES OF INSULT
Congruous insult. An insult produced intentionally by the insulting group and recognized by the insulted group as an offense.
Futile insult. An insult that is produced intentionally by the insulting group but is not recognized as and insult by the insulted group.
Attributed insult. An insult that is not intentionally produced by the insulting group but is claimed as intentional by insulted group.
Potential insult. An insult that is not intentionally produced by the insulting group and is not recognized by the insulted group.

DYNAMICS OF INSULT
Transfer of insult. An increase in the scope of an insult by involving more in-group members in its construction.
Sensitizing. Enlightening of in-group members about meaning of an out-group insult and its impact on the in-group's image so as to increase motivation to protect the identity, self-esteem, and social position of the in-group.

Learned insult. Discovery of the potency of a particular insult based on the observation of reactions of other in-group members.

Generalization of insult. The actions and words of out-group perceived as an insult based on their similarity to a previous insult.

Conglomeration of insult. The impact of an insult's frequency on the perception of its effects. The more often an insult is repeated, the more it is perceived as offensive and abusive.

Delayed insult. The recognition of an insult some time after it was enacted. Nevertheless, it contributes to conglomeration and generalization processes.

Diffusion of insult. A loss of the offensive effect of an insult over time.

Reactivation of insult. Reactivation of insultThe reappearance of a perception of offense long after the insult was performed; often a product of public revalidation of past experiences.

SELECTED BIBLIOGRAPHY

Andersson, L. M., and C. M. Pearson. "Tit for Tat? The Spiraling Effect of Incivility in the Workplace." *Academy of Management Review* 24 (1999): 452.

Bordens, K. S., and I. A. Horowitz. *Social Psychology*. New York: Psychology Press, 2012.

Branscombe, N. R., and D. L. Wann. "Collective Self-Esteem Consequences of Outgroup Derogation When a Valued Social Identity Is on Trial." *European Journal of Social Psychology* 24 (1994): 641.

Brewer, M. B. "The Many Faces of Social Identity: Implications for Political Psychology." *Political Psychology* 22, no. 1 (2001): 115.

Brewer, M. B. *Intergroup Relations*. 2nd ed. Philadelphia: Open University Press, 2003.

Cairns, E., and M. Hewstone. "Embitterment and Forgiveness in the Context of the Conflict in Northern Ireland." In *Embitterment*, ed. M. Linden and A. Maercker. Vienna: Springer, 2011.

Canidu, M., and C. Reggiori. "Discrimination of Low-Status Outgroup: The Role of Ingroup Threat." *European Journal of Social Psychology* 32 (2002): 501.

Cartwright, D. *Studies in Social Power*. Ann Arbor: Research Center for Group Dynamics, Institute for Social Research, University of Michigan, 1959.

Caza, B. B., and L. M. Cortina. "From Insult to Injury: Explaining the Impact of Incivility." *Basic and Applied Social Psychology* 29, no. 4 (2007): 335.

Cohen, D., R. E. Nisbett, B. F. Bowdle, and N. Schwarz. "Insult, Aggression, and the Southern Culture of Honor: An 'experimental Ethnography.'" *Journal of Personality and Social Psychology* 70, no. 5 (1996): 945.

Crosby, F. "The Denial of Personal Discrimination." *American Behavioral Scientist* 27, no. 3 (1984): 371.

Culpeper, J. *Impoliteness: Using Language to Cause Offence*. New York: Cambridge University Press, 2011.

Davis, J. A. "A Formal Interpretation of the Theory of Relative Deprivation." *Sociometry* 22 (1959): 280.

Deutsch, M., and H. B. Gerard. "A Study of Normative and Informational Social Influences upon Individual Judgment." *Journal of Abnormal and Social Psychology* 51, no. 3 (1955): 629.

Enaharo, K. *Race Code War: The Power of Words, Images, and Symbols on the Black Psyche*. Chicago: African American Images, 2003.

Eribon, D. *Insult and the Making of the Gay Self*. Trans. M. Lucey. Durham, NC: Duke University Press, 2004.

Felson, R. B. "Aggression as Impression Management." *Social Psychology* 41, no. 3 (1978): 205.

Festinger, L. "A Theory of Social Comparison Processes." *Human Relations* 7, no. 2 (1954): 117.

French, J. R. P., and B. Raven. "The Bases of Social Power." In *Studies in Social Power*, ed. D. Cartwright. Ann Arbor: Research Center for Group Dynamics, Institute for Social Research, University of Michigan, 1959.

Frijda, N. H. *The Emotions*. Cambridge, UK: Cambridge University Press, 1986.

Gabler, I., and A. Maercker. "Revenge after Trauma: Theoretical Outline." In *Embitterment*, ed. M. Linden and A. Maercker, Vienna: Springer, 2011.

Gabriel, Y. "An Introduction to the Social Psychology of Insults in Organizations." *Human Relations* 51, no. 11 (1998): 1329–54.

Galam, S., and S. Moscovici. "Towards a Theory of Collective Phenomena: III. Conflicts and Forms of Power." *European Journal of Social Psychology* 25 (1995): 217.

Grant, P. R., and R. Brown. "From Ethnocentrism to Collective Protest: Responses to Relative Deprivation and Threats to Social Identity." *Social Psychology Quarterly* 58, no. 3 (1995): 195.

Greer, T., M. Berman, V. Varan, L. Bobrycki, and S. Watson. "We Are a Religious People; We Are a Vengeful People." *Journal of Scientific Study of Religion* 44, no. 1 (2005): 45.

Hauser, M. *Moral Minds*. New York: HarperCollins, 2009.

Hendrix, B. A. "Moral Error, Power, and Insult." *Political Theory* 35, no. 5 (2007): 550.

Herz, J. H. "Idealist Internationalism and the Security Dilemma." *World Politics* 2, no. 2 (1950): 157.

Hornsey, M. J., M. Trembath, and S. Gunthorpe. "You Can Criticize Because You Care: Identity Attachment, Constructiveness, and the Intergroup Sensitivity Effect." *European Journal of Social Psychology* 34 (2004): 499–518.

Irvine, W. B. *A Slap in the Face: Why Insults Hurt—and Why They Shouldn't*. New York: Oxford University Press, 2013.

Issues in Social Psychology and Conflict Resolution: 2011 Edition. Atlanta: Scholarly Editions, 2012.

Jackson, J. W. "The Relationship between Group Identity and Intergroup Prejudice Is Moderated by Sociostructural Variation." *Journal of Applied Social Psychology* 32, no. 5 (2002): 908.

Jones, W. K. *Insult to Injury: Libel, Slander and Invasions of Privacy*. Boulder, CO: University Press of Colorado, 2003.

Kashima, Y., K. Fiedler, and P. Freytag, eds. *Stereotype Dynamics: Language-Based Approaches to the Formation, Maintenance, and Transformation of Stereotypes*. New York: Psychology Press, 2007.

Kawakami, K., and L. K. Dion. "The Impact of Salient Self-identities on Relative Deprivation and Action Intentions." *European Journal of Social Psychology* 23 (1993): 525.

Kelman, H. C. "Compliance, Identification, and Internalization Three Processes of Attitude Change." *Journal of Conflict Resolution* 2, no. 1 (1958): 51.

Kelman, H. "Reflections on the Social and Pyschological Processes of Legitimization and Delegitimization." In *The Psychology of Legitimacy: Emerging Perspectives on Ideology, Justice, and Intergroup Relations*, ed. J. T. Jost and B. Major. New York: Cambridge University Press, 2001.

Linden, M., M. Rotter, K. Baumann, and B. Lieberei. *The Post-traumatic Embitterment (PTED)*. Bern: Hogrefe & Huber, 2007.

Mackie, D. M., L. Silver, and E. R. Smith. "Emotion as an Intergroup Phenomenon." In *The Social Life of Emotions*, ed. C. W. Leach and L. A, Tiedens. New York: Cambridge University Press, 2004.

Maitner, A. T., D. M. Mackie, and E. R. Smith. "Evidence for the Regulatory Function of Intergroup Emotion: Emotional Consequences of Implemented or Impeded Intergroup Action." *Journal of Experimental Social Psychology* 42 (2006): 720.

Maitra, I., and M. K. McGowan, eds. *Speech and Harm: Controversies over Free Speech*. New York: Oxford University Press, 2012.

Matsibekker, C. L. Z. *The Snob Effect: The Psychology of Negotiation Tactics in the Salesroom*. Ann Arbor: ProQuest, 2008.

Matsuda, M. J., C. R. Lawrence III, R. Delgado, and K. W. Crenshaw. *Words That Wound: Critical Race Theory, Assaultive Speech, and the First Amendment*. Boulder, CO: Westview Press, 1993.

McKee, I. R., and N. T. Feather. "Revenge, Retribution, and Values: Social Attitudes and Punitive Sentencing." *Social Justice Research* 21, no. 2 (2008): 138.

Miller, W. I. *Humiliation: And Other Essays on Honor, Social Discomfort, and Violence*. Ithaca, NY: Cornell University Press, 1995.

Moscovici, S. *Social Influence and Social Change*. New York: Academic Press, in cooperation with European Association of Experimental Social Psychology, 1976.

Neu, J. *Sticks and Stones: The Philosophy of Insults*. New York: Oxford University Press, 2009.

Newman, L. S., and R. Erber, eds. *Understanding Genocide: The Social Psychology of the Holocaust*. New York: Oxford University Press, 2002.

Orbach, I. "The Victim's Reaction to an Attack as a Function of His Perception of the Attacker Following a Verbal Insult." *European Journal of Social Psychology* 8 (1978): 43.

Orth, U., L. Montada, and A. Maercker. "Feelings of Revenge, Retaliation Motive, and Posttraumatic Stress Reactions in Crime Victims." *Journal of Interpersonal Violence* 21, no. 2 (2006): 229.

Rothbart, D., and K. Korostelina, eds. *Identity, Morality, and Threat: Studies in Violent Conflict*. Lexington, KY: Lexington Books, 2006.

Runciman, W. G. *Relative Deprivation and Social Justice: A Study of Attitudes to Social Inequality in Twentieth Century England*. New York: Penguin, 1972.

Rydell, R. J., D. M. Mackie, A. T. Maitner, H. M. Claypool, M. J. Ryan, and E. R. Smith. "Arousal, Processing, and Risk Taking: Consequences of Intergroup Anger." *Personality and Social Psychology Bulletin* 34 (2008): 1141.

Sharp, G. *The Politics of Nonviolent Action*. Boston: P. Sargent, 1973.

Smith, A. D. *Ethno-symbolism and Nationalism: A Cultural Approach*. New York: Routledge, 2009.

Smith, E. R., C. Seger, and D. M. Mackie. "Can Emotions Be Truly Group-Level? Evidence regarding Four Conceptual Criteria." *Journal of Personality and Social Psychology* 93 (2007): 431.

Tajfel, H., ed. *Differentiation between Social Groups: Studies in the Social Psychology of Intergroup Relations*. New York: Academic Press, 1979.

Tajfel, H., and J. C. Turner. "The Social Identity Theory of Intergroup Behaviour." In *Psychology of Intergroup Relations*, ed. S. Worchel and W. G. Austin. 2nd ed. Chicago: Nelson-Hall, 1985.

Tanter, R., and T. R. Gurr. "Why Men Rebel." *Midwest Journal of Political Science* 14, no. 4 (1970): 725–728.

Tilly, C. *Identities, Boundaries, and Social Ties*. Boulder, CO: Paradigm, 2005.

Turner, J. C. "Explaining the Nature of Power: A Three-process Theory." *European Journal of Social Psychology* 35 (2005): 1.

Turner J. C., M. A. Hogg, P. J. Turner, and P. M. Smith. "Failure and Defeat as Determinants of Group Cohesiveness." *British Journal of Social Psychology* 23, no. 2 (1984): 97.

Volkan, V. D. *Blind Trust: Large Groups and Their Leaders in Times of Crisis and Terror.* Charlottesville, VA: Pitchstone, 2004.

Volkan, V. D. *Bloodlines: From Ethnic Pride to Ethnic Terrorism.* Boulder, CO: Westview Press, 1998.

Walker, I., and T. F. Pettigrew. "Relative Deprivation Theory: An Overview and Conceptual Critique." *British Journal of Social Psychology* 23, no. 4 (1984): 301.

Weinstein, E., and P. Deutschberger. "Some Dimensions of Altercasting." *Sociometry* 26 (1963): 454.

INDEX OF NAMES

Abdullayev, Elman 85, 90
Abe, Shinzo 108
Abrahamyan, Hovik 89
Adenauer, Konrad 146
Adwan, Sami 149
Akhmedov, Ali 83, 86
Alasgarov, Fuad 87
Aliyev, Ilham 10, 76, 77, 84, 86
Alizadeh, Zardusht 82
Alyokhina, Maria 43, 48
Ashton, Catherine 86
Aslanov, Elnur 90
Astakhov, Oleg 64
Azumi, Jun 112

Bandera 56–58, 67
Bar-on, Dan 149
Basseley Nakoula, Nakoula 3
Ben Ali, Zine El Abidine 4
Bikini Kill 38
Bjork 51
Borutsky, Svyatoslav 61
Bouazizi, Mohamed 4
Bratmobile 38
Bratstvo 67
Bush, George W. 120
Byung-see, Yun 130

Carney, Jay 129, 130
Clapper, James 130

de Gaulle, Charles 146
de Waal, Thomas 85
Donilon, Tom 130

Emperor Gojong 96
Empress Myeongseong (Queen Min) 96

Femen 51
Fujimura, Osamu 99, 100, 102, 103, 105, 111

Gaddafi, Muammar 37
Gaderli, Erkin 82
Gang, Qin 101, 104
Gasparian, Hamlet 81
Gemba, Koichiro 99, 106, 110, 111
Goffman, Erving 14
Golub, Alexander 62
Gudkov, Dmitry 50
Guliyev, Vilayet 84
Gurbanli, Mubariz 87

Hagel, Chuck 126–127
Hakubun, Shimomura 97
Homistkiy, Andrei 66
Huseynov, Rafael 87

Ikeda, Yukihiko 108
Ishihara, Shintaro 10, 99, 102–103, 105

Jiechi, Yang 105
Jinping, Xi 102, 104

Kak-soo, Shin 110
Kelman, Herbert C. 163, 164
Kerry, John 127, 130, 131
Ki Moon, Ban 108
Kim, Il Sung 121
Kim, Jong-Il 120, 125
Kim, Jong-Un 37, 121–131
Kingston, Jeffrey 101
Kirill I 1, 31, 33–36, 40–42, 46, 53
Kocijancic, Maja 86
Kodama, Kazuo 105

Koga, Tetsushiro 97–98
Koga, Zenji 97–98
Kojima, Kenichi 101

L7 38
Le Tigre 38
Lei, Hong 102, 126–127
Lukin, Vladimir 43

Madonna 50
Mammadov, Farhad 99
Margaryan, Gurgen 78–79, 81–83
McCain, John 130–131
McCartney, Paul 51
Medvedev, Dmitry 31, 33
Meiji Dynasty 95
Miller, James 126
Ming Dynasty 103
Moo-hyun, Roh 109
Muto, Masatoshi 110
Myung-bak, Lee 10, 27, 109, 110, 111, 126

Nalbandian, Edward 88
Navalny, Alexei 50
Nihonseinensha 98
Niwa, Uichiro 99, 100
Noda, Yoshihiko 100–102, 105, 110–112
Novruzov, Tahmasib 83
Nuland, Victoria 130

Obama, Barak 86, 121, 124–125, 129, 131, 133
Ono, Yoko 51
Oruj, Zahid 84–85

Peaches 51
Prophet Muhammad 3
Putin, Vladimir 1, 9, 31–34, 37–53

Qing Dynasty 94–95

Red Hot Chili Peppers 50
Rice, Condolezza 120
Riot Grrrl' movement 38
Rodman, Dennis 124

Safarov, Ramil 10, 78–92, 144, 160
Samutsevich, Yekaterina 43, 46–48
Sargsyan, Serzh 76, 87, 89–90
Sasae, Kenichiro 101
Sin'kova, Anna 67–68
Sleater-Kinney 38
Smith, Patti 51
Stalin, Joseph 56–57, 60–62, 65, 70, 77
Stevens, Christopher 3
Sung-hwan, Kim 113
Syrova, Marina 48

Tai-young, Cho 111
Tolokonnikova, Nadezhda 43, 45, 47–48

Verhovna Rada 9, 58

Weimin, Liu 99, 100
Winnefeld, James 126

Xiaoping, Deng 98
Xinhua, Lu 106

Yachi, Shotaro 108
Yamaguchi, Tsuyoshi 112
Yanukovich, Victor 58, 59, 72
Yeltsin, Boris 31
Yuan, Luo 106
Yukio, Edano 97
Yushchenko, Victor 58–59, 72

Zahirov, Vilayat 84–85

INDEX OF SUBJECTS

acknowledgement 12, 16, 18, 23, 36, 44, 45, 70, 79, 131, 151, 162, 199
Afghanistan 1, 6
agonistic dialogue 133, 151, 152, 165
Amnesty International 43
Arab Spring 1
Armenia 20, 22, 34, 73–93, 136, 140, 144, 145, 153, 160
attributed insult. *See* types of insult
Azerbaijan 1, 10, 22, 73–93, 135, 136, 139, 140, 143–145, 152–153, 160, 164

Balkans 132, 144
beliefs 3, 6, 13, 14, 17, 20, 25, 27, 48, 57, 64, 68, 71, 135, 138–141, 143, 147, 149, 151–153
bias 18, 149
Boxer Protocol 95
Breguet watch 36–37

Cairo 1
Cairo declaration 104
Cathedral of Christ the Saviour 1, 9, 31, 40, 47, 48, 49
China 10, 29, 94–95, 97–107, 114–117, 119, 120, 130, 136–137, 143, 145, 149, 157, 161–162, 165
chosen trauma 29
collective axiology 138, 140–143, 154, 165
  axiological balance 141–143
  generality 141
  mythic narrative 29
  normative order 22
concepts of national identity. *See* national identity, concepts

civic 151
  ethnic 2, 57, 141, 151, 154, 155
Conference for Security and Cooperation in Europe (CSCE) 74, 75
conflict
  analysis 3, 11, 54, 68, 73, 92, 93, 117, 133, 135, 137
  dynamic 1–3, 8, 11, 12, 30, 69, 71, 72, 92, 94, 133, 135, 137, 165
  ethnic (*see* conflict, ethnic)
  resolution 3, 11, 53, 70, 71, 72, 74, 92, 111, 140, 153, 157–158, 160, 162, 164–165
conglomeration of insult. *See* dynamics of insult
congruous insult. *See* types of insult
Court of International Justice (ICJ) 110, 112, 113, 117
culture 3, 4, 5, 9, 13, 26, 33, 39, 46, 47, 51, 86, 92, 139, 141, 163
culture of honor 26

delayed insult. *See* dynamics of insult
Democratic People's Republic of Korea (DPRK)
deprivation 69, 77
  fraternal 19
  relative 23, 24, 25, 63, 65
dialogue 93, 128, 131, 138, 144, 146, 148, 151, 152, 154, 156, 163, 165
  agnostic 138, 151–152, 165
  identity 138, 154, 156, 163, 165
Diaoyu 10, 97, 99–101, 103, 105
diffusion of insult. *See* dynamics of insult
dignity 6, 15, 83, 112, 123
discrimination 147, 154, 155

divergence insult. *See* forms of insult
Dokdo 10, 30, 107–110, 113
dominant group 5, 26, 159
   identity 154
dynamics of insult
   conglomeration 2, 29, 62, 68, 71, 107, 113, 116, 118, 129, 135
   delayed 2, 29
   diffusion 2, 30
   Generalization 2, 28–29, 30, 67, 71, 112, 115, 118, 135
   learned 2, 4, 28, 29, 30
   reactivation 30, 104, 109, 115, 116, 118, 137
   sensitizing 2, 27–28, 62, 64, 139
   transfer 2, 26–27, 29, 43, 50, 52, 53, 62, 64, 68, 69, 81, 135, 136, 139

education 28, 29, 154. *See also* history education
Egypt 3
embitterment 5, 6
empowerment 159
Erevan State University 34
ethnic
   cleansing 56, 85, 90, 92, 139, 160 (*see also* conflict, ethnic)
   conflict 55, 56, 57, 72, 74, 75, 77, 85, 88, 90, 92, 94, 139, 147, 160 (*see also* cleansing, ethnic)
   identity 57
ethnocentrism 148
European Union 1, 4, 62, 71, 86

forms of insult
   divergence 9, 17–18, 23, 25, 30, 42, 45, 52, 53, 59–62, 68–71, 100, 114, 117, 135–136, 138, 149–152, 165
   identity 3, 6, 7, 10, 15–16, 23–25, 28, 30, 35–37, 41–43, 45, 47–48, 51–53, 68, 81, 83, 88, 91, 92, 135, 136, 137–143, 164, 165
   legitimacy insult 2, 9, 10, 22–23, 25, 27, 35, 37, 38, 39, 41, 42, 43, 47, 48, 50, 51, 52, 53, 62–72, 88, 91–93, 99–101, 103, 104, 107, 109, 111–117, 124, 131–133, 135, 136, 138, 139, 159–164, 165
   power insult 2, 4, 10, 11, 12–14, 20–22, 23, 25, 26, 101, 106–107, 110–118, 121–127, 129, 131–133, 136–138, 156–159, 165
   projection 2, 16–17, 25, 30, 80–83, 85, 87, 90, 91–92, 104, 107, 111, 113, 115–116, 123, 132–133, 143–145
   relative 2, 19–20, 25, 62, 63, 65, 66, 69, 70, 71, 90–92, 152–154
forgiveness 118, 138, 145–147, 149, 165
futile insult. *See* types of insult

generalization of insult. *See* dynamics of insult
genocide 61, 90
Google 4, 20
Great Patriotic War 57–59, 63, 64, 139, 140, 152, 153. *See also* World War II

Harlem Globetrotters 124
history education 138, 147–149, 165
holocaust 3
human rights 38, 41, 47, 52, 88, 92, 139, 142, 146, 151, 154, 156, 160, 161
humiliation 95, 101, 104, 114, 121, 161
Hungary 1, 10, 20, 22, 55, 83–86, 88–90

identity
   common 72, 155, 164
   dialogue 138, 151, 154–156, 163, 165
   dominant 154
   ethnic 57
   gender 12
   insult (*see* forms of insult)
   national (*see* national identity)
   negotiation (*see* national identity, negotiation of)
   regional 57
   superordinate 7
identity reconstruction workshop 163
impoliteness 5, 7, 17
imposition 18, 21, 30, 59, 63, 68, 69, 70, 72, 135, 138, 149, 150, 151, 152
incivility 5, 6–7
ingroup
   favoritism 15, 20, 70, 140
   loyalty 16, 114
   support 15, 20, 21, 70, 114, 135

intergroup
  comparison 19, 21, 143
  conflict 6, 7, 8, 11, 12–15, 27, 30, 70, 141, 143, 152, 159, 163
International Court of Justice (ICJ) 110, 112, 113, 117
Internet 1, 4, 8, 20, 37, 68
Israel 3, 44

Japan 1, 10, 11, 18, 22, 27, 29, 30, 94–118, 120, 127–128, 130, 136–137, 143, 145, 149–150, 157, 161–162, 165
Japan Sea 1, 10, 11

Korean War 119–120
Kosovo 6, 76

learned insult. See dynamics of insult
legitimacy insult. See forms of insult
Lennon Ono Grant for Peace 51
LGBT rights 37–38, 41, 52
Libya 3, 37
London 3, 20, 110

majority–minority position 13, 19, 30, 31, 70, 81, 138, 162, 156. See also position, relative
Makuden (Manchurian) incident 95
mass media 9, 57, 67, 76, 81, 82, 83, 91, 101, 102, 113–114, 117, 136–137, 144, 150
meaning of identity 23, 142
mediation 138, 158, 159, 164, 165
  problem solving 159
  transformative 159
minor differences 18
Minsk conference 74
Moscow 1, 9, 31, 37–40, 45, 74, 77, 130
Muslims 3, 20, 44, 77, 78, 82, 155
mythic narrative 29

Nagorno-Karabakh 10, 72, 74–79, 81, 85, 87–88, 90–93, 140, 143–145, 153, 160
Nanking Massacre 95
national identity 27–28, 32, 49–50, 52, 53, 54, 60, 64, 100, 139, 146, 151, 163–165
  concepts 139, 151, 155, 163, 164

  formation 155
  negotiation of 80, 162–165
nationalism 54, 58, 59, 60, 64, 65, 68, 69, 150
NATO 1, 10, 78, 85, 87, 88, 143
Nazi 9, 23, 55–58, 61–64, 66–67, 69–70, 150
negotiation of national identity. See national identity, negotiation of
North Korea 11, 17, 37, 95, 119–134, 136–137, 143–146, 156–157, 159, 162, 165
nuclear 11, 119, 120, 122–133, 144, 156, 157
  bomb tests 11, 17, 119–120, 133, 144, 162
Nuclear Nonproliferation Treaty 120

Okinawa 97, 127
Orange Revolution 57
Organization of Ukrainian Nationalists (OUN) 56–58, 61, 63
orthodox faith 9, 33, 35–36, 41–45, 48, 51–52, 137, 139, 160
outgroup threat 142

Paris Peace Treaties 56
patriotism 27, 48, 50–54, 100, 117, 135, 136, 139
potential insult. See types of insult
power
  balance of 2, 13, 14, 21, 24, 25, 127, 131, 133, 156, 157
  coercive 2, 21, 25, 26, 46, 138, 156, 159
  insult (see forms of insult)
  legitimate 21, 22
prejudice 18
process tracing 8
projection insult. See forms of insult
Pussy Riot 9, 18, 27, 31–54, 134, 137, 139, 149–150, 159, 160, 161, 165

racism 5, 88
reactivated insult. See dynamics of insult
recategorization 22, 138, 160, 164
reconciliation 86, 97, 104, 118, 138, 143, 145, 146–149, 165
red
  army 16, 23, 56, 58, 62–64, 68–69, 140, 152, 153

Index of Subjects [199]

red (Cont.)
　flag 9, 19, 23, 29, 54, 57–66, 68–71, 92, 149, 150
regime change 37, 53, 56
relative
　deprivation 23, 24
　insult (see forms of insult)
　position 13, 19, 25, 66, 138 (see also majority–minority position)
Republic of Korea (ROK) 1, 10, 11, 17, 18, 22, 27, 29, 30, 94–97, 107–118, 119–122, 124–132, 136–137, 144–145, 149, 156–157, 161–162, 165
restorative justice 5, 146
revenge 5–6, 44, 79, 80, 165
Ribbentrop-Molotov Pact 56
Russia 13, 28, 31–54, 55–72, 74, 78, 86, 120, 149, 150, 159, 161
Russian Federation 34, 50, 64, 65, 66
Russian Orthodox Church 1, 9, 18, 27, 31–34, 37, 39, 41–53, 135, 137
Russky newspaper 41

salience of identity 7, 17, 154
San Francisco Peace Treaty 108
security dilemma 17, 157
self
　conception 15, 142
　esteem 2, 15, 16, 23–30, 137, 138, 140, 143
　image 2, 7, 13, 14, 16, 18, 24, 25, 27, 140, 142, 143, 144
Senkaku Islands 10, 97–106
sensitizing. See dynamics of insult
September 11 3
shared society 138, 154–156, 165
Sino-Japanese relations 95, 97, 99, 101, 114, 117, 157, 161
Sino-Japanese War 94
social boundary 2, 6, 8, 12, 15, 18, 28, 42, 45, 48, 52, 53, 61, 68–71, 100, 114, 117, 138, 150, 151, 152, 189
social change 4, 11, 19–20, 151
social identity theory 15, 163
social status 7, 15, 18–19
South Korea. See Republic of Korea (ROK)

Soviet Union 34, 56, 59, 61, 62, 65
stereotypes 5, 6, 78, 148, 154

Takeshima 9, 30, 107, 110–113
threatened egotism 3
Tomb of the Unknown Soldier 1, 9, 55, 63, 67, 68, 140 (typo on pg. 140)
transfer of insult. See dynamics of insult
trauma healing 147–149
Truth and Reconciliation Commission 146, 148
Tunisia 4, 17, 28
Tunisian Revolution 1
types of insult
　attributed 2, 24, 25–26, 59, 60, 61, 62, 68–69, 71, 78, 137, 139, 165
　congruous 2, 24, 25, 62–65, 67, 68, 69, 70, 124, 189
　futile 2, 24, 25
　potential 2, 5, 24, 26, 62

Uganda 6
Ukraine 1, 9, 13, 16, 18–21, 23, 29, 30, 33, 55–72, 135–137, 140, 149–150, 152–153, 159, 161, 165
Ukrainians 18, 56, 57, 60, 61, 63, 140
Ukrainian Insurgent Army UPA 9, 23, 56–58, 61–63
United Stated (of America) 3, 6, 11, 17, 86, 96–97, 104, 119–134, 136, 143–146, 156, 157, 160, 162, 165
USS Pueblo 120

Victory Day 9, 23, 55, 57–72, 91, 105, 110, 137, 149, 152–153, 159

Waffen Grenadier Division of the SS Galicia 56
"we-ness" 156
World War II 1, 9, 18, 21, 30, 42, 55–57, 59, 60, 62–64, 67, 69, 71, 95–97, 104, 105, 117, 140, 162. See also Great Patriotic War

Zrinyi Miklos National Defense University 78

[200]　*Index of Subjects*